The
Fragrant
Year

Books by
Helen Van Pelt Wilson

House Plants for Every Window
  (*in collaboration with Dorothy H. Jenkins*)

The Complete Book of African Violets (1951)

The Joy of Flower Arranging

Perennials Preferred (1952)

Climbing Roses

Geraniums—Pelargoniums (1957)

Roses for Pleasure
  (*in collaboration with Richard Thomson*)

The New Perennials Preferred (1961)

The Flower Arrangement Calendar (1947-1967)

The New Complete Book of African Violets (1963)

The Joy of Geraniums (1965)

The Gardener's Book of Verse: Poems for Five Seasons
  (*an anthology*)

with Léonie Bell

The Fragrant Year

The Fragrant Year

*SCENTED PLANTS FOR YOUR GARDEN
AND YOUR HOUSE*

by Helen Van Pelt Wilson and Léonie Bell

with drawings by Léonie Bell

William Morrow & Co., Inc. New York

Designed by Millicent Fairhurst

Published simultaneously in Canada by
George J. McLeod Limited, Toronto.

Printed in the United States of America.

Library of Congress Catalog Card Number 67-15150

Fragrance:
Our Mutual Delight

Some years ago when I had a garden in suburban Philadelphia, Léonie Bell and I, who had worked on many projects together, discovered our mutual enthusiasm for fragrant plants. We agreed that even the most beautiful flowers lacked something for us if they were scentless. We read and discussed all the books we could find on the subject of scent, and regretted that the very best, *The Fragrant Path* by Louise Beebe Wilder, was so out-of-date horticulturally.

Comparing our impressions of various scents—the delicate ones discovered only by the searching nose, the freer ones that floated out on the air—we tried to analyze and classify. We often disagreed. To Léonie, a flower might have decided fragrance; to me, the odor might be weak. To her, it might smell of roses, to me of lemon. We found that other gardening enthusiasts also held divergent opinions on some scents, *but not on all*. Gradually we discovered a wide area of unanimity in identifications, at least enough to make possible the nine classifications that we have used here as the basis for our descriptions of fragrance.

This book on the subject of our keenest garden pleasure has been ten years in the making, through several books of mine and three children of Léonie's. Her garden is near Conshohocken, outside Philadelphia. There she has slowly gathered a collection of plants of every sort, learning with experience which were best scented. She now grows almost two hundred roses, most of them old, and of all fragrant plants, these are surely dearest to her. On a June day their mingled perfumes are lovely beyond words. She has recorded many in pencil, as the illustrations in this book indicate, always trying to capture a flower's evanescent beauty while cleaving to its botanical distinctions.

My present garden by a brook is close to Long Island Sound in Westport, Connecticut. Here on a couple of acres there is plenty of room for the scented trees, shrubs, and vines I have long admired. Winter temperatures do not often go below zero and summers are only briefly hot and humid. Despite distance, Léonie and I are both in the southern part of Zone 6, and so grow plants under about the same conditions. Blooming dates in Westport are sometimes a little later than in Conshohocken—more a matter of microclimate than miles, we have decided.

To avoid awkward and shifting reference from one garden to another, we have had recourse to the time-honored editorial *we,* writing of our two gardens as if they were one. In botanical nomenclature we have followed, as far as possible, *Hortus Second.* Some of this material has appeared in *Flower Grower, the Home Garden Magazine.*

We hope this book will increase your pleasure in plants and introduce you to the many fragrant ones that add a delightful fourth dimension to the garden. Because we see our visitors' enjoyment in these gardens where there is so much emphasis on fragrance, we are eager to have more plants of notable scent. We hope that hybridizers will move away from size toward scent, and that landscape designers will be as aware of the fragrance of plants as they are of their forms, flowers, and seasons. For all of you, we chronicle here our own delightful discoveries of the "pleasures of the nose."

HELEN VAN PELT WILSON

Westport, Connecticut
January 1967

Contents

Contents

List of Illustrations

List of Illustrations

xii

1

This Fragrant World

On a May morning our world is sweet with scent, so pervasive and far-reaching that even strangers linger by the road arrested by the fragrance. But we do not wait until May for such delight. In propitious years, we enjoy the fragrant vernal witch-hazel in January, wintersweet in February, and in March, *Daphne Mezereum*. At the end of that month or early in the next one, the winter honeysuckle, *Lonicera fragrantissima*, perfumes the air for yards around. April comes with a deluge of sweetness from hyacinths, andromeda, sweet violets, and star magnolias, and so it goes from month to month. Ours is indeed a fragrant year, and as Beverly Nichols remarked, "to be overpowered by the fragrance of flowers is a delectable form of defeat." Actually there are only a few weeks in the dead of winter when we are without something scented in the garden. And if the outdoors fails us, we enjoy our sunny windows where sweet-olive, heliotrope, star-jasmine, and many other plants offer scented blooms or fragrant leaves.

"PLEASURES OF THE NOSE"

Appreciation of fragrant plants is not a modern enthusiasm, and we are certainly not unique in our desire to fill our gardens mainly with flowers of sweet scent. As Rosetta Clarkson has noted in her book, *Magic Gardens,* "In ancient Greece the living rooms opened on beautiful gardens where the most fragrant plants were planted near the windows in the belief that the scent had a salutary effect on the occupants of the house. In medieval monasteries the monks planted near the infirmary sweet-smelling herbs for the benefit of their patients, and now modern science has given us reason to believe that health-giving ozone is developed from the sun's shining on the aromatic plants."

During the early seventeenth century, the Elizabethans began to devote plots to flowers alone. This innovation was given various names by garden writers of that time. Gervase Markham called it the "Garden for flowers and sweet smells." Plants of pleasant odor were especially desirable in those unsanitary years.

In 1600, Richard Surflet noted that "The Garden shall be divided into two equall parts; the one shall containe the hearbes and flowers used to make nosegaies and garlands . . . The other part shall have all the sweet smelling hearbes, whether they be such as beare no flowers, or if they beare any, yet they are not put in Nosegaies alone, but the whole hearbe with them . . . and this may be called the Garden for hearbes of good smell." (And "hearbe" here means any herbaceous plant.)

These scents that pleased the seventeenth-century Englishman and were used "for perfuming shoes, gloves, . . . linens, tobacco, snuff, candles, soap," are mainly the ones the English favor today—the light "clean" scents of violets, lavender, and rosemary. Latins usually prefer the heavier fragrances of lilies, tuberoses, and jasmine. Patchouli, sandalwood and ginger appeal to Indian peoples. The Victorians were sentimental about fragrances—"smells" they did not mention—and they loved the nosegay flowers, moss rose, lily-of-the-valley, and the sweet-leaved geraniums. They developed a language of flowers and wrote at length of the refreshment of the senses experienced when sweet odors were inhaled.

POWERS OF FRAGRANCE

If our gardens today were more often planned as fragrant retreats and our rooms were frequently perfumed with bowls of spicy pinks, bunches of aromatic herbs, vases of fragrant roses, and jars of potpourri, perhaps we would not have to depend so much on tranquilizers to hold us together in this frantic, fast-paced world. For there is sound evidence of the therapeutic value, physical and emotional, of sweet odors, especially those of aromatic herbs. It is more than hearsay that sleep comes more readily between sheets scented with lavender, which is also said "to comfort and clear the eyes." Whether the smell of rosemary does "keep thee youngly" may be open to question, but we agree it keeps us happily. Herbs smelling of mint and lemon are ever refreshing and were once used for strewing along with rue, the favorite for this purpose. There were herbs to make us merry, to cure depression, and to strengthen memory.

According to F. A. Hampton, author of a delightful book, *The Scent of Flowers and Leaves,* published in England in 1925 and now unfortunately out of print, our ancestors "invented the first antiseptic by pouring balsam into their own wounds, and the old 'Friar's Balsam' (an alcoholic solution of gum benzoin and balsam of Peru) still finds a place in the Pharmacopoeia. The antiseptic power is stronger in the leaf oils than in the flower attar . . . Eucalyptol, which occurs in nearly all scented leaves, is a powerful antiseptic, and is closely followed by oil of Thyme, Verbena, Cloves, and several others.

"Their antiseptic value faintly justified the use of Rue and Rosemary at the Old Bailey as protection against jail fever, and of the cinnamon and camphor in the doctor's gold-headed cane. 'Four Thieves' Vinegar' was an infusion of aromatic herbs and Garlic used by four robbers to protect themselves while they stripped the dead during the plague year at Marseilles in 1722 . . . It may well be that these prophylactics had a real value, not in destroying germs, but in keeping off the bugs and lice that carried them. The black plague and the purple fever have withdrawn to less civilised countries than ours, together with their attendant vermin, and the sprigs of Rue and Rosemary only persist at the Old Bailey out of our pleasant respect for old tradition. But the vermin reappeared with the relapse of civilisation in the Great War, and were proven carriers of trench fever; and once again the essential oils were used to ward them off."

The great sixteenth-century French philosopher and essayist, Montaigne, wrote of the emotional effect of pleasant odors: "Physicians might in mine opinion draw more use and good from odours than they doe. For myself have often perceived that according unto their strength and qualitie, they change and alter and move my spirits and worke strange effects in me which may prove the common saying that the invention of insense and perfumes in churches, so ancient and so far dispersed throughout all nations and religions, had a special regard to rejoyce, to comfort, to quicken, to rouse, and to purify the senses, so that we might be the apter and readier unto contemplation."

Mr. Hampton tells of the effect the beanflower had upon him: "I remember once being in the train beside the open window; I was reading, and quite absorbed in a very interesting book; presently I became aware that my heart was beating and I had my 'beanfield feeling.' I was just saying to myself, 'This book is as exciting as a beanfield,' when I looked out of the window and saw we were passing a beanfield! The effect passed off as soon as we were out of the scent zone, which proved it was not the book. It was a most delightful sensation, and the excitement pleasurable; a sort of happy, buoyant ecstasy."

MEMORIES THROUGH SCENT

"Smell is the most memoristic of scents," E. F. Benson has pointed out, and we compare recollections: "The scent of a certain old-fashioned white rose inevitably recalls to me the great bush that grew by the back door of the house where I was born and of how my little sister looked when she was just four years old. The scent of Madonna lilies brings back the picture of my first garden and how it appeared in the moonlight the June night of her death. Honeysuckle conjures up a swing made immobile by its rampant canopy, a place for confidences with my first 'best friend.' The smell of baking bread recalls my mother's graham gems that we ate hot from the oven with butter and molasses, and the batch she let burn one day in her excitement over the delivery of the grand piano; the scent of wisteria brings back the time I had chickenpox and was presented with a great flowering branch from the decorations of a party I had to miss."

That gifted chronicler of scented plants, Louise Beebe Wilder, remarks in *The Fragrant Path* that fragrance "speaks more clearly to age than to youth. With the young it may not pass much beyond the olfactory nerve, but with those who have started down the far side of the hill it reaches into the heart. No other of the five senses is more subtle in its suggestions than the sense of smell or more unmistakably reminiscent of a time and state in which one was something else and possibly something better."

ANOSMIC OR HYPEROSMIC

Then there are those to whom fragrance speaks not at all, so undeveloped is their sense of smell. We call them *anosmic*—"noses they have but smell not." Like those who are blind to color, the anosmic are insensitive to smell. Surely our friend was anosmic if in April she could stand beside our balm-tree that poured forth the aromatic fragrance of unfolding spring leaf buds and "smell nothing." The *hyperosmic* have a sharp sense of smell, not always a blessing. They "smell a rat" very quickly and are rabid about sewers. The hyperosmic make excellent perfumers and buyers of wine, tobacco, coffee, and

5

spices. However, even the hyperosmic can disagree on quality and quantity of scent.

The sense of smell can be educated. Once you become aware of scents, you will notice many that you overlooked before. It is a matter of attention and use. Appreciation comes, as it does for music by listening, for art by looking. You may begin to classify the fragrances of your garden as basically like a rose, a lily. Some flower scents will remind you of fruits; some may defy identification because they are a blend; some you won't like at all. They have a "stuffing" smell, you will say of a flowering hedge of privet or certain species of lilac, or the scent of boxwood is "disturbing." You will find that perception waxes and wanes; it is "fatigued" especially by some scents, as that of violets.

Helen Keller called the sense of smell "a fallen angel." To her it was enormously useful and she relished not only its angelic aspects but less attractive sensations. She could detect St. Louis from miles away by its brewery odors, Peoria by whisky fumes. She found Mark Twain's conversation "fragrant with tobacco."

PURPOSE OF SCENT IN PLANTS

Why, we wonder, do plants have fragrance or, in some cases, distinctly unpleasant smells? Apparently strong scents protect plants against browsing animals which are repelled by the pungency of leaf oils; or they may be for the mitigation of heat. In hot dry places, as in the Mediterranean foothills, lavender, rosemary, myrtle, bay, citrus, sage, and thyme grow in abundance and, under the hot sun, as in our own herb gardens, their scent is strong. Perhaps the vapors of their essential oils produce a kind of air conditioning. Certainly we feel cooler when we walk among our mints on a hot day.

One theory expounded by Mr. Hampton is that the purpose of fragrance in a flower is to attract the "nectar-feeding insects which fertilise it. The colour, form, and scent of the flower are adapted to

the one end of attracting or guiding insects . . . to secure cross fertilisation, and flowers do not occur except in association with these insects." Bees and butterflies often have odors much like those of the
plants dependent on their visits for fertilisation—and hence for survival. Thus stapelia smells like carrion and attracts carrion flies, and
the sickly smell of most hawthorns and pears draws other flies. Many
sweet-scented flowers—jasmine, hyacinth, honeysuckle, tuberose, narcissus—attract moths and butterflies that also have sweet scents.

In his book *In My Vicarage Garden and Elsewhere,* the Rev. Henry
A. Ellacombe, a twentieth-century student of fragrance, remarks that
"there are, of course, cases of flowers being attractive to more than
one family of insects, and there are insects, such as bees, which do not
confine themselves to one flower only, but they all work within certain fixed limits, and there are cases when, if the particular insect does
not come, the flower cannot perfect itself. The common red clover is
a well-known case in point, which so much requires the help of humble-
bees—and no other bee can help it—that Darwin believed that if humble-
bees became extinct in England the red clover would wholly disappear;
and in New Zealand it was necessary to ship a large quantity of humble-
bees from England before red clover produced any seed."

FACTORS OF TIME AND COLOR

When is the fragrance of flowers most noticeable? We observe that
the hours of strongest scent are not the same, even for the same plants.
It depends on the essential oils, which are present in varying amounts
at different times of day and night; they evaporate at different speeds and
at different temperatures. Most roses smell sweetest on a mild damp
morning as the sun strikes them, reach a crescendo at noon, and may
be scentless by night. The same flowers may pour out a stronger perfume in a protected corner than in the open, and exposure to sun, as well
as to weather, affects them. Drought and heat often rob flowers of sweetness, and flower scents vary slightly from youth to age.

Then there are the night-blooming flowers that show restraint by day—stock, nicotiana, some day-lilies, and many others. What joy their sweetness brings at twilight and through the evening hours when they are planted near a terrace or below a bedroom window. Indeed, whole gardens can be devoted to these plants for the delectation of those whose leisure time does not occur till evening.

The fragrance of most plants offers pleasure for the day. To enjoy boxwood—and many of us do while to others it is unpleasant—you must walk beside it when the sun shines full upon it and the heat releases the oils. The herb garden also is most aromatic in full sun. Leafy scents are released when we brush great plants of lavender and rosemary, or tread upon thyme growing in the interstices of flagstones, or pinch the leaves and rub our fingers with rose-geranium, mint, or lemon-verbena. Some plants are noticeably sweeter after rain. Wet leaves of boxwood have a different scent than when the sun shines full upon them, and the damp foliage of the sweetbrier or eglantine rose is richly apple-scented.

A cold spell in autumn, even a touch of light frost, sharpens some fragrances, or perhaps our perception is keener when so few scents remain as autumn closes in. We think of the sharp clear scent of sweet alyssum, particularly the purple kind, and of chrysanthemums. Francis Bacon noted that "the Nouember Rose is the sweetest, having been less exhaled by the sun."

Arbitrary association of certain kinds of scents with flower colors is almost useless in this day of widening color range in every genus. White flowers, often thick-petaled and night-blooming, have the most distinctive, intense perfumes, and moths are aware of this. Pastel-colored flowers were once thought to be dependably sweeter than dark-hued flowers, but no longer. Often, green or yellow-green blooms like those of *Cestrum Parqui, Aquilegia viridiflora,* and *Narcissus viridiflorus* compensate for their leafy colors with pronounced fragrance. The scented flowers of winter seem to be mostly yellow or cream in color and, recalling lilacs, irises, grape-hyacinths, and violets, we cannot

8

fault blue or purple. Where petals carry the essential oils, doubling of petalage results in increased fragrance and longer-lived flowers (as petals evolve from anthers). However, when the anthers contain the scent, doubling causes it to disappear, as in the full-petaled offspring of *Rosa multiflora* and many of the pompon-flowering cherries.

The connoisseur of fragrance will do well when he buys trees, shrubs, vines, even perennials, to select plants while they are in bloom in a nursery so their scent can be personally tested. There is a tremendous difference in strength of scent among specimens even of the same species. We have smelled almost scentless fringe-trees, but the one that graces our front entrance is marvelously sweet and perfumes the whole downstairs in June when the front door is open.

Fragrant plants add a fourth dimension to any garden. Why a scentless climbing rose, when 'City of York' will flood your summer bedroom with delectable scent? why *Jasminum nudiflorum* when, in the same place and for the same season, you could have Chinese witch-hazel? why a scentless silverbell when Russian olive can bewitch your walk in June? It seems to us that a garden is not complete until there is added the enchanting quality of fragrance.

2

Classification of Scents

For the gardener, there is no more delightful classification of scents than that of Francis Bacon in his essay "Of Gardens," written in the late sixteenth century. "And because the breath of flowers is far sweeter in the air (where it comes and goes like the warbling of music) than in the hand, therefore nothing is more fit for that delight, than to know what be the flowers and plants that do best perfume the air. Roses, damask and red, are fast flowers of their smells; so that you may walk by a whole row of them, and find nothing of their sweetness; yea though it be in a morning's dew. Bays likewise yield no smell as they grow. Rosemary little; nor sweet marjoram. That which above all others yields the sweetest smell in the air, is the violet, specially the white double violet, which comes twice a year; about the middle of April, and about Bartholomew-tide. Next to that is the musk-rose. Then the strawberry-leaves dying, with a most excellent cordial smell. Then the flower of the vines; it is a little dust, like the dust of a bent, which grows upon the cluster in the first coming forth. Then sweet-briar. Then wall-flowers, which are very delightful to be set under a parlour or lower chamber window. Then pinks and gilliflowers, specially the matted pink and clove gilliflower. Then the flowers of the lime-tree. Then the honeysuckles, so they be some-what afar off. Of bean-flowers I speak not, because they are field flowers. But those which perfume the air most delightfully, not passed by as the rest, but being trodden upon and crushed, are three; that is, burnet, wild-thyme, and watermints. Therefore you are to set whole alleys of them, to have the pleasure when you walk or tread."

For the most part, Bacon's analysis holds, even after four centuries, and we forgive his slight to roses because autumn Damask and cabbage-rose were unknown to him. As for us, honeysuckles need not "be somewhat afar off." Bacon might have added that many herbs are "free" in full sun, and that flowers "fast of their smells" in the garden are often free indoors.

In the eighteenth century, the great Swedish botanist Linnaeus—that inveterate classifier—was the first to attempt placing flower odors into categories with appropriate examples. Canon H. N. Ellacombe lists them for us: AMBROSIACA, as musk, sweet-scented geranium; FRAGRANTIA, as pinks, jasmine, violets, and the leaves of lavender, thyme, balm; ARO-MATICA (similar in taste and smell), as cinnamon, camphor, orange; GRAVEOLENTIA, subdivided into ALLIACEA, as onions, garlick, asafoetida, and HIRCINA, as Herb Robert; TETRA, as hemp, elder; NAUSEOLA, pro-ducing sickness as veratrum, tobacco.

These divisions amuse us now, but they were a beginning. By the twentieth century it became obvious that plant scents came from chemical substances. Count Kerner von Marilaun in 1893 devised groups according to predominating essential oils, six of them, but these too became invalid as more was learned of floral chemistry.

THE HAMPTON CLASSIFICATIONS

In his book on scents, Mr. Hampton improved upon von Marilaun's scheme with one of his own—more complicated, admittedly "tentative and rather rough," yet important as another step in the evolution of our own arrangement. His groups, with descriptions and examples, included: INDOLID OR FOETID, Stapelia; AMINOID, stale or fishy, Hawthorn; HEAVY, very sweet, Jasmine; AROMATIC, spicy, which he divided into BALSAMIC, Hyacinth, and CLOVE, Carnation; ANISE, Cowslip; VANILLA, Azara; ALMOND, Twinflower; HAWTHORN, Choisya. Next came VIOLET as in sweet Violets, sweet but less heavy than flowers in preceding groups; ROSE, sweet but not heavy as in certain Roses; LEMON, light, fresh, Bullbay Magnolia; FRUIT-SCENTED, fruity, Little-leaf Mock-orange; ANIMAL, goatlike, unpleasant, Lizard Orchid; and MUSK-HONEY, sweet, often rather dry, dusty, Musk Orchid.

Enthusiastic about Hampton's groupings at first, we came to realize they would not do for us. His examples were often of obscure plants, possibly English natives, seldom grown in this country. His term "balsamic," used to describe hyacinth, flowering tobacco, night-scented stock, bore no relation to our idea of balsam, the resinous aroma of pine or fir. His inclusion of noxious odors, two whole groups of them, seemed to give repulsive smells undue attention. Furthermore, we hesitated to delve too deep into the fascinating mystery of flower fragrances; labeling each component with a chemical name somehow ruins the pleasure of experiencing an exquisite blend—as if French *parfumeurs* were to identify their creations by formulae!

FRAGRANCE RECLASSIFIED

Why bother, then, to classify at all? Because we feel it is the only way to lift some of the subjectivity from the act of smelling and to discover how floral scents are related to one another. If five people give five disparate descriptions of the same fragrance, the excuse is invariably, "But scent is subjective! Everyone gets something different." Yet without necessarily liking them, we all agree on the tastes of orange, chocolate, and celery, and we identify the smells of bacon, cheese, cloves, because we have experienced them all our lives. With experience, we come to agree on garden odors, too, for in the limited floral world, every distinguishable scent arises from a particular compound, wherever and whenever it occurs.

More than nineteen hundred years ago Lucretius noted that odors, though invisible, had actual substance. Scorned for centuries, his theory has now been proved. Scent comes from molecules that are perceived by olfactory cells in two nerve-rich pads in the roof of the nose.

A flower with stable fragrance, like apple-blossom or lily-of-the-valley or gardenia, smells the same throughout its brief life, season after season, despite physical factors. Scented leaves are consistent and so are most flowers, like simple notes of music. It is the blends—or chords—that confuse, but once basic odors are committed to memory, their elements become recognizable. Educating a sense of smell takes time and persistence, but the quest is a daily adventure. While we are attempting to memorize scents, we must be willing to poke a nose into everything, to be open-minded to new smells, even risking occasional unpleasant ones—for they are part of the learning process, too.

This reclassification, then, attempts to arrange fragrances as objectively as possible. Many opinions besides our own have been sought and recorded with the gratifying discovery that we are not alone: other experienced noses have the same reactions as ours. *Preferences are still subjective, but identification of the odors themselves is consistent.*

We do not expect to find heavy perfume in a rose, nor the bouquet of fruit in a violet. The many blends are unaccounted for but involve two or more of our nine basic types. The types themselves may overlap and as far as it is practical, this is indicated in the sequence.

MODERN CLASSIFICATIONS OF FRAGRANCE

Balsamic. This type of fragrance is found only in leaves that contain essential oils as menthol, eucalyptol, balsam, camphor, wintergreen. SOME BALSAMIC-SCENTED PLANTS: mints (*Mentha*); lavender (*Lavandula*); sages (*Salvia*); rosemary (*Rosmarinus*); wormwood (*Artemisia*).

Spicy. Found in leaves *or* flowers, often blended with the Heavy types or with one of the Balsamics—scents as clove, cinnamon, pepper, anise, nutmeg. SOME SPICY-SCENTED PLANTS: carnation (*Dianthus Caryophyllus*) and pink (*Dianthus*); azalea (*Rhododendron*); fennel (*Foeniculum vulgare*); nasturtium (*Tropaeolum*).

Heavy. Not one example, but several, typified by the flower names they bear; all have a free and penetrating perfume, possibly unpleasant in confinement, and often apparent in blends with other types and in other genera besides their own. We tend to think of the Heavy-scenteds as tropical, as indeed most are. SOME HEAVY-SCENTED PLANTS: auratum lily (*Lilium auratum*); jasmine (*Jasminum officinale* var. *grandiflorum*); orange-blossom (*Citrus Aurantium*)—*not* the same orange scent as listed later in the Fruited group; gardenia (*Gardenia jasminoides*); jonquil (*Narcissus Jonquilla*); cestrum (*Cestrum nocturnum*).

Sweet. Found in many flowers, and in some grasses and ferns. This fragrance progresses from a gentle lightness through the sugariness of watermelon to the strength of either honeysuckle or heliotrope (splitting, as it were, toward either the Heavy-scented, above, or the Honeyed, below). The scent of vanilla belongs here, too. SOME SWEET-SCENTED PLANTS: clover (*Trifolium*); fringe-tree (*Chionanthus virginica*); elder (*Sambucus canadensis*); honeysuckle (*Lonicera*); heliotrope (*Heliotropium*); crinum (*Crinum*).

Honeyed. Possibly the largest group, it is divided into three sub-categories:

(a) Dry, musty, almondlike, sweet. PLANTS: hawthorn (*Crataegus Oxyacantha*); trailing arbutus (*Epigaea*).

(b) Yeasty, from sweet to offensively strong. PLANTS: barberry (*Berberis verruculosa*); Oregon holly-grape (*Mahonia Aquifolium*); broom (*Cytisus praecox*).

(c) Musky, fermented, sweet. PLANTS: Bechtel's crabapple (*Malus ioensis* 'Bechtel's'); hybrid musk roses (hybrids of *Rosa moschata*).

Fruited. Found in either flowers or foliage; subdivisions are listed more or less in the order they occur in blends with the Honeyed and Violet-scented types:

(a) Grapelike. PLANTS: mignonette (*Reseda*); grape (*Vitis*); grape-hyacinth (*Muscari*); the flowers of box (*Buxus*).

(b) Pineapple-orange or mango. PLANTS: magnolia (*Magnolia*); broom (*Cytisus Battandieri*); polyanthus narcissus (*Narcissus Tazetta* 'Soleil d'Or').

(c) Nectarine, plum, peach, apricot. PLANTS: sweet-olive (*Osmanthus fragrans*); hybrid tea roses.

(d) Lemon, orange. PLANTS: geraniums (*Pelargonium*); lemon-verbena (*Lippia citriodora*); passion-flower (*Passiflora*).

Violet. Perhaps an extension of Fruited(a); so pure and characteristic, it cannot be mistaken. SOME VIOLET-SCENTED PLANTS: sweet violet (*Viola odorata*); Siberian crabapple (*Malus baccata*).

Rose. The attar of perfumes, rosewater, syrups, confections. All roses do not contain this; it predominates in the old European garden sorts, and is found also in root-woods. SOME ROSE-SCENTED PLANTS: roses (*Rosa*); a few peonies (*Paeonia*); winter honeysuckle (*Lonicera fragrantissima*); leatherleaf mahonia (*Mahonia Bealei*).

Unique. Comparable to Heavy, but refined; may be found in pure form in other genera than their own but seldom in blends. SOME UNIQUE-SCENTED PLANTS: lily-of-the-valley (*Convallaria*); sweet-pea (*Lathyrus odoratus*); some irises (*Iris*); wisteria (*Wisteria*); common lilac (*Syringa vulgaris*).

3

Fragrant Possibilities
for the Winter Garden

Winter sets in for us, regardless of the calendar, when frost checks the outdoor garden—not the early "tomato frost" from which many plants recover to go on blooming, but the "killing frost" that usually occurs well before Thanksgiving. This terminates our outdoor year which is not resumed until work is possible toward the end of March or early April. Then we consider that winter has passed. In November the smell of dry leaves and smouldering leaf piles gives way to the dry crisp smell of winter, and when this has a certain bleak overtone, it presages snow to the weatherwise. After the hurly-burly of the final garden cleanup, we turn gratefully to fireside hours with books; we enjoy the fragrant burning of well-seasoned fruit woods—apple and pear, plum and cherry—and we throw into the blaze faggots of aromatic lavender, wormwood, and costmary that we have saved for this cold-weather pleasure, and pine cones, too, gathered on late walks in autumn.

Outside, the winter garden—optimistically planned—still offers us flowers with various shrubs to brighten the dull months, their blooming not certain every year but worth planting for the successful seasons, the time of their appearance dependent, of course, on the weather. And we have sweet violets in October and November, four crocus species in a December-into-February series, with the spring snowflake for January. From year to year we are challenged by other fragrant plants that just might come through if we could find enough sunny out-of-the-wind spots for them or build that walled garden so prominent in the dreams of every true gardener. But for dependable cold-weather color and fragrance, we count particularly on the witch-hazels, daphnes, wintersweet, and fragrant guelder, and we appreciate the seasons when the leatherleaf mahonia and sweet-box also make it.

THE FRAGRANT WITCH-HAZELS

Three fragrant witch-hazels bloom in the cold—*Hamamelis virginiana, H. vernalis,* and *H. mollis,* in that order. You can have others if you like, but we choose these for their excellent scent.

The native common witch-hazel, *H. virginiana,* a small tree, brightens moist woodlands throughout the East. It is the last hardy shrub to bloom and a handsome sight indeed. After its golden leaves have fallen in late October, a profusion of lemon-yellow, spidery clusters open to cheer us with one last bright fling before winter. These have a sweet musty scent and are followed by capsules from which seeds are forcibly ejected. In a brown pottery pitcher with pine, this yellow witch-hazel makes a lovely bouquet. On a thinly wooded slope on the far side of a brook, it grows with hemlock, laurel, and azaleas in a spot open to the sky, for it requires full light for good blooming. Here it is fully seen from the house and much appreciated in the dull landscape.

The smaller vernal witch-hazel, *H. vernalis,* grows near a seat at

Hamamelis mollis

the edge of the Round Garden. There in good years it is a golden, late-February surprise or a welcome harbinger of spring. Another clump of *H. vernalis* flourishes outside a ground-floor north window that we wanted to screen. The first year there the soil was improved with peatmoss; now, ten winters later, growth has reached as many feet. On the first mild day of January, branches are covered with short yellow or orange curls that last two whole months. When pieces are cut for a vase indoors, the scent permeates a room with a sweet yeasty aroma like that of risen bread dough.

The Chinese witch-hazel, *H. mollis,* usually grafted on *H. vernalis,* requires some four years to develop flowering wood. Velvety buds are set by August, but do not unfurl until a warm spell in February or even March. Their fragrance is unbelievable, the pure delicious perfume of jonquil, and it carries many yards. If the weather turns cold, the ribbons roll right up again like the noise-makers of children's birthday parties. In rare years of unusual cold, buds do not survive the first month of the year, but the risk is worth taking for the odd years of success. Usually this Chinese witch-hazel blooms after the wintersweet but sometimes they come together.

WINTERSWEET

The cherished wintersweet, *Chimonanthus praecox (Meratia praecox)*, long considered winter-hardy only in the South, is a fragrant fact much farther north. In Philadelphia some plants have come through many harsh winters, as large and ancient specimens attest. Where temperatures go much below 10 degrees F and stay there, however, wintersweet suffers. The flowers begin as little balls easily detected in early fall in the leaf axils of five-year or older plants. First they swell to fat golden peas; when open, their overall color is sheer yellow, so transparent that the shadow lines of outer sepals are visible within. Flowers are stemless, perched snugly against gray twigs, opening up-

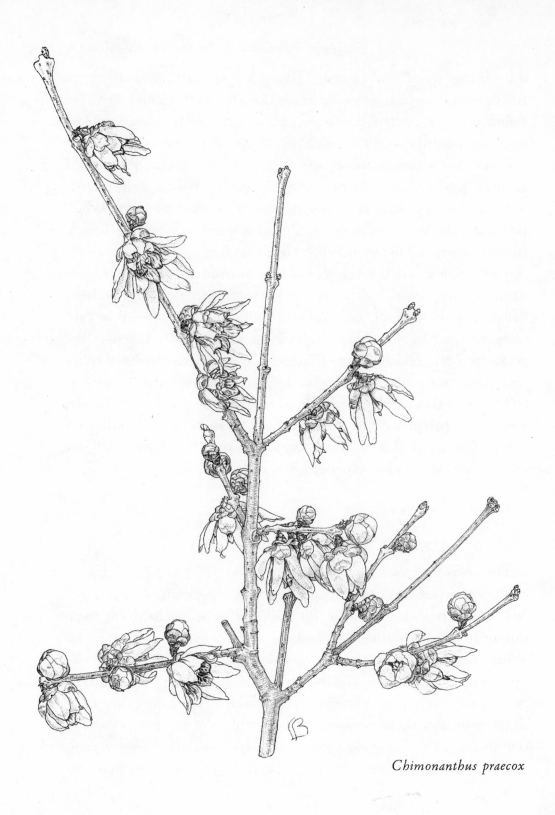

Chimonanthus praecox

side-down more often than not. To some the fragrance suggests honey-suckle; we find it like poets jessamine—far-carrying, never heavy, exquisite, a perfume of which we cannot get enough. Seedlings give rise to plants that differ in small ways, though all have the intense fragrance. Two "improved" forms, var. *grandiflorus,* with flowers half again as large and wider sepals, and var. *luteus,* a prolific opaque yellow, do not tempt us whose main desire is off-season fragrance, for they have some but not enough.

Location is important, particularly protection from wind in January and February. Plant wintersweet to receive afternoon sun, if you can, to insure that buds set and wood hardens. Either acid or sweet soil is satisfactory. Like many of the most fragrant shrubs, winter-sweet hardly makes a handsome specimen and for many months could well be out of sight in a corner like ours where in time the plants can be espaliered. In a large garden, in an area where the temperature does not go below zero, wintersweet does well in a high sunny spot. There, like its relative, sweet-shrub (*Calycanthus floridus*), it could grow to 8 feet. To prune, shorten the new flowerless growth by about half and trim back the side shoots that have bloomed to 2 to 3 inches. But if you have been regularly perfuming your winter rooms with cuttings from a big plant, that is pruning enough.

AZARA AND APRICOT

Two other woody winter-blooming plants are of borderline hardiness but worth a try for their fine fragrance. *Azara microphylla,* with no common name, comes from Chile. Cold seems not to harm it so much as wind and early morning winter sun, so plant where it can thaw slowly. Tall and rangy to 10 feet or more, azara makes an attractive espalier, and out of the wind it is hardy at least to Washington, D. C. In a cool greenhouse, plants bloom from February through April. The little greenish-yellow blossoms, mostly stamens, nestle under small lacquered leaves. Although flowers are hardly noticeable, their perfume is extraordinary; you cannot walk in the vicinity of a plant without being overwhelmed with the scent of pure vanilla— even a few sprigs fill a room with sweetness.

The Japanese apricot, *Prunus Mume* (pronounced mū'meh), is more tree than shrub and familiar from Chinese paintings. If peaches succeed in your area, no doubt *P. Mume* will too. The wood is hardier than the flower buds whose urge to open in the first warmth of the new year sometimes destroys them. The snowy bloom suggests jonquil fragrance and is perceptible far away. However, it may be that the scent differs from one variety to another, for it has been likened to hyacinth and clove, even to lilies, and a few clones with doubled flowers have little or no scent. *P. Mume* is uncommonly hard to find so seek the assistance of your nurseryman.

DAPHNES FOR WINTER

Among the lovely daphnes, treasured wherever they can be grown, are two scented species for possible cold-weather bloom. The spreading winter-daphne, *Daphne odora* (declared the most powerfully fragrant plant in the world and surely it is one of them), with its variegated form, var. *marginata,* may reach 3 feet in ten years. It sometimes flowers by late November but more often not until early March. The upright February daphne, *D. Mezereum,* easily 3 to 4 feet, always waits until late March and often the two come charmingly together. In some years, there are also final flowers in December on the rose-daphne, *D. Cneorum,* that from May on offers intermittent sweetness.

Most of the daphnes are marvelously free of their fragrance. That of *D. odora* suggests the old-fashioned dessert, ambrosia, orangey with a strong undercurrent of coconut. Just a few flowers richly perfume the air for some distance and three weeks of bloom are a good possibility. In the mild Northwest, *D. odora* is a common dooryard plant and cultivars like 'Rose Queen', of deeper color than the usual cream-and-pink, are available there. In the East both *D. odora* and var. *marginata,*

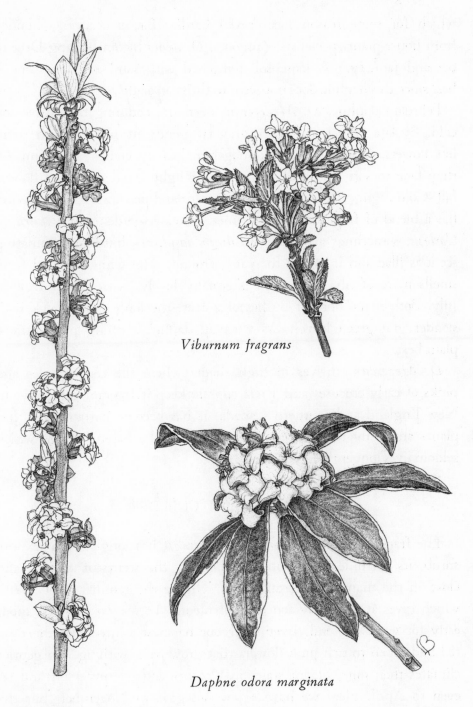

Viburnum fragrans

Daphne odora marginata

Daphne Mezereum

which for some reason has proved hardier for us, can be obtained from house-plant specialists. (Indoors, *D. odora* blooms during December and January.) A loose soil lightened with sand and limestone is best since this daphne does not seem to thrive in acidity.

February daphne, *D. Mezereum,* needs no coddling but thrives on cold. By late March the thick gray twig-ends are massed with stemless flowers. Opening a frank magenta, heavily creped and dimpled, they fade to soft rose, and then tufts of light green appear as flowers fall. Cold nights allow three weeks of color and perfume. *D. Mezereum* has a blend of fragrances—sometimes the clove-gardenia of *Viburnum Carlesii,* sometimes a breath of *Lilium auratum*—but the dominating scent is lilac and it carries for yards around. The white-flowered form smells more of lily alone, and is equally lovely, with amber fruit in July. Both make upright bushes of 4 feet, the long shoots thick with slender gray-green leaves. As with all daphnes, young plants transplant best.

D. Mezereum thrives in high shade, where the cool purples and pinks of early crocuses and *Viola odorata* keep it fragrant company. In New England and southern Canada, it has become naturalized. New plants are easily raised from seed to replace the parent shrub, which seldom lives longer than ten years.

THE FRAGRANT GUELDER

The fragrant guelder, *Viburnum fragrans,* has long been a favorite shrub, its perfume mysteriously combining the scents of wisteria and clove in the manner of certain lilacs. Unlike the familiar *V. Carlesii,* which gives at best only ten days of bloom, *V. fragrans* flowers modestly for weeks on end. Even after our harshest winters, all the rosered buds open to rich pink flowers that grow paler with age. In gentler climates than ours, bloom starts in October and continues off and on even to April. Here we have a few nosegays in November, but the main display comes in March.

Viburnum fragrans, brought from China by Reginald Farrer some fifty years ago, grows to 6 feet or more and develops a well-rounded form with branches to the ground. To encourage side shoots that terminate in flower buds, pinch out the tips of new growth in May. Soil type is not important. This lovely shrub has proved hardy in both exposed and sheltered positions. We have one plant in the open, another at a corner of the house where casement windows can be "cracked" to enjoy it when weather permits.

The rosy bloom of fragrant guelder is not easily shattered. In mid-March we saw a plant in full bloom in a friend's garden in Toronto but covered one day with snow. Next day, when the snow had melted, the flowers were still scented and beautiful. This bush stood by a great bowed plant window and leaned somewhat toward it, making a lovely open background for the green foliage plants and pots of daffodils and hyacinths within.

LEATHERLEAF MAHONIA AND SWEET-BOX

The well-considered garden, from early to late March, has many other fragrant tenants, among them two evergreen shrubs. Both of these are plant-hardy for us even through severe cold, but they do not bloom reliably. We think them worth having for the two years in three when they do flower. Leatherleaf mahonia, *Mahonia Bealei,* enters winter with a crest of budded stems in a nest of fiercely prickled leaves at the top of every "trunk." In late February or early March the 6-inch strings of beads swell into lemon-yellow bells, hundreds of them, perfumed with roses and lily-of-the-valley. Quite astounding is this sweet assault in a garden still wearing the look of winter. Leatherleaf blooms a full month before the familiar *M. Aquifolium,* and it grows slowly, perhaps 6 inches a year. You can readily keep it below its possible 6 to 8 feet by pruning back the stout canes of umbrella foliage in early spring.

Creeping sweet-box, *Sarcococca Hookeriana humilis,* seldom exceeds 15 inches and seems to us unique in providing rich and shining black-green foliage in complete shade. Best bloom follows deep snow, and the scent is the musk-grape bouquet of mignonette, which is also apparent in the flowers of the related *Buxus microphylla.*

SWEET VIOLETS

Sweet violet, *Viola odorata,* is the last scented perennial of autumn, and even in the coldest gardens, the first of spring. One warm day in March draws up buds and another sees them open. The fragrance reaches out to snare you into stopping, marveling. Pick a few to inhale their goodness close up—three or four deep sniffs are all you'll get—"sweet, not lasting, the perfume and suppliance of a minute, no more". The essence of violet has a soporific effect on olfactory nerves, which means the fragrance isn't used up, but you are unable to smell it for awhile. The hothouse violets sold by florists seem to have no scent.

The end of the growing season for most plants is really the beginning for violets since short cool days are needed to trigger bud formation. In a greenhouse or well-insulated coldframe or a coldframe with an electric cable, you can have bloom from September to April. In the open garden without protection, you can also enjoy sweet violets, but briefly in fall, then for a longer time late in winter. Or if, like us, you consider this natural season of cold-weather blooming too brief, you can compromise, cover clumps in mid-October with a commercial cloche or homemade glass-topped box, and have an extra fall month of scented violet blooms as well as an earlier start in February.

Sweet violets must have *full sun in fall and winter.* They are often recommended as groundcovers in shade where the *plants* will do well but won't bloom much. However, the summer shade of trees or bushes that leaf out late will do, if all your sunny sheltered corners

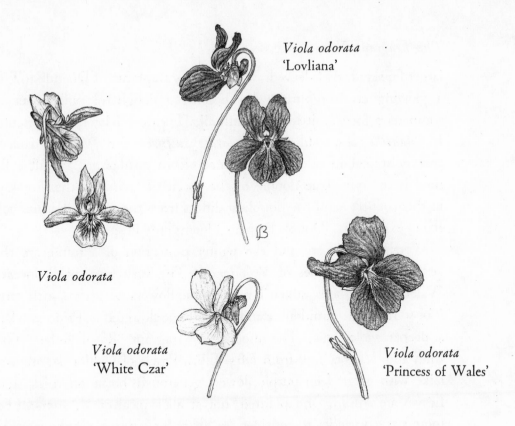

Viola odorata
'Lovliana'

Viola odorata

Viola odorata
'White Czar'

Viola odorata
'Princess of Wales'

are filled up. To get larger flowers with longer stems, work in plenty of well-aged compost and a little ground limestone. If soil is acid, scratch in more lime every year, for sweet violets *do not thrive in acid loam,* though they may exist there. As buds form, water well with a soluble plant food.

Among the small-flowered, richly scented color variants of the wild *V. odorata* we find several that are easy to grow and lovely for naturalizing. The incredibly fragrant *V. odorata semperflorens* is "everblooming" only where summers are cool and moist; for us it blooms in October and briefly in March. It has seeded freely in full sun even on poor soil. Flowers are small, intensely purple, and appear by the hundreds over 4-inch mounds of leaves. Old, beloved var. *rosina* is the mauve-pink version of this, but 'Rochelle' is better, really rose-pink with no grapey overcast. White 'Palustris', which blooms only in spring, is not the American species of this name (*V. palustris*), but a typical soft-leaved *V. odorata* with small pure white flowers. 'White Czar' is

27

larger-flowered, dark-leaved. The intensely fragrant 'El Duende' ('Elf'), a glowing crimson-purple, has become a delightful bulb cover and companion for the little early daffodil, 'Trumpet Major' (Buttercups). *V. glabella,* also sold as *V. odorata sulfurea* and 'Vilmoriniana', is creamy apricot in color and does not bloom until April. 'Double Russian' is the only true double of the species *V. odorata* that we know in this country, and the doubling differs from that of the Parma violet. In our experience, 'Double Russian' blooms only in spring.

Worth special care and the winter protection of a frame are these large-flowered varieties of *V. odorata:* The very fragrant 'Princess of Wales' bears superb, silken lavender-blue flowers, at least 1 inch across. Not so fragrant, semidouble and just as large-flowered is 'Princess Mary', a deeper violet-blue. The moderately fragrant 'Royal Robe', 'Giant Elk', and 'Victory', all from Mrs. Edith Pawla of California, are much alike with great deep purple flowers generously borne on thick stems. Leaves are shining and pointed, not at all typical of *V. odorata.* Four more sweet varieties to consider are, first, for autumn emphasis, 'Texas Tommy' ('Blue Bird') with long-stemmed light-blue flowers; the exceedingly sweet 'Lovliana', a warm purple; 'Little Papoose', a grayed rose; and 'Australian Red' as close to red as any.

Sweet violets have three enemies, not the least of which is our invasive dooryard kind, *Viola papilionacea,* which has no fragrance whatever. It will seed right in the midst of sweet violets and soon smother the low-growing *V. odorata* with its taller shining pointed leaves. In lists of perennials, the two are often confused; a large white, 'Snow Princess', quite scentless, is often sold for fragrant 'White Czar'. Slugs are to be watched for and routed; and in dry summer weeks, red spider must be avoided with frequent hosings.

The intensely fragrant Parma violets, with glossy pointed leaves, are so distinct as to appear another species, though they are a form of *Viola odorata* var. *pallida plena,* the Neapolitan violet. The long-stemmed, long-lasting double flowers with large rounded, ruffled petals come mostly in lavenders. One is pure white, the magnificent

'Swanley', which as 'Comte De Brazza' was a great favorite in the Edwardian era. 'Neapolitan'—lavender paling to a white center, 'Duchesse de Parme' (or simply 'de Parme')—another silky lavender, and 'Marie Louise'—rich lavender-blue, are the *three most fragrant violets in existence*. The tender Parmas may bloom half the year, but take long to recover from even a little frost. Yet they thrive in cold air that is seldom over 50 degrees F. If you have a greenhouse kept just above freezing, or a well insulated—and well tended—coldframe, you can have six months of exquisitely scented Parma violets—a goal worth some effort.

A WINTER IRIS

The Algerian iris, *Iris unguicularis* (*Iris stylosa*), is another tantalizing winter-blooming plant that makes gardeners here wish for Decembers a few degrees warmer. In California and the South it blooms outdoors from November to March with a scent of honey and cowslips, the epitome of spring. Getting it to survive and bloom here is a challenge.

New divisions are difficult to establish but, once roots go deep, a cold frame should bring plants safely through our worst weather. Transplanting in late summer when new roots form is recommended, but as this is too late here, we have potted pieces to grow in the cold window with house plants or in a coldframe with violets. By spring they are ready to plant outdoors in a sun-pocket. A mulch of wood ashes discourages slugs.

Blooming begins on warm days in January or February, the buds emerging from the center of a tangle of leaves. The beardless flowers are lavender of a shimmering quality, beautifully veined and patterned. To enjoy them fully, unflawed by slugs, gently break off buds when stems are about 4 inches high and place in water, to watch unfurl slowly and to breath their enchanting scent.

CROCUS AND SPRING SNOWFLAKE

Toward the end of October, and in exciting succession into February, our garden is graced by four musty-honey scented crocuses, all in tints of lavender with brilliant orange stigmata revealed when the cups are fully opened. *Crocus longiflorus* is the sweetest one. Newly planted bulbs bloom in early December, established clumps usually before the end of October and for two weeks or longer. *C. laevigatus Fontenayi* appears any time from early December to late January. Grow it through a dense mat of *Phlox subulata* and it will bloom even in the depth of winter. *C. Sieberi* will not show color in snow but wait for a mild open day. Sometimes the spread of lavender appears as early as January. *C. Imperati* produces the largest and latest bloom of this quartet in the first warm days of February, with a few flowers opening at a time.

For late winter, from January on, the spring snowflake, *Leucojum vernum,* a sweet bellflower with dangles of white bloom is a treasure. Plant as many bulbs as you can so there will be some to spare for picking. On a cold day the vaguely violet scent is truly enchanting. Select a spot easily observed, and with morning sun. Mix in sand and wood ashes for these dependably hardy bulbs.

With the advent of the snowflakes and the blooms of *Crocus Imperati,* the progression of outdoor scented winter plants—so deeply appreciated for they are all too few—gives place to the great perfumed multitudes of spring.

4

Spring Scents of
Shrubs and Trees

Every year spring knocks at our door in the same unmistakable fragrant way. We know the winter is gone the morning our great honeysuckle shrub casts its sweetness on the March air and makes that day so different from the one just past. Our most devastating winters cannot hurt the dormant buds, only delay their opening, and bloom even by the end of February is possible. Any warm day brings out more of the little flowers, stubby replicas of the summer honeysuckles, a translucent cream turning buff-yellow. It is no brief pleasure that this early shrub affords, for it continues to enchant us—and everyone else—for two months or more. A diary note of May twenty-third reads, "The honeysuckle is almost over; still fragrant if you sniff the branches but the strong delectable perfume that reached the back door is gone now." And the back door is a full 30 feet away.

This winter honeysuckle, *Lonicera fragrantissima*, can grow to 15 feet. Supposedly a straggler, it becomes a handsome cascade if properly pruned, or it can be trained flat against a house wall and around windows. We grow it this way, too, and it is decorative well into December for the oval leaves stay green that late. How to describe the fragrance? Plants differ, as do noses, but it seems to us pure geraniol, the irrisistible far-reaching scent of some roses. *L. Standishii* grows half as high and blooms about the same time with thinner flowers. The hybrid, *L. ×Purpusii,* makes a small bush for garden use, the bloom more showy than that of either parent, and just as fragrant. Even so, *L. fragrantissima* remains our favorite for gracing leafless winter walls. In some years, the winter *Daphne odora* and February *D. Mezereum* bloom with it, and the blend of sweetness is then so marvelous we do not stir from home.

THE SCENTED SHRUBS

Indeed the scents of April and early May assail us on every hand. This is one of the best of seasons for those who enjoy fragrant plants. Now many shrubs broadcast delectable perfumes, hyacinths and narcissus offer their sweet blooms, while overhead fruit trees burgeon and the colorful pageant of crabapples and magnolias begins.

The buds of andromeda, *Pieris japonica,* swell in late March and continue for a month. A large shrub festooned with drooping braids of papery bells, it has a far-reaching vinous bouquet of mignonette. Toward the end of flowering, the leaf whorls sprout three or four glistening amber shoots that give the look of a second lilylike blooming. Since plants differ in fragrance and also in foliage coloring, it is worth waiting to select *Pieris* in a nursery in late April.

Andromeda does not require extreme acidity so long as soil has been lightened with peatmoss and sand and is adequately moist. High shade with a little sun is best. Flower buds form in early fall and hang like bunches of little knotted strings, on some plants remaining green, on others turning a deep rose. The umbrella leaves keep their good green all winter, never bronzing. Indeed there is never a day when a flourishing

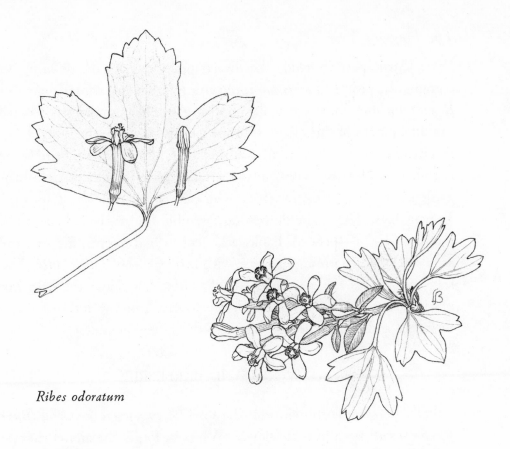

Ribes odoratum

andromeda is not worth admiring. The popular name, lily-of-the-valley shrub, refers to the flowers, not to the scent. The variegated form, *P. japonica variegata,* less hardy than the type, can be grown indoors.

By mid-April the too-little appreciated clove currant of the Midwest, *Ribes odoratum,* is as showy as forsythia but with the scent of a thousand pinks. In *The Garden's Story,* George H. Ellwanger remarks, "A shrub will perfume a garden, a bunch of it a hall, and its bouquet is as spicy as that of the yellow St. Peray wine . . . the favorite of Dumas pérè. The bees crowd around its yellow blossoms and its honey should be worth its apothecary weight in gold." We realize that *Ribes* is the alternate host of white pine blister-rust, although our own nearby pines have not been affected. However, distance between the two is indicated.

Beyond the Rockies grows *R. aureum,* golden currant, often confused with clove currant but lacking its vigor and intensity of scent. Fragrant

West Coast species include the dwarf, pink-flowering *R. cereum,* wax currant; the pink *R. malvaceum,* blooming in fall and winter there; and *R. sanguineum,* with spectacular crimson April bloom modestly scented; a prolific variant of this, 'King Edward VII', is offered in the East.

The Korean "white forsythia," abelialeaf (*Abeliophyllum distichum*), is a small shrub of too recent introduction to have found a place in many gardens, but rewarding for those who cannot get enough of spring in its first days. The white flowers do resemble forsythia in their form— four-parted, curly-petaled. If pieces are cut in bud to open indoors, they are a soft pink, charming in a vase with little stems of *Puschkinia.* Their fragrance carries far, a warm scent of honey that draws the bees from nearby crocus and squills. Abelialeaf is as easy to grow and as hardy as forsythia, and quickly becomes an attractive 5-foot mound.

BOXWOOD AND BARBERRIES

We have great enthusiasm for the smell of evergreen boxwood, *Buxus sempervirens,* both leaf and flower. Who can forget the aroma that pervades a town like Williamsburg where boxwood is so freely planted? Whether diffused by rain or volatilized in hot sun, the leaves suggest, as Oliver Wendell Holmes wrote, "the fragrance of eternity, for this is one of the odors which carry us out of time into the abysses of the unbeginning past; if we ever lived on another ball of stone than this, it must be that there was Box growing on it."

Some noses cannot abide box "inasmuch as it is of a naughtie smell." Parkinson did not care for "the ill sent that Boxe hath." According to Mrs. Earle, in her book *Old Time Gardens,* ". . . the unique aroma of Box, cleanly bitter in scent as in taste, is . . . almost hypnotic in its effect. This strange power is not felt by all, nor is it a present sensory influence; it is an hereditary memory, half-known by many, but fixed in its intensity in those of New England birth and descent, true children of the Puritans; to such ones the Box breathes out the very atmosphere of New England's past." In spite of such descriptions as clean, bitter, warm, aro-

matic, even sweet, box smells sour, feline, pleasantly but definitely of cat
—and we love it.

In April, box blooms with countless tiny, inconspicuous yellow-green
flowers. They have a distinctly sweet bouquet of their own, a melding
of honey and grape-flower or mignonette that catches our attention in
passing to trace the origin of the mysterious sweetness. Littleleaf box,
B. microphylla, lacks the pungent leaves but has even stronger floral
perfume on a low, hardy mound.

Barberries open now, and the strong scent of the most of them is certainly not perfume, but there are two that do smell sweet, both good-
looking evergreens. The hardy dwarf *Berberis buxifolia* with tiny rounded
leaves is hung with golden bells, heavy with a honey musty fragrance out
of all proportion to their size. Fiercely prickled *B. verruculosa* is our
favorite with its pale yellow globes dangling beneath arching twigs; the
smell is extremely sweet and yeasty, the marvelous smell of fresh-baked
bread.

Oregon holly-grape, *Mahonia Aquifolium,* is a handsome plant with
a gleaming red-touched evergreen leaf; it bears chartreuse tufted blooms,
fermentedly sweet. You must come close to enjoy the scent since it is
not spilled out. Flowering continues for a month under dining-room windows in a northwest location with laurel and hyacinths. We find mahonia
charming in bouquets of lavender lilacs for it accents their fragrance and

Berberis verruculosa

lightens the coloring. Leaves resemble holly and the decorative summer clusters of blue-bloomed berries do look like grapes, hence the popular name for Oregon's state flower.

THE GREAT VIBURNUM CLAN

Every viburnum has scent, too often an effluvium; the truly perfumed few come from the Orient. We have already spoken of the possible winter pleasure of the fragrant guelder, *Viburnum fragrans.*

Words fail us when we try to express our admiration for another Oriental, *V. Carlesii.* We are always adding plants of it to be sure no part of the garden will be without the tantalizing blend of carnation and gardenia that this flower dispels so freely. In March, bud clusters swell and redden; usually by late April or early May the flowers begin. Such a red-letter day is this! We keep an eye on the plant all morning as one side of the bush opens in the warm sunshine. In two days more, the other side is out, and at 50 feet through day and night the fragrance of that one bush covered with coral brooches is strong and enchanting. Since it stands beside the window of a guest room, its supreme sweetness gives great pleasure to the week-end sojourner. We are also training *V. Carlesii* as espaliers for each side of the big south window of the plant room and at the front entrance close by. Even with cold nights, *V. Carlesii* lasts only ten days, not long to be sure, but we who love the plant accept its brief appearance. We nip back long shoots to pairs of leaves to induce twiggy growth and more flowers. By August next year's fat buds are set.

Hybrids of *V. Carlesii* vary in foliage and scent. Burkwood viburnum, *V. ×Burkwoodii,* opens about two weeks later. Smaller heads of bloom, smooth dark green slender leaves and a tall loose-branched habit make it look altogether different from *V. Carlesii,* nor is its fragrance quite so spicy. In *V. ×Chenaultii* the fragrance is strongly gardenia and the plant super-hardy, delaying bloom until the end of May.

Viburnum
×*Carlcephalum*

Viburnum Carlesii

Bright foilage in fall and a heavy crop of black seeds make it superior to Burkwood.

The most notable *V. Carlesii* hybrid, *V. ×Carlcephalum,* originated in England where it has been disparaged as "clumsy" with its over-sized heads of bloom and tremendous basal shoots. That may be, but those heads, with their polished greenish-pink buds and slow-opening flowers, provide a continuance of *V. Carlesii* fragrance just as that beauty is fading. *V. ×Carlcephalum* begins a week later and lasts more than two weeks; its scent cannot be distinguished from that of *V. Carlesii,* the same bouquet of carnation and gardenia that carries farther, per-haps because there is more of it. The shrub does require shaping and responds immediately to pinching back in mid-June by sending out many side shoots that set cluster buds. Our plant set to the north of the house in open shade produced no bloom for two years after plant-ing. The third year even in this untoward location there were notably big blooms of fine fragrance. We have seen a magnificent plant trained as an espalier, reaching up to first-floor eaves and spreading 8 feet each way. The clusters of creamy bloom were astounding. We know they *can* measure 6 inches through, but pinching results in more clusters with a modest, 3-inch spread.

A tender species worth noting is sweet viburnum, *V. odoratissimum,* hardy only in the lower South. There it becomes a small tree, ever-green, with long, polished leaves. These make a rich setting for the apricot-scented plates of white bloom in May.

DELECTABLE SPRING DAPHNES

It is easy to become enamored of the daphnes once you have suc-ceeded with one or two. As a genus they are not easy to grow where summers bake. Almost every one of these handsome small shrubs is incredibly fragrant; only *Daphne Genkwa* disappoints. *D. odora,* as we have said, is for the cool window garden, or a protected spot in the winter garden where it perfumes March along with hardy *D. Mezereum*.

Garland daphne, *D. Cneorum,* is irresistible in forced clumps in the spring garden marts, its scent resembling that of *Viburnum Carlesii* but with the lilac quality of the big *D. Mezereum*. The little domes of pure pink in their gray-green ruching are the epitome of daintiness, and one sniff is enough to win new admirers. *D. Cneorum* comes in several forms, the white-flowered and the variegated-leaved too miffy to recommend, but the var. *eximia* is larger in every way, with inch-and-a-half heads of rose-pink stars on a vigorous plant. 'Ruby Glow' is new, with a more upright growth, long leaves, and sumptuous rose-red flowers. Garland daphne will not accommodate you. It is the other way around, so plant in full sun in a deep stony root-run of limestone, coarse sand, and old compost. And this is essential, and somehow psychologically difficult: *shear the tops way down after the first flowers have fallen*. You will be rewarded by two more good crops. Even a declining plant will try to bloom three times, greeting frost with more clusters heading up.

Also worth growing is *D. ×Burkwoodii* 'Somerset', a hybrid of *D. Cneorum*. It is an upright grower to 4 feet and to bloom it needs half a day of sun. Pale pink flowers are borne all through May, occasionally later, and the gray-green plant responds well to occasional shearing. Its sweet fragrance differs from garland daphne, and is more like the scent of rubrum lily.

Other daphnes are mountain folk, dwarf treasures for the collector with the means to please them. They can survive the winters, but not our hot dry summers. Many thrive in Washington state and Oregon where they flower in May and again in fall. They have large flowers rosy or ivory to three-quarters of an inch wide in close clusters against rosettes of evergreen foliage, and demand perfect drainage, midday shade, and a cool, deep root-run. *Daphne arbuscula, D. retusa, D. ×Mantensiana* 'Manten', and *D. alpina* are the perfumed cream of an exquisite genus.

39

FRAGRANT EXTRAS

There are other possibilities for the fragrant spring garden. *Fothergilla* is an adaptable genus of the southern Appalachians. Usually by late April every twig is tipped with a bottlebrush, cream-white and deliciously honey-sweet. Best is the spreading *F. monticola* with the largest spikes, at least 2 inches long; *F. Gardenii* is smaller in every way, needs seashore conditions, but is easier to obtain. *F. major* makes a tall pyramid with grayish leaves. They color gorgeously in fall.

About the same time in late April the beautifully designed *Akebia quinata*, a vine that makes a screen like a mosaic of maidenhair fern, blooms to cast its fragrance of grape and chicle for many yards around. The strange flowers droop in little clusters from every node: the male with gray-magenta capsules that split in three to reveal the stamens, the female with large fleshy plum-purple shells centered with glue-tipped pistils. Akebia can be magnificent if isolated and kept within bounds; left alone, the wiry shoots can throttle any shrub.

SPRING'S SCENTED CANOPIES

The first bold color and fragrance in trees comes from the French pussywillow, *Salix Caprea*. In February the forced branches decorate shop windows; outdoors by late March this medium-high tree releases a delicious honeyed fragrance from fat silver-velvet catkins, much larger than those of our wild pussywillow. Later these are hidden by a thick brush of lemon stamens more than 2 inches long. While one tree in full sun is a luminous sheath of pale yellow, wonderfully fragrant of honey and grape-flower, a hedge is magnificent. Bought branches develop roots in a vase of water, and can be set out in loose soil. In five years each will become a creditable tree, broadly columnar and single-trunked, catkin-laden every spring.

A resinous fragrance from unfolding bronze leaf buds is the spring gift of the balsam poplars. It is a fine, astringent, far-reaching odor that pervades the month of May here and mingles agreeably with the many sweeter flower scents, giving their bouquet a sharp but pleasing accent. Balm-of-Gilead, *Populus candicans,* has proved a mighty grower. Fifteen years ago we respected each other at a mutual five feet. Now it looks gracefully down from forty feet, and the end is not yet. The similar *P. Tacamahaca* of Montana is true balsam poplar. We think either one of these large resinous trees is indispensable for this unique and free leaf fragrance. Balm-of-Gilead usually forms a rather broad top; *P. Tacamahaca* is pyramidal and extremely durable.

THE MAGNIFICENT MAGNOLIAS

Magnolias are, without question, among the most beautiful and impressive of all flowering trees, and to blossoms that smell of tropical citrus and melon they add the charm of handsome gaudy seed-filled cones. American species bloom after leaves have emerged; some from the Orient open then, too; but most magnolias flower abundantly on leafless branches in spring. All grow best in acid soil and full sun.

After pussywillow catkins puff to pale gold, *Magnolia stellata,* the star magnolia, is the first large-flowered tree to bloom. After only one week, it may daringly open its ribbon-petaled 4-inch flowers that smell sweet of watermelon or honeydew blended with Easter lily. Frost can brown them but two years out of three the show is good. Trained to a single trunk, *M. stellata* becomes a 15-foot tree but usually we see it as a broad shrub with branches to the ground. Once we had a great pair of star magnolia bushes flanking the broad brick entrance walk to the front door. While these were in bloom we noticed that none but smiling faces greeted us, so great was the pleasure of mailman, delivery boy, and visitor in the unexpected fragrance that assailed them inside our gate. Several forms and hybrids share this delightful perfume. 'Waterlily' is more double, palest pink before opening; 'Royal

Magnolia Kobus

Malus sylvestris

Star' is similar, but by waiting usually foils frost by an extra week; var. *rosea* is utterly lovely, every slender petal pure pink outside, white within, in three ranks; the petal reverses of var. *rubra* are deeper rose.

Following *M. stellata* by a few days is *M. Kobus* with larger, fewer petals. This has been disparaged because it does not bloom when young, nor abundantly when old, and along with *M. stellata,* it is susceptible to scale but a late winter, miscible-oil spray controls this. While the creamy, kid-textured flowers may not put on the show of *M. stellata* or the later *M. ×Soulangeana,* they are undoubtedly the most fragrant of early magnolias, distilling the ripe mango aroma of orange and pineapple softened by a note of lily, a perfume noticeable many yards away. Later the glossy leaves and gray twigs, crushed, have the spiciness of bayberry and the surface-spread yellowed roots carry a cedar pungence.

M. ×Loebneri 'Merrill', a hybrid of *M. stellata* and *M. Kobus,* with petals of heavier substance than those of *M. stellata,* is almost as fragrant as the more vigorous parent, and plants begin to flower as early as *M. stellata,* when only a few years old. These three, even in full bloom, transplant easily in spring if roots are balled and burlapped.

Saucer magnolia, *M. ×Soulangeana,* has only faint scent, although both parents, *M. liliflora* and *M. denudata,* are fragrant; var. *Lennei* is good. When newly opened, the purple-flushed flowers of *M. liliflora* smell of raspberries.

The magnificent Yulan tree, *M. denudata* (*M. conspicua*), has the mango bouquet of *M. Kobus,* though it is not so rich. The Yulan can be a majestic tree reaching 50 feet. There is one that tall not far from us, and to see it in April, clothed from top to bottom with great milky cups, wide-petaled, upright, never reflexing, is to stand in veneration. In China, ancient, gnarled Yulan trees are called Jade Orchid, the flowers a symbol of purity. Only one other flower-before-foliage species rivals it: the very tender, fragrant, luscious pink *M. Campbellii,* with flowers of similar size and form.

43

FRUIT TREES

Every cherry and plum, fruiting or ornamental, has some odor, but only one, the Japanese apricot, *Prunus Mume,* has exquisite scent, and we hope for this at winter's end in the garden. Some edible plums and flowering cherries exhale a pleasing fragrance like that of English hawthorn. Others, including native trees and handsome evergreen shrubs, bear long fluffy, small-flowered racemes, upright or drooping, that are heavily endowed with a buckwheat-honey-and-almond bouquet.

Plum blossoms are small, white, and gold-hazed by many stamens. Since all the fruiting plums are sweet-scented, select those whose fruits appeal to you, making sure they will cross-pollinate. We have found pleasing 'Stanley Prune', 'Yellow Egg', and 'Shiro'—which took nine years to bloom—but best of all is the Hansen hybrid, 'Toka', a cross of Manchurian apricot and American plum. In late April it perfumes an entire acre. Added to its honeyed-almond is the refinement of wild-grape, a blend that delights us more each year. All the very hardy Hansen introductions are worth investigating; the bush-cherries, cherry-plums, and apricot-plums have scent as well as delicious fruits and they are much easier to grow than the old European and Japanese varieties.

Our East Coast beach plum *Prunus maritima,* the Western sand plum *P. Besseyi,* and Manchurian cherry *P. tomentosa,* are bushes loaded with warmly-scented white-gold bloom in April and they bear edible fruit.

Several Japanese cherries, cultivars of *P. serrulata,* open around the first of May with a hawthorn fragrance, though it is less strong, more flowery, and perceptible only nearby.

The European bird cherry, *Prunus Padus,* a sizeable tree, produces countless fat white tassels in early May. In Canada and our coldest states, the var. *commutata* is known as May Day Tree. It is planted not only for the honey-scented flowers but also for black fruit that lures birds. Our own wild black cherry, *P. serotina,* source of that wonderful wild-cherry candy flavor and the wood of treasured furniture, produces long hanging racemes that are pleasantly scented. The choke-cherry of hedgerows, *P. virginiana,* has gone over to rankness, tolerated only for the wildlife it supports; and the evergreen species *P. ilicifolia, P. Laurocerasus,* and *P. lusitanica* are on the borderline.

Late in April or early in May the round buds of the various apple-blossoms open to fill the garden with one of the best of spring scents. It is soft and pervasive as mist, the fragrance of a thousand sweet violets, but more lasting for it is *there* (violet perfume soon fades), all day and all night, inescapable in its brief season. The flowers of sweet apple, *Malus sylvestris,* have a faint odor more dusty than violet, good to breathe in hand and lightly present in still air.

We turn to the crabapples—the many species and their hybrids— for really superb fragrance. Siberian crabapple, *Malus baccata,* taller than most apple trees, even to 30 feet, with small pure white flowers, is the earliest to appear, sometimes by the third week of April. The flowers last only a week, for apple blossoms of every kind are fragile and go quickly with the first hot wind. The form easiest to find is the large-flowered var. *mandshurica;* var. *columnaris,* which is especially lovely but better suited to small gardens, is pyramidal.

Brought to this country before 1800, each of the natural crosses of *M. baccata* with the common apple of Europe seems as entrancingly violet-scented as the Siberian. These are often encountered along country roads in late April, laden with pink-stained buds and cupped white flowers then, and with little amber-and-red apples later. The fruits of *M. baccata* are less than half an inch, a treat for birds in early fall.

Hybrids, well endowed with the ineffable perfume of parent *M. baccata,* include *M. Arnoldiana, M. ×robusta,* and *M. ×Zumi calocarpa.* The Kaido crabapple, *M. ×micromalus,* is of restrained upright form, and 'Hopa' belongs here, too.

One clone that appears closely related to Siberian crabapple is 'Dolgo', handsome in flower, magnificent in fruit, and possibly the most perfumed of all. Pure white buds and flowers open a few days after *M. baccata,* diffusing a vapor of pronounced violet with something else, the musky bouquet of the wild grape in June. Bury your face in the hanging snow, or breathe it far off, the scent is softly hypnotic; you are compelled to stillness, to let the cloud enclose you. It permeates the air for a hundred feet around; with age branches bend, making a great mound 15 to 20 feet high, a brilliant sight late in August when the bloomy garnet-red fruits are ripe.

Several other Oriental species have this perfume to a degree. Some are good to smell close-up, others seem scentless yet emit thin puffs that your nose catches in passing. The mounding Japanese flowering crabapple, *M. floribunda,* is one; tea crabapple, *M. hupehensis,* is another. *M. Sargentii,* growing in our shrubbery border, is smallest, more a wide, single-trunked bush than a tree. In mid-May the dainty snow-white buds and flowers look like a lacy veil and are delightfully sweet.

HAWTHORNS

Of countless species of hawthorn, all laden with bright fruit in the fall, apparently only one has flowers good to smell, *Crataegus Oxyacantha,* the English hawthorn or May (Maytree). The rest smell of fish, hardly fresh, an effluvium they share with the deceivingly lovely, red-stamened blossoms of pear. It is not obvious, we are relieved to report, only noticeable close-up. English hawthorn is uniquely different with a pronounced fragrance of honey and almond, not the almond of paste or flavoring, this, but the bite of prussic acid in apple seeds and peach pits. It is a far-reaching scent, one we have encountered often in plum blossoms and certain cherries, simple, refreshing, not a true perfume. Like that of the musk rose, it is produced by the stamens, for double forms are odorless.

The tree grows to perhaps 18 feet, densely twigged and thorny, the trunk gnarled in age. In England, hedgerows of "moonlight-coloured May" mark boundaries. Close-set saplings, sheared to form a thick mesh, will still bloom. There are a number of varieties of *C. Oxya-cantha* with pink, rose, or crimson flowers but best is the species itself, with single white flowers. We delight in our one tree at the corner of the terrace and prune to keep open horizontal lines through which we can glimpse the brook. Fragrantly adorned with spring blossoms, this Maytree is irresistible, but we also appreciate the autumn berries and the shapely leafless form. On a white, winter day of snow and sleet, the brilliant cardinal stops there mindful of the lingering supply of tiny crimson fruits.

5

From Early Bulbs
and Small Perennials

Unfailing and sweet year after year, valued far and wide for their early beauty, are narcissus, the colorful mainstay of the spring garden. Well chosen and planted in massed beds or naturalized, they can make a whole property fragrant in April and May. But before their encompassing splendor occurs, the modest Lebanon-squill takes a bow and the too-little-appreciated Dutch hyacinths continue the scented procession that began on our window sills at Christmas with the tender French-Romans. Broad stretches of the excellent small grape-hyacinths are another of April's many joys. Among tulips, there is little scent and that from only a few varieties. Some of the first perennials delight us now with their sweetness—violets, primroses, the smaller kinds of phlox—and, of course, lily-of-the-valley that comes around Mother's Day and gives pleasure in so many gardens.

LEBANON-SQUILL

Sometimes before March is over, and always in sweet evidence by early April, Lebanon-squill, *Puschkinia scilloides,* opens its modest blooms on stems at most 6 inches high. The fine perfume of mignonette comes from flowers that face out and up in many-budded racemes. Through each white petal runs a pure blue line from tip to center, inside and out, giving the effect of fine porcelain. The all-white form is charming, too, but not so lovely as the patterned blue-on-white. The first spring the bulbs are in the garden, buds sometimes try to open even before they emerge from the ground, but a year of acclimation restrains their impatience. Our puschkinias are set out in a large patch under and about the "white forsythia" (*Abeliophyllum distichum*) because they bloom at the same time and are attractive companions outdoors or in.

HYACINTHS

For us, hyacinths with their heady sweetness are the very essence of spring. Because they bloom while it is still fairly cold and we do not wander often to the far reaches of the garden, we crowd them in to every spot near the house—at the back door, under the kitchen casements, beside the terrace where we sit on the steps for a moment on pleasant mornings, and strewn along the driveway bed for everybody's pleasure. These are the sturdy Dutch hyacinths, descendants of the graceful wild blue jacinth of Greece and Asia Minor. To avoid the sometimes formidably chunky flowers that need staking, we do not buy the largest show-bloom bulbs but seconds (by name) or Cynthellas (by color alone).

Of course, our first concern is fragrance, for some hyacinths have an unpleasant smell. This is not merely an intensification of type hyacinth, but disagreeable even at a distance. Since hyacinths are a long-

Hyacinthus 'L'Innocence'

time investment, you should sniff discerningly to suit yourself, and exhibits at flower shows offer good opportunity.

Admittedly, white hyacinths are our favorites; unsurpassed are 'L'Innocence', 'Edelweiss', and 'Carnegie'. Two creamy yellows, 'City of Haarlem' and 'Prince Henry', are delightful; 'Gypsy Queen', a salmon blend, harmonizes with them. Aside from the double 'Chestnut Flower', 'Pink Pearl' is the one pink that is very sweet. 'La Victoire', rose-pink, has a rank odor in shade yet is good in full sun. There are countless fragrant blues: 'King of the Blues' and 'Ostara', both tall, rich, deep-toned; 'Grand Maitre', a handsome medium violet; and the heavenly light-blue 'Cote D'Azure', unsurpassed for fragrance as well as form and color. 'Royal Mulberry' has the vinaceous tones of old purple roses, a lovely shade in a hyacinth. All these are best bought in second sizes by name.

You may also want to try some of the lovely large doubled hyacinths. In cool seasons they last a possible three weeks, well into May. 'Mme. Sophie' and 'Ben Nevis' are superbly fragrant whites and 'Chestnut Flower' a delectable light pink, but the splendid 'Scarlet Perfection' has no noticeable odor.

Together, hyacinths and grape-hyacinths fill April with rich-scented blues.

GRAPE-HYACINTHS

This smaller-flowered "hyacinth" derives its popular name not only from the racemes which, upside down, resemble clusters of grapes, but from the pronounced spicy-grape bouquet of the flowers—the perfume of clove and sun-warmed Concord grapes of late September. Of the half-dozen or more species available, three are pervasively sweet, while the others, *Muscari botryoides, M. neglectum, M. paradoxum,* and *M. racemosum* have only modest scent when held in hand.

Old 'Heavenly Blue', from whatever species it may have been derived, can still be found in Southern lists. In September it sends up grassy leaves from which rise blue spearheads to 6 inches in mid-April, filling spring-clean air with a marvelous perfume. In England forty years ago the Rev. Joseph Jacob wrote: "I must put in a plea for the aroma that comes from a large bed of 'Heavenly Blue' on a blazing hot day in April or early May. It is worth living for. Make a mixture of the spicy scent of the real old clove carnation and the ecclesiastical odour of the night-scented stock into one, and . . . you get a sort of idea of the delight that will be yours . . .". Clove and lily are indeed there, but grape contributes, too.

51

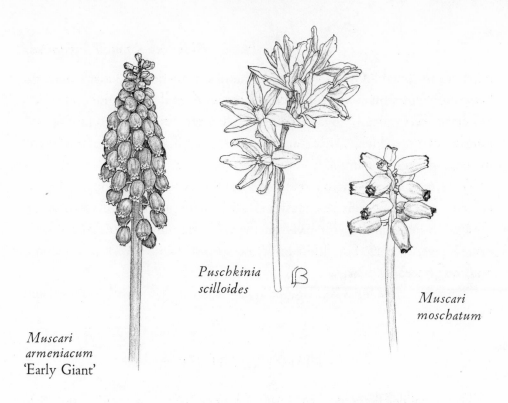

Puschkinia
scilloides

Muscari
moschatum

Muscari
armeniacum
'Early Giant'

The vibrant blue racemes of *Muscari armeniacum* 'Early Giant', about 9 inches, provide a succession from mid-April to mid-May. They have the grape bouquet softened with a cloviness that distinctly freights the air. Gerard's "yellow muscarie," *M. moschatum*, charms us with its glow of pale yellow and its potent scent that varies from year to year, from blends of goldband lily and grape, to lily and clove, to all clove, and back again; whatever the bouquet, one stem offers the equivalent of dozens of 'Heavenly Blue'.

THE VARIED NARCISSUS

The splendid yellow and white flowers of narcissus alone could make April and May months of delightful sweetness in the garden. More than three hundred years ago Parkinson admired them while scorning those "idle and ignorant Gardeners" who confused narcissus and daffodil, for "as all know that know any Latine that Narcissus is the Latine name and Daffodill the English of one and the same thing."

Today, "daffodil" usually refers to the trumpets and large-flowered garden forms, while "jonquil" includes the very fragrant small-flowered sort. "Narcissus" does nicely for all the rest.

In the sweet-smelling kinds, five odors predominate, with slight variations: the exotic, little-goes-a-long-way odor of paperwhite; the fruited bouquet of 'Soleil d'Or', repeated to some extent in all the *Narcissus poetaz* group; the essence of *Lilium auratum* in *N. poeticus;* the exquisite and distinctive perfume of *N. Jonquilla;* and the light sweetness of many large-flowered hybrids, not strong but distinctly daffodil.

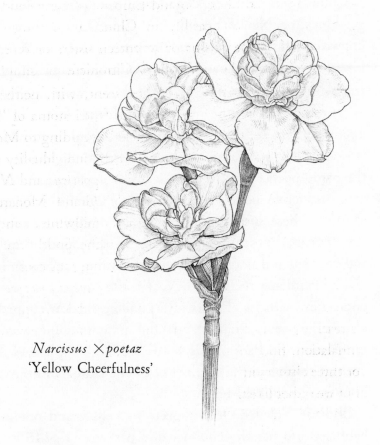

Narcissus ✕ *poetaz*
'Yellow Cheerfulness'

NARCISSUS TAZETTA—ITS FORMS AND HYBRIDS

Most ancient and widespread are the strongly scented cluster-heads, the *N. Tazetta* group, named for their shapely cups or *tazza*. Among them the paperwhites have long been window favorites. Where they are hardy, the forms of *N. Tazetta* brighten dry pastures from Spain and Morocco to Palestine and Persia, ornament centuries-old Chinese porcelains and silks, and belong to the dynasty of flowers that have accompanied history—lily, laurel, rose, lotus, oleander.

Botanists divide *Narcissus Tazetta* into three series: yellow-to-orange-and-white bicolors, all whites, and all yellows. The kind known here as Chinese sacred-lily or 'Grand Emperor' (orange and white) is called good-luck or New Year-lily in China. In our own South another, known as cluster-narcissus or seventeen-sisters or even Chinese-sacred, is really venerable 'Grand Primo Citroniere' or simply primo, lemon and white. These two have a fine scent, with neither the oppressive sweetness of paperwhite nor the tutti-frutti aroma of 'Soleil d'Or', but a pleasant blend of the two, jasminelike according to Mr. Bowles. Surely it is as delicious as jasmine, yet with the individuality of narcissus. All the hardy poetaz group (hybrids of *N. poeticus* and *N. Tazetta*) share this distinctive bouquet and include 'Grand Monarque' and 'Scilly White'. These insist on blooming in midwinter, and so are not for our climate, but through January in the South they are a glorious sight in beds and along driveways, perfuming the cool air far away.

The familiar paperwhite (*N. Tazetta* subsp. *papyraceus*) of the second series, with its clusters of crystalline shallow-cupped blossoms, has a reaching scent, strange and unpleasant to some who, after the first inhalation, find Parkinson's word "stuffing" applicable. More than two or three clusters in the confines of even a large room try their endurance, but we rather like the heavy scent.

Brilliant 'Soleil d'Or' of spectrum yellow and orange opens late in February and has the bouquet of a basket of ripe fruit; as George Ellwanger observed, "here is spring incense enough to fill a cathedral at

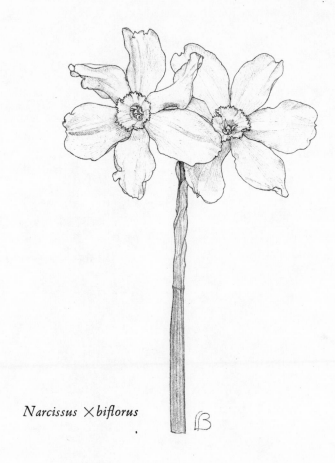

Narcissus ✕biflorus

Easter-tide. Is there any odor more delectable than the mingled essence of pineapple, orange, and banana, which this form of the poet's flower exhales?" A recent double, 'Golden Rain', is an incredible treasure, with long-lasting tufted flowers of stunning fragrance.

Hybrids of *N. Tazetta* share the fragrance and clustering of *N. ✕poetaz.* Oldest is Gerard's "primrose peerlesse," *N. ✕biflorus,* still vigorous but masquerading in the Deep South as twin-sisters and April narcissus, farther north as May narcissus and even as poets narcissus. The stems carry two flowers, ivory with a flat, ruffled cup of lemon-yellow. The lovely perfume resembles the fruit bouquet of 'Soleil d'Or'. Perfectly hardy, it blooms here in the first half of May and naturalizes with a will.

55

Narcissus Canaliculatus

Canaliculatus (a trade name for a form of *N. Tazetta* subsp. *lacti-color*) is one of the smallest of the race, a dwarf form of *N. Tazetta*. The little white-and-gold flowers open almost as soon as buds are above soil. In the garden, this plant disappears after a few years so we prefer to grow it in pots indoors. The fragrance, a powerful aroma of apricot as delicious as that of sweet-olive, fills a window enclosure but tends to be lost out-of-doors. Other diminutive *N. Tazetta* hybrids lack perfume.

A cross of *N. Tazetta* with *N. triandrus* produced the magnificent 'Silver Chimes'. Heads of six to ten flowers are usual, though very large bulbs give a possible eighteen, and these pour out a gardenia perfume, strange and delightful in a narcissus. 'Silver Chimes' blooms in the

Southern garden toward the end of April, but seldom thrives this far north—for us it is another to cherish indoors.

POETS NARCISSUS

Narcissus poeticus is one of the latest to open, captivating with bright-eyed whiteness and rich perfume. Mr. Bowles observed that "there is a great deal of nutmeg odour about it that is delightful in the open air, but on a dinner table is disastrous to the palate, causing all delicate flavours to partake of nutmeg." To us the fragrance seems precisely that of *Lilium auratum,* a scent apparent in many flowers but memorably so in poets narcissus. Modern versions are handsome, yet few have the free, exotic pungence of the nearly wild var. *recurvus* (the old pheasants-eye) that opens in early May. Bulbs grow best in dark woodsy loam and full sun, yet naturalize well in high shade.

Many small-cupped garden hybrids close to *N. poeticus* share the scent in dilution, are late blooming, and vigorous enough for naturalizing. *N. poeticus* ancestry does not guarantee fragrance, unfortunately; some that appear similar, like 'Actaea', are all form, show-flowers without scent.

Narcissus poeticus 'Flore Pleno', the doubled poets narcissus—called gardenia-flowered, Albus Plenus Odoratus, even sweet-Nancy—is ages old, as temperamental today as ever. The small rather shapeless flowers, white with a fleck or two of orange and yellow, will open only in cool dry weather; humid heat cooks them. Extra bonemeal underneath the bulbs at planting time seems to give them needed substance, and nipping the sheath tip helps. If flowers do open, their fragrance is magnified lily, free and intense.

We now know *N. poeticus ornatus* only in its double-flowered sport 'Daphne', the most unappreciated of all sweet-scented narcissus. This small beauty, hardly 2 inches across, is as shapely as a formal, ice-white camellia. 'Daphne' shares with 'Silver Chimes' a fragrance of gardenia with a hint of clove, so the little flowers smell very like *Viburnum Carlesii* that opens at the same time.

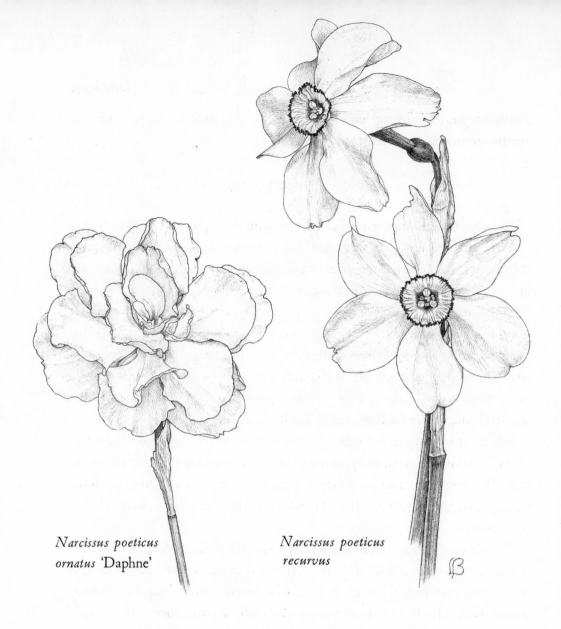

Narcissus poeticus
ornatus 'Daphne'

Narcissus poeticus
recurvus

JONQUILS

The true, chive-leaved jonquil has the most penetrating fragrance
of all narcissus, a delicious piercing sweetness found in few other flowers.
It defies description but seems midway between grape-flower and jasmine, so free that one stem of the dainty blossoms perfumes a room.
Narcissus Jonquilla and a few related species, all sweet-scented, are
properly called jonquils.

In the last few days of April the nickel-big blooms of *N. Jonquilla* (erroneously but persistently called *N. simplex* by the trade) open, a few long-tubed flowers per stem, not much to look at but with a scent out of all proportion to size. *N. Jonquilla* and its kind come from the parched mountain-meadows of Spain, Portugal, and North Africa, and need full sun, lime, and sharp drainage to prosper an ocean away from home. It can be stingy; more dependable and as typically fragrant are late 'Baby Star' and 'Helena'; the latter, from a Southern garden and nursery-distributed, is particularly vigorous and carries the luscious scent to the end of May.

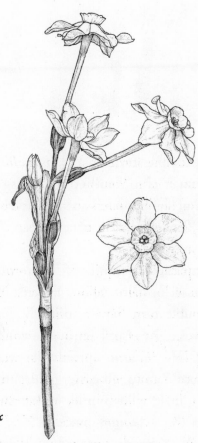

Narcissus Jonquilla simplex

Narcissus ×odorus rugulosus

The double form of *N. Jonquilla* is a fairy flower treasured for the heirloom it is in Southern gardens—their Queen Anne's jonquil. This tiniest of double narcissus is marvelously perfumed but does not thrive here. 'Pencrebar', the true Queen Anne's jonquil, is double and lacks the great scent.

Campernelle jonquil, *N. ×odorus*, is earliest and most prolific with clusters of brilliant yellow flowers. *N. ×odorus*, its var. *rugulosus*, and the double form have a mild *N. Jonquilla* perfume; mostly, they are just sweet. By April tenth the countless bobbing flowers open. In the South, *N. ×odorus* spreads like weeds and there are slight variations with local names, all early, gold, and fragrant.

Two little wild hybrids repeat the jonquil form in pale citron. The smaller *N. ×tenuior* precedes *N. Jonquilla* by a few days, while the larger *N. ×gracilis* starts when 'Helena' does and smells more of wisteria than of jonquil. Both multiply well and have individuality among the many golds. Another species, smallest of the group, is quaint *N. juncifolius,* with two or three late-season flowers on 3-inch stems and with a different, spicy aroma. All jonquils have the round hollow leaves of *N. Jonquilla* that pierce the ground in October with their first dark tips. *N. juncifolius, N. ✕gracilis,* and *N. ✕tenuior* have been interbred as well as crossed with larger narcissus and most of the hybrids are sweet-scented though not with jonquil purity. These are excellent: 'Baby Moon'; 'Kidling'; 'Trevithian', tall and very fragrant; 'Nirvana'; 'Sweetness'; and 'Orange Queen', strongly scented with a syrupy stuffiness that bothers us but may please other noses.

ROCK GARDEN MINIATURES

For the rock-gardener many early narcissus species have charm but little scent. The miniature trumpets, numerous *N. cyclamineus* hybrids, even the dainty angel's-tears, *N. triandrus albus,* are treats for the eyes, not the nose. The hoopskirt or petticoat daffodils have a bouquet of the fruity *N. Tazetta; N. Bulbocodium* subsp. *obesus, N. cantabricus* var. *foliosus* and var. *monophyllus* and the hybrid 'Nylon', all in starched and pleated white, are pleasantly sweet. Several large-flowered *N. triandrus* hybrids have excellent fragrance, as the tall 'Thalia' and 'Liberty Bells'. 'Tresamble' waits until May to open its four to six crimped cups, which are loveliest of all.

DAFFODILS

The wild *Narcissus Pseudo-Narcissus* was ". . . a crowd, a host, of golden daffodils" in Wordsworth's poem, the Lent-lily of England and Europe. This carpets our Southern grasslands and thin woods, too, but offers only the mild sweetness characteristic of countless sturdy hybrids. Here, Lent-lily is known as Early Virginia, Trumpet Major, and Buttercup, and was probably brought over by settlers in the seventeenth century. It naturalizes beautifully, even spreading by seed, and is charming grown with purple *Viola odorata,* for their seasons overlap.

Daffodils—all those one-per-stem, trumpet narcissus—seldom have impressive fragrance. Some have none at all, others an odd pungence like dandelion bloom. The great golden 'King Alfred' has good scent, and so have enough others for a wide selection, as 'All Glory', 'Carlton', 'Golden Smile', 'John Evelyn', 'Mt. Hood', and 'White Nile'.

The large doubled narcissus seldom have good form and the buds blast in muggy weather. Mrs. Wilder grew sweet-smelling old *N.* ×*incomparabilis* sorts (our large-cupped group) with delectable names like 'Codlins and Cream', 'Primrose Phoenix', and 'Butter and Eggs', but these are found only in old country gardens.

The Copeland hybrids are fairly scented, 'Mrs. Copeland' best. The newer 'White Lion' smells odd to us, but good to others; 'Snowball' has little odor nor has 'Inglescombe'. 'Golden Ducat' (the multi-perianthed version of 'King Alfred') and 'Golden Castle' have pleasant fragrance while 'Mol's Hobby' has novel form as well as delicious perfume; 'Papillon Blanche' is similar, an ivory jewel.

A few narcissus often described as fragrant have proved disappointing, even 'Louise De Coligny' and all the other pink daffodils, as well as the early, antique *N. moschatus,* and 'Silver Bells' (or 'Swan Neck').

FEW TULIP POSSIBILITIES

The flamboyant tulips are such vivid spring flowers we wish they were not so generally scentless. Best of the early tulips for scent are the clear yellow 'Bellona', orange-and-scarlet-streaked 'De Wet', large vermilion 'Doctor Plesman' and 'Prince of Austria'; the gaily striped red-and-yellow 'Prince Carnival', too bizarre to go with anything but yellows or reds; and the soft coppery orange 'Princess Irene'. These smell more of freesia than of poppy, and large plantings fill the air with soft sweetness.

Tulipa sylvestris

A few tulip species have close-up fragrance, as the candy-striped *Tulipa Clusiana,* the rose-edged creamy *T. Marjolettii,* and the very late, bronzed orange *T. patens* (*T. persica*), golden within. Sweetest is *T. sylvestris,* the wild tulip of Europe, an enameled lily-flowered yellow. It blooms for three weeks from late April into May with a medium-strong freesia perfume that persists indoors when flowers are set close to a table lamp.

HARDY VIOLETS, PRIMROSES, AND PHLOX

The great perfume of the violets belongs, of course, to European *Viola odorata.* Among native violets, only a few white-flowered species produce any scent—the bearded mite *V. pallens,* the larger *V. blanda,* and rare *V. primulifolia* said to be "pungently fragrant." When fragrance is found in garden violas, it must come from the perennial *V. cornuta,* the tufted pansy of the Pyrenees, with perky lavender-blue flowers. This, crossed with garden pansies (*V. tricolor hortensis*), gives us the charming violas of spectrum brilliance and six-months bloom. Among them can be found some with remarkable scent on the order of primrose, far better than the millipede odor of the much larger pansies. In pansies, fragrance seems to predominate in warm colors—yellows and apricot are best, with carnelian reds and whites next. Do not expect size in these, for it is the little 1-inch flowers that smell sweetest. To establish them in your garden, grow a packet from seed in August; or in May select the best-perfumed, potted clumps at a roadside nursery. The large-flowered pansies now come in a fragrant strain, Read's New Century Scented, with thick, long-lasting blooms.

Many primroses have a light sweet scent, mostly the honey-and-grape-flower bouquet of *Primula veris,* and the fragrance seems to pick up strength in the hybrids. Polyanthus primroses, in the strains known as Colossal and Giant-flowered, vary from having no odor at all to a delightful aroma of ripe peach. Rose-red and blue shades are deficient in fragrance, but sniffing among the medium-sized yellows reveals a few outstanding individuals. *P. vulgaris,* the wild yellow English primrose, has a sweet breath, as do the "reckless" multicolored auricula primroses. In the bog-loving *P. involucrata,* the perfume is intense, so also in the lilac-blue *P. marginata.*

Phlox is a native American genus and countless are its forms as they grow all over the country, from mountains to prairie to woodland and seashore. Those small forms of our springtime gardens have scent in varying amounts but hardly the pervasive sweetness of big summer *Phlox paniculata.* April's moss-pink, *P. subulata,* has a decided honey sweetness in some forms, and so has the pale lilac ten-point phlox, *P. bifida,* with its deep cushions of needled leaves.

A mass of blue phlox (wild sweet-William), *P. divaricata,* has

64

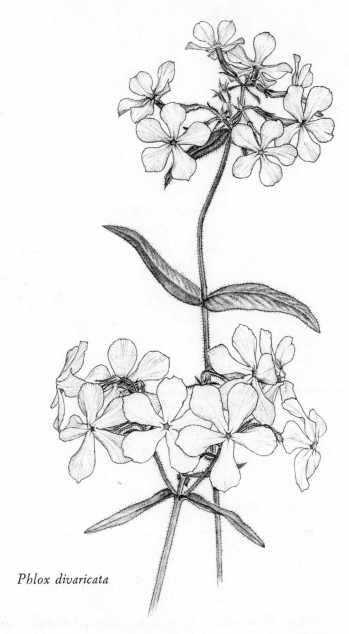

Phlox divaricata

a light odor, like the low note of a few very fragrant irises without their ameliorating sweetness. We do not care for it, but to a few of our visitors the scent is often a true perfume. Creeping evergreen phlox, *P. stolonifera,* has the best scent, the heady but modified perfume of *Lilium auratum,* sometimes more noticeable at a short distance than close up. 'Blue Ridge', 'Lavender Lady', and 'Pink Ridge' are lovely hybrids.

65

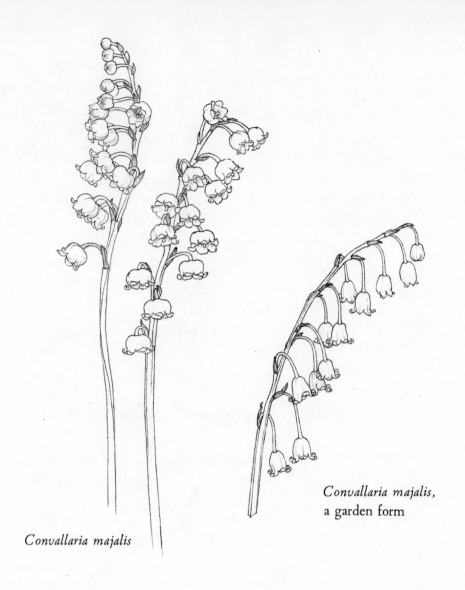

Convallaria majalis

Convallaria majalis,
a garden form

LILY-OF-THE-VALLEY

When lily-of-the-valley (*Convallaria*) blooms, usually the first three weeks in May, we decide, *this* must be our favorite, the little Muguet of exquisite scent. The fragrance is never cloying, always refreshingly new and springlike, a scent that wears well. On still days a bed in bloom may fill the air above with perfume, but usually it is a private thing, to be inhaled intimately and long. Few other flowers share this distinctive sweetness, but we recognize it in *Neomarica, Mahernia,* and *Sansevieria trifasciata Laurentii.*

By early April, hard purple-stained points stud the soil and even then the flower-buds show. We grow most of our lilies-of-the-valley in loose, rich soil in light open shade, but the patch that is most prolific covers a parched slope in full sun (where we found it); there, in sweet soil, we have counted up to seven pips per square inch, every one bearing buds. The ropey roots are strong enough to push through old asphalt. Indeed, the modest "Liriconfancie," as Gerard knew it, is a formidable plant, best grown in a bed to itself or with large ferns and periwinkle that can hold their own among the crowding roots.

One species, *Convallaria majalis,* is found in the woodlands of Europe as well as in our eastern mountains. Our form has up to

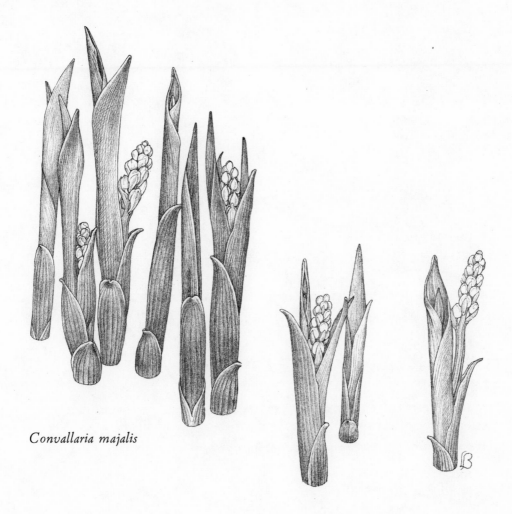

Convallaria majalis

twenty fat flowers, exactly like 'Fortune's Giant'; but a slender sort grows in gardens nearby. Var. *rosea* has small mauve-pink flowers and almost no fragrance. These begin about May first, plants in shade blooming later and longer. Last to open is var. *plena* 'Double White', whose flowers are monstrosities but with the true scent; and this sets large berries more dependably than the type.

6

Sweetest Shrubs
for Early Summer

From mid-May through June the fragrant garden is a place of enchantment, a "place of peace" drawing us away from the impinging turmoil of the world. Now "every aspect pleases"; July heat and humidity are not yet upon us, and everywhere subtly different scents assail the discerning nose. Now the sweetest of shrubs are in full beauty, all wonderfully free of fragrance; above our heads trees suspend their perfumed panicles, and the great clan of spicy gilliflowers—we call them pinks today—are rampant in garden beds where well-chosen peonies and iris add to the bouquet carried on the early summer air.

EARLY LILACS OF FINE FRAGRANCE

First to give pleasure in this season are the lilacs. May belongs to them as June to roses. Although lilac-time begins before April ends and continues through June, the lilacs of ineffable scent bloom in May alone.

The season opens with Lemoine's Giraldi Hybrids and the Oblata Hybrids of Dr. F. L. Skinner of Manitoba, Canada. About a week later comes *Syringa vulgaris* with its fascinating offspring, the so-called French Hybrids, the singles lasting two weeks, late doubles going on into June. At the same time, other enchanting sorts bloom—*S. ✕chinensis, S. ✕persica, S. laciniata, S. microphylla,* and *S. pubescens.* Before May ends, the late hybrids commence but these have a rather disagreeable privet heaviness. The latest for good scent is the new little *S. velutina (S. Palibiniana)* or its pale blue form, 'Miss Kim', in flower through the heart of June. Two that bloom even later, *S. amurensis* and its var. *japonica,* are not admitted to our fragrant garden under any circumstances.

Lilacs thrive on sweet soil and are almost immune to scale and mildew if enough lime is present. In summer, cut back the faded clusters to strong shoots, particularly on young specimens and thin-wooded species like *S. microphylla* and *S. laciniata.* Set out new plants in fall.

The first hybrids came from *S. Giraldii,* which Lemoine considered only a geographical variation of *S. vulgaris.* They are indistinguishable from *S. vulgaris* except that they bloom about a week earlier and sucker less. All have abundant large open clusters, great vigor, and lovely fragrance. Here, April 27 to May 12 finds them in full color, when *Malus floribunda* and *M. spectabilis* are also at their best and can use cool tones to dramatize their rosiness.

Of the single-flowered ones, we particularly like the lavender-pink 'Lamartine', the deep violet 'Louvois', soft magenta 'Montesquieu', and 'Pascal', duplicates of common lilac with a much larger cluster of unshaded lavender and a treelike plant. 'Turgot', light mauve-pink fading to white, is perhaps the most fragrant of all, the scent purest lilac, somehow even sweeter than 'Old Purple'.

The only double-flowered Lemoine Earlies are the lavender-pink 'Vauban' and light violet-blue 'Claude Bernard', the latter extremely tall and prolific, a loosely arranged version of the much later 'Olivier des Serres'. We long to have 'Claude Bernard' but it seems impossible to locate. These date from the 1900's. Clarke's 'Blue Hyacinth' of 1942 is similar, a single light blue that resembles the hyacinths blooming at the same time, and is almost as sweet.

The cross of *S. vulgaris* with *S. oblata dilatata,* the earliest species to bloom, gave true hybrids. The long-tapered leaves of *S. oblata,* the short panicles, and red coloring in stems and foliage distinguish them from Lemoine's production.

Dr. Skinner has produced such fragrant clones as 'Excel', 'Evangeline', and 'Pocahontas'. His 'Minnehaha', rich reddish-purple, the immense clusters borne with abandon, is outstanding, with a perfume that carries for yards around. 'Charles Nordine' is a large, single pale blue with big open panicles. When good early blues like this and 'Claude Bernard' exist, with their handsome clusters and superior scent, it is hard to understand why the small-flowered 'President Lincoln' continues to be offered as "the best blue."

COMMON LILAC AND FRENCH HYBRIDS

A general favorite is the old *Syringa vulgaris* that years ago grew next to every New England kitchen door and porch, barn and springhouse. By late May whole villages are perfumed with a scent that Edward Bunyard called "the very heart and soul of memory." Mrs. Wilder wrote that "Next to Box and Wild Grape it seems to me the most memory-stirring of all the fragrances." Longfellow firmly declared "I shall not go to town while the Lilacs bloom," nor did he.

About 1875, the French plant wizard Victor Lemoine bred from these old lavender and white lilacs and a tiny-flowered double form what we now know as French Hybrids. Some say they lack scent, that only the common lilac carries the typical perfume. It is true that a few like 'Lucie Baltet', 'Montesquieu', 'Firmament', and 'Candeur' are deficient. Others, including magnificent 'Olivier des Serres', 'Leon

Syringa vulgaris clones, individual flowers

Gambetta', 'Henri Martin', and 'Decaisne' have one of those strange odors that are delightful to some noses, to others oppressive and unbearable, particularly indoors.

The fact is that French lilacs—and there are many American-bred varieties among them—vary in fragrance as much as in flower form and color. However, by far the greatest number have the scent of common lilac, although it may be stronger, or refined in some way by the addition of other flowery notes. As Gertrude Jekyll observed, doubling of flowers increases fragrance because of the extra petals. Furthermore, double flowers, usually sterile with center petals replacing stamens, last longer than single ones, and the very sweet double lilacs retain their goodness with their color, perfumed to the end.

Some gardeners claim that lilacs must be well established before they produce characteristic odors; those we have grown have all been sweet from the first season. Of course, fragrance varies with weather, and few flowers can still produce scent at the end of a hot windy day.

Of the French Hybrids we have found consistently fragrant, most are doubles. Some are hard to find, for lilac specialists are disappearing, but so long as superior varieties exist in arboretums, there is the chance they will be propagated. These are French Hybrids that we highly recommend for both fragrance and beauty:

WHITE. There are three particularly fine doubles: the pure white 'Mme. Lemoine', still best for scent; the cream-white 'Mme. Casimir Perier' with true lilac scent; and the ivory-tinted 'Edith Cavell' with far more scent than the much praised 'Ellen Willmott'. Other fairly fragrant whites include 'Hiryo', 'Marie Finon', 'Alice Harding', and the luscious heavy-textured 'Siebold'.

LAVENDER-PINK to MAGENTA. Again we like three fine doubles: 'Mme. Antoine Buchner', at first pure pink, fading to cool pink and deliciously sweet; 'Paul Thirion', sometimes called red, is magenta-rose; 'Perle Von Stuttgart', amazingly sweet, a true aristocrat. 'Glory' is a single with deepest coloring, a purplish-rose with glorious perfume.

LAVENDER. There are two doubles: 'Victor Lemoine', a two-toned pink and blue with the effect of lavender, begins late, lasts long, and has superb scent; 'Belle De Nancy', the clear lavender of common lilac, opens at the same time and is deliciously sweet.

LAVENDER-BLUE to VIOLET. 'President Grevy', a double in tints of blue has the pure *S. vulgaris* scent. 'Marechal Lannes', a double of medium violet-blue, flowers late, is sweet-scented, and lasts for three full weeks. 'Boule Azurée', a single, is a uniquely lovely blue, best of the light blues with a fragrance that is enchanting; 'Cavour', also single, is deep violet with a rich fragrance that develops by the end of the first week; 'Thunberg', a medium-violet double with dark reddish buds, opens to cool lavender with good lilac fragrance even after two weeks.

DEEPEST TONES. These four singles bring rich dark colors to the garden picture: 'Mrs. W. E. Marshall', a pure purple, richly scented; 'Klager Dark Purple', intense plum color with incredible scent; 'De Miribel', deepest violet, intense color and fine hyacinth fragrance; and 'Congo', intense red-purple fading to magenta, with a lasting scent.

Syringa ×chinensis

CHINESE, PERSIAN, AND CUT-LEAF LILACS

The lilac called Chinese (*S. ×chinensis*) actually originated in Rouen, France, about 1777, not in China, and is invariably sold as Persian. But the old name of Rouen Lilac is more appropriate for this truly wonderful shrub with white, lavender, or "lilac-red" flowers. It makes a tremendous plant, 10 feet high and almost twice that wide at maturity, a great mass of limber stems, bending gracefully with the weight of enormous multiclustered panicles. The fragrance is quite sweet, more like *S. vulgaris* than *S. ×persica* but without the sharp identities of either. Indoors, it is never oppressive.

74

Persian lilac, *Syringa ×persica,* has been in gardens for centuries. In 1640 Parkinson described it precisely, noting the variations of leaf-form—some "with a whole without any division therein, resembling a Privet leafe, or both and divers will be halfe like or wholly like the ... divisions of the Catalonian Jasmine [*Jasminum officinale*] resembling it so neerely that thereby it came to be called a Jasmine ..." The type is tinted pinkish-lavender with something of the *S. laciniata* daphne-wisteria bouquet, though hardly so intense or fine, while var. *alba,* a definite white set off by dark foliage, is sweeter and prettier than the mauve, which has a faded neither-nor look.

Young plants of *Syringa laciniata,* once thought to be a form of *S. ×persica* but now considered a distinct species, lack real hardiness for us, and often branches lose their buds in a late April frost, but with age come resistance and profuse bloom. What a fascinating species this is. No one can believe it is *Syringa.* The leaves, only 1 ½ inches long

Syringa ×persica

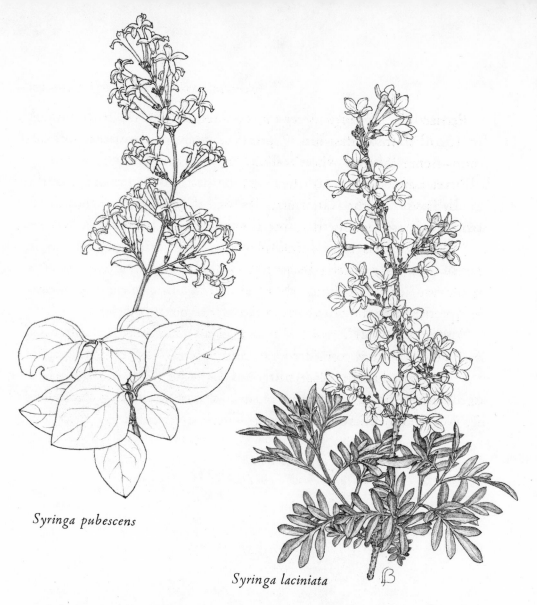

Syringa pubescens

Syringa laciniata

and deep-cut into five or seven fingers, give the effect of fern tips. Tiny flowers of lavender-blue mass the whip-ends; clusters appear at every node. From the time they open, about May 7, until they begin to fall two weeks later, in any weather, morning or night, these emit one of the most heavenly perfumes of any deciduous shrub. There is little of common lilac in it. The fragrance fills the air for yards around, and there is no escaping it. At first it seems like *Daphne Mezereum,* itself a tantalizing blend, then white Chinese wisteria. It is a sophisticated perfume that lingers on even in dry flowers. These do not brown but hold their gentle mauve, a treasure for dry potpourri.

76

Littleleaf lilac, *S. microphylla,* is a charming plant with minute flowers of palest pink. The perfume at its best is a simple sweetness to breathe in over and over again. Select in-bloom plants in a nursery where you will discover that the scent varies, with possibly too much privet for your taste. This is true of the var. *superba* or daphne-lilac, which lacks the littleleaf's good proportions of 1-inch heart-shaped leaves and sprigged clusters of pink stars.

White lace-tree would be a more appropriate name for *Syringa pubescens* than hairy lilac, for tree it is, with a single trunk or two or three diverging widely near the ground. When in bloom these bend beneath a froth of snowflakes. Weather must be just right for *S. pubescens* to release any scent. Walk past on a still day in mid-May and you are caught in a cloud of exotic fragrance with the headiness of *Lilium auratum,* and then you understand why this has been declared the most perfumed of all lilacs.

THE LATE LILACS

The Korean lilac, *Syringa velutina* (*S. Palibiniana*), is that rarity, a late lavender-flowering species of good scent on a plant modest enough to complement rather than dominate the star-performers of June. The compact shrub seldom reaches more than 3 feet. The dark leaves turn bronze-red in fall, most unusual in lilacs. A form presently offered as 'Palibiniana' has small clusters of lavender flowers covering the plant. We have already mentioned 'Miss Kim', which is almost identical with light violet sprigs fading milk-white. We cannot think of any other bluish flowers of delightful scent that come from June fifth to twentieth except the herbal garden sage and the first lavenders.

For bloom in northern areas where heavy May frost can ruin the season for *S. vulgaris,* many late-flowering hybrids are either scentless or smell to some degree of privet. A few like the pink 'Handel' and lavender-rose 'Floreal', also *S. Sweginzowii* and its hybrid 'Pink Pearl', are pleasantly sweet and can be used at close quarters, but by early June here, we are ready to bid lilacs farewell and go on to the old roses.

The later that lilacs bloom the worse they smell, it seems. We mention the tree-lilac, *Syringa amurensis* and var. *japonica,* only because they are offered, and warn that they *must be avoided* in the fragrant garden. Their scent is stronger than the worst privet and so intense it carries far. (Lindens are the only trees of good scent in late June.)

CAROLINA ALLSPICE

Native to many Eastern woodlands is *Calycanthus floridus*. It is a plant of happy memories and many names—allspice, sweet-shrub, strawberry-bush—a favorite of pioneer women. The large rugose leaves, the stems, even the big fig-shaped seedpods have a spiciness reminiscent of sassafras or bayberry. Best though are the long-petaled red-brown flowers, sweetest just as the center petals part. They smell of green tea and Damson plum preserves and occasionally of strawberries—"a perfume of distinction." Quality of scent does vary from year to year, even on bushes known to be fragrant. Once again nursery selection is important. One clone, 'Mrs. Henry', has proved vigorous, prolific, and delightful to smell.

Strawberry-bush is adaptable but best in acid soil and moisture. Established plants bloom from early May into July; in hot June sun, an old specimen can make its presence known some distance away. Children love to pick the flowers, to sniff many times their fruity goodness. Mrs. Wilder recalled how as a little girl she used to knot one in the corner of her handkerchief and how, years later, "one sniff of the spicy, exhilarating odor, and open flies the gate long closed upon a joyous childhood, and with the brown talisman tightly held within my palm I am free to pass through a land of perpetual revels, where all wonders are possible and where faith in life and its great promises is as firm as the walls which guard the garden."

Rhododendron roseum

RHODODENDRONS AND AZALEAS

Rhododendrons are a mother-lode of fragrance. Most of the many species are native to the mountains of China and India, but more than two dozen grow in our Eastern woodlands from Florida to Maine, among them some of the most beautiful azaleas of all. An acid soil, cool moisture, and high shade are essential. If you have these, as we do along our brook, go in for azaleas heavily—not for the flamboyant, scentless Kurumes and Kaempferis, but the many charming scented natives and their magnificent hybrids, all deciduous, all highly colored in fall. Flowers come in every tint of crimson, scarlet, orange, pink, yellow, as well as white; early kinds begin to bloom by late April, others not until July, but the main show is usually mid-May.

There is no simple way to distinguish rhododendrons from azaleas: botanically, both belong to the genus *Rhododendron* (there is no "Azalea" genus) and can be evergreen or deciduous. For fragrance, in our frigid winters, the deciduous azaleas are the more rewarding. Scent varies, but basically it is clove, light or intense, often with enough of something else for a delicious blend. A little clove with a lot of

79

honeysuckle is a frequent combination but even within a species there is diversity. We marvel at two plantings of our favorite azalea, *Rhododendron roseum:* one is of mature nursery seedlings, the other, an arboretum collection. Colors range from warm white through luscious pinks to rich rose, and odors are as various. Every degree of clove is there from faint sweetness to a kind so rank it lost all appeal in spite of near-crimson coloring.

EARLY FRAGRANT AZALEAS

First of the good-to-smell azaleas is the hardy *R. canescens,* the Southern pinxterbloom or Piedmont azalea. As April draws to a close, clusters of rosy-tubed white or pale pink flowers open before the leaves, with a bouquet of spice and honeysuckle. Next opens the tall, amazing *R. austrinum,* quite hardy this far north, in butter-yellow, gold, or apricot, even a light vermilion, with a pleasant spiciness, mild but definite. Closely allied to *R. austrinum* and flowering in early May, is the East European Pontic azalea, *R. flavum* (*A. pontica* and *R. luteum*). This, gold with the strength of a spotlight, has a strong, delicious honeysuckle-clove bouquet that has been passed on to numerous hybrid offspring.

FOR MAY, JUNE, AND JULY

By May eighth in our Zone 6, the glory of the azaleas is upon us beginning with our favorite, the intensely clove *R. roseum.* Rose-shell azalea is its popular name and it reaches to about 6 feet. Color varies from palest pink to light crimson; the prettiest form is clear pink brightened by rose-red tubes and stamens, broad petaled and many budded, the fragrance pure carnation sweetness. Try to select nursery plants in bloom, for variations are considerable. *R. roseum* is the ideal shrub to underplant with blue phlox in high shade. Coming at the same time but with only faint sweetness is pinxterbloom,

R. nudiflorum, sometimes called honeysuckle-azalea, with white or pale pink flowers in thin clusters. If a catalogue stresses rich pink plus strong fragrance, the plant is *R. roseum,* not *R. nudiflorum;* they are often confused and both are hardy.

A charming, little-known hardy species that suckers into a low gray-green hummock is coast azalea, *R. atlanticum.* In mid-May it is sprigged all over with rondels of white bloom with a strong blended fragrance, gardenia and clove as delicious as that of *Viburnum Carlesii;* some noses have found rose-attar in it, but this note has eluded us. *R. atlanticum* is occasionally light pink, but we love the white.

Found wild only in Alabama, the 3- to 4-foot *R. alabamense* is hardy only to Philadelphia and most lovely, massed in mid-May with wide-petaled white flowers, yellow-marked, their fragrance mild clove with an accent of auratum lily. Taller versions open earlier with clusters

Rhododendron atlanticum

in sherbet pastels—yellow, apricot, pink—and these are probably hybrids of *R. canescens* and *R. austrinum*.

Toward mid-June, when the last of the brilliant hybrid azaleas have faded, the natives carry on. The 10-foot sweet azalea, *R. arborescens,* beside the brook opens pure white clusters with rosy filaments that emit a very sweet version of clove like clethra or heliotrope. Later, the 10- to 15-foot swamp azalea, *R. viscosum,* graces our flowerless July woods with little white flowers that smell as richly of clove as *R. roseum.* A remarkable hybrid of this, a Mollis azalea, is the easy-to-find *R. ×Daviesii,* a very old clone with the gray-green foliage of *R. viscosum* and clusters of handsome yellow-marked white flowers, rewardingly sweet. It blooms during the last ten days of May into June and is usually listed with the Ghent azaleas. We make it the center of a picture with laurels, hemlock, and white birches, under-planted with ferns and narcissus.

In cool gorges and steep woodlands of northern California, the superb Western azalea, *R. occidentale,* opens in June and July—great white and pink flowers with a perfume far-carrying and deli-cious, the clove masked with the sweetness of honeysuckle and clethra. Hardy at least to Philadelphia, this is difficult in the East because it needs cool summers. Easier and earlier are the Occidentale Hybrids. crosses of Western azalea with Mollis Hybrids. Best and earliest is 'Irene Koster', white, washed coral-rose, and powerfully fragrant.

GHENT, MOLLIS, AND KNAP HILL HYBRIDS

The first great hybrid strain of fragrant azaleas was the so-called Ghent azalea that brought together the American *R. calendulaceum, R. nudiflorum,* and *R. viscosum,* and the European *R. flavum.* Tall, hardy plants, they bloom the last half of May, the flowers small, and almost without exception perfumed with clove, sometimes honey-suckle. Colors cover a wide range with pastels smelling sweetest. They are still desirable and a few fine singles are offered. Even one 6-foot shrub can perfume the air of a whole garden. Look for 'Nancy Waterer', 'Unique', 'Fanny', and 'Bouquet de Flore'.

Double Ghents and the Rustica Flore Pleno group are visually identical; the few offered are in such demand lately that they must be ordered in advance. These are delightful plants in soft blendings of color that are a pleasure to work into a garden scheme; the small flowers have a delicate air lacking in the latest hybrids and, with doubleness, have even more perfume than the singles. These are the only scented, hardy, double azaleas, and we hope more of them will become available again. 'Milton', 'Narcissiflora', 'Aida', 'Corneille', 'Il Tasso', 'Norma', and 'Freya' appear on current nursery lists.

An account of the great fragrant hybrid groups begins with the one called Mollis, which is a marriage of the hardy flame-colored *R. japonicum* with the tender straw-yellow *R. molle*. The innumerable offspring are predominantly *R. japonicum,* for their foliage has an unmistakable odor of skunk, particularly when newly expanded in May. The air near a large planting is puzzling until you realize the fume is shed by the leaves not the flowers. Mollis bloom is individually large and the colorings gay yet soft, from light yellow through orange to blood red, including delectable pinks without hint of blue. Flowers open the second week of May and have a pronounced spiciness, clove with a piercing quality unlike the pure carnation of the American species and *R. flavum,* all with foliage of polecat pungence. We think a little skunk on moist evening air is a good country smell, and it is one we do not mind in Mollis, so lovely are the flowers.

With the advent of the Knap Hill Hybrids, the only Mollis offered are sometimes unnamed seedlings rather than named clones, but these excellent hybrids are still available: 'Hortulanus H. Witte', 'Christopher Wren' ('Goldball'), our great favorite 'Directeur Moerlands' ('Golden Sunlight'), 'Adriaan Koster', and 'Chevalier A. de Reali'. They provide a palette of golds, from orange-yellow to light buff fading white. 'Spek's Orange', 'Floradora', 'Dr. M. Oosthoek',

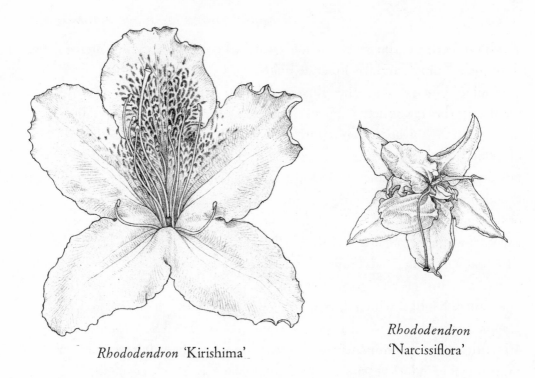

Rhododendron 'Kirishima'

Rhododendron
'Narcissiflora'

and 'Koster's Brilliant Red' cover the orange-to-reds, while 'Mevrouw G. van Noordt' is a superb salmon.

The newest deciduous azaleas are the Knap Hill Hybrids that bring together after many decades the flame-colored species, *R. japonicum* and *R. calendulaceum,* and two of our loveliest scented natives, *R. occidentale* and *R. arborescens.* Every azalea color is here, in great heavy-textured flowers, rivaling the largest rhododendron bloom. Some plants grow bushy, others tall, and flowers open with the Ghents from the middle to the end of May.

Fragrance varies from almost none through every degree of clove to scents too strong for pleasure. Nurseries now feature budded plants; if the Knap Hill Hybrids appeal to you, smell among the assorted beauties for the most captivating. Exbury and Ilam strains are the same as Knap Hill, and American seedlings selected by the Robert Bovees of Portland, Oregon, include exceptionally lovely whites as well as low spreading plants well adapted to our many soils and weathers.

EVERGREEN AZALEAS AND RHODODENDRONS

Few of the evergreen azaleas in cultivation have the gift of fragrance. Two semi-evergreen species from the Orient have it to some extent. The Chinese snow azalea, *R. mucronatum* (*R. ledifolium album*). has the breath of auratum lily in several of its forms, those with less attractive off-white flowers usually sweetest and scenting the air at some distance more noticeably than near the plant. The most popu-lar is pure white 'Indica Alba' opening with the Kurumes in the first week of May. Our favorite, 'Sekidera' ('Magnifica', 'Damask Rose', and bought as 'Kirishima'), opens very large flowers a week or two later, white, heavily speckled magenta-rose, with pronounced perfume. At least one Glenn Dale azalea, 'Pixie', has similar scent.

Korean azalea, *R. yedoense poukhanense,* is the single-flowered form of the familiar, double Yodogawa azalea. The warm lavender flowers, crimson-spotted, cover the low mounding plants in mid-May, and puzzle the questing nose with the odor of lilies at a great dis-tance, while close up they seem scentless. In milder climates, snow and Korean azaleas retain their dull leaves until new ones emerge, but plants are deciduous here. An excellent substitute for bud-tender *R. mucronatum* is the hose-in-hose, chartreuse-stained Gable azalea, 'Rose Greeley', with the same subtle perfume but handsome rich green foliage.

Of large-leaved evergreen rhododendrons, three species have grand fragrances of vanilla or clove or honeysuckle, even gardenia, with blends of these, but the vanilla sweetness predominates. These are *R. decorum, R. discolor,* and *R. Fortunei,* all hardy here, with 3- to 5-inch flowers, seven-lobed, in translucent pinks; their hybrids are only beginning to be marketed. 'Skyglow' ('Dexter #9') and 'Caro-line' are outstanding. In the mild environs of San Francisco grow gorgeous species, like *R. bullatum, R. crassum, R. Dalhousiae, R. Maddenii, R. formosum, R. megacalyx,* and *R. taggianum,* each large-flowered, with pervasive, wonderful perfumes.

85

THE MOCK-ORANGES

With our extremes of weather, we may not have fragrant jasmines and gardenias in our gardens, but we do have mock-oranges. However, so few clones are offered that gardeners have no idea of the assortment of perfumes the white flowers of *Philadelphus* can pour out. First to grace gardens was European *Philadelphus coronarius,* which Gerard and Parkinson called syringa. Its fragrance is still the type for this group, a delicious blend of orange fruit (not blossoms) and jasmine. Gerard found the scent "troubling and molesting the head in a very strange manner," but we have never known anyone who did not like it. Superficially, the flowers resemble orange blossoms with their column stamens and broad white petals, four instead of five. Old *P. coronarius* in time makes a 10- to 12-foot shrub sprigged with scented bloom from the last week of May well into June. Flowers of seedlings vary in quality. A double form, var. *duplex,* has been known almost as long as the single. Golden mock-orange, var. *aureus,* is primarily a foliage plant.

To avoid disappointment, it is well for the fragrant-minded to realize that many philadelphus have no perfume, "scentless, or souless . . . beautiful and dumb" in Mrs. Wilder's words. Today, the only scentless ones likely to be encountered are 'Atlas', *P. grandiflorus,* and *P. pubescens.* Particularly handsome are *P. ×splendens* and *P. pekinensis,* saved from ignominy by a little of the *P. coronarius* bouquet. Then a few are even more richly endowed than *P. coronarius; P. purpurascens* from China is sparse-flowered but intensely fragrant of sweet-peas; *P. argyrocalyx,* with the aroma of ripe pineapple, comes from New Mexico and is a taller version of the gem of the race, *P. microphyllus.*

This littleleaf mock-orange, *P. microphyllus,* denizen of shady canyons through the dry Southwest, is hardy here only in sheltered sun pockets. Flowers are small but a compote of pineapple and orange, the ripest mango, is faint compared to a branch of them. Lemoine, recognizing the possibilities, crossed it with *P. coronarius* to create

86

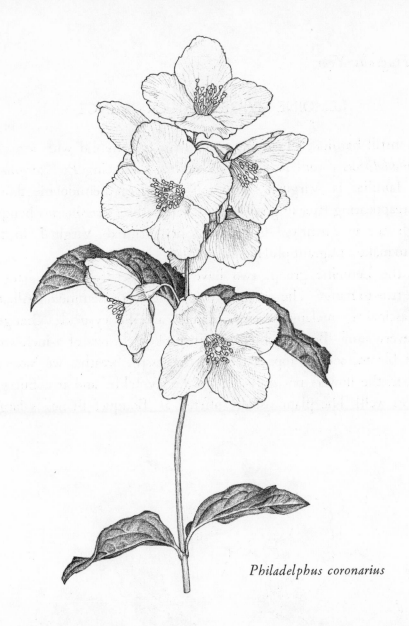

Philadelphus coronarius

the Lemoine Hybrids. 'Avalanche' comes closest to *P. microphyllus*, but is hardier and far more prolific, a 4-foot mound of tight little clusters duplicating the tropical-fruit bouquet. The perfume of the small, single-flowered 'Mount Blanc' is a blend of orange and rose, but far off has a tutti-frutti aroma; the 6-foot mound is one of the most potently fragrant of hardy shrubs, but we have been unable to find it *true* in nurseries. Others of this parentage include 'Girandole', the low 'Manteau D'Hermine', and 'Innocence' which has not proved vigorous here.

87

LEMOINE HYBRIDS—MOCK-ORANGE

To instill hardiness, Lemoine crossed his first hybrid with a second of *Philadelphus coronarius* × *P. pubescens,* producing *P.* ×*virginalis.* Most familiar is 'Virginal', very tall with large semidouble flowers often reappearing later in good seasons. It has the *P. coronarius* bouquet though not in quantity; Constance Spry planted 'Virginal' in two rows, to make a fragrant philadelphus walk.

Of the Lemoine group, two have superb scent but are hard to locate true-to-name. The fragrance of the 6-foot aneminoid 'Albatre' is a fascinating melange of iris, orange, and honeysuckle, changing with every sniff. 'Bouquet Blanc', with packed clusters of 1-inch semi-double bloom, seldom tops 4 feet; in successive breaths, we have detected in the flowers not only orange, honeysuckle, and iris, but gardenia as well! The plant usually offered as 'Bouquet Blanc' is larger,

Philadelphus ×*purpureo-maculatus*
'Belle Etoile'

mounding, and single-flowered. 'Pyramidale', with perhaps the most charming form of these doubles, the small bloom centered with pompons of crinkled petals, has a relatively simple *P. coronarius* perfume. 'Minnesota Snowflake' is only mildly sweet. 'Enchantment' smells but weakly of *P. coronarius*.

Lemoine brought color to the cream and ivory whites of mock-orange by merging the tender Mexican *P. Coulteri* with his hybrids. The resulting hybrids (*P. ×purpureo-maculatus*) are single, large-flowered, spotted with rose, but they are the least hardy of all his creations. 'Belle Etoile' is deservedly popular with its thick-textured, cerise-eyed flowers and graceful arching branches. Bloom begins the second week in June and lasts well into July, longer than the usual two weeks of mock-oranges. The fragrance is astonishing, predominantly gardenia with a note of orange, so free it carries to the far corners of the garden. Dr. J. H. McFarland declared, "that if it still froze every winter I should still want to grow it with whatever care was necessary because of the richness of its gardenia odor." 'Sybille' is extremely lovely, with fringed petals, pink centers, heavily fragrant; 'Beauclerk' makes a 3-foot mound with flowers that smell of grape lollipops!

OTHER SCENTED MOCK-ORANGES

In Canada, Dr. Skinner sought greater hardiness by using the sweet-scented Manchurian mock-orange *P. Schrenkii*. His three named clones may be dwarf in Manitoba but reach 6 to 7 feet here. 'Patricia' blooms with *P. coronarius* late in May; 'Mrs. Thompson' has thousands of small flowers; 'Purity' opens by May's end with magnificent 2-inch flowers on a modest shrub. All are delightfully fragrant but 'Purity' is outstanding, like an intense *P. coronarius*, and they are much hardier than the Lemoine hybrids, ideal for very cold gardens. A few from other sources deserve mention. *P. ×Burfordensis* opens by mid-June, even later than 'Belle Etoile', with the fragrance of *P. coronarius,* not overpowering but quite good. 'Silver Showers' releases a delightful perfume at the very end of the season.

Philadelphus requires little care; full sun and, to keep plants productive, removal of third-season canes, either in bloom or when spent. All grow best in sweet soil, though they are adaptable and the addition of lime is seldom necessary. Cut branches first thing in the morning when still in bud, mash the ends with a hammer, and let stand in a pail of water all day before arranging them. Constance Spry discovered that the removal of most of the leaves prolonged the life of the flowers.

MORE SHRUBS FOR EARLY SUMMER

Something new to add to the wealth of June is a Moroccan broom, *Cytisus Battandieri.* Most brooms with their bright green stems, tiny leaves, and winged yellow bloom have some scent of honey, ranging from the heavy rank odor of *C.* ×*praecox* and the light clover-honey scent of *C. scoparius* to the delicious lemon-and-mead of tender, March-flowering *C. canariensis,* the florist's "Genista." Short cones of bright yellow *C. Battandieri* release a fragrance entirely different, a tropical bouquet of ripe pineapple, cantaloupe, and orange, similar to that found in littleleaf mock-orange. Fairly hardy in coastal Maryland, this unusual broom is worth trying inland in sandy soil. Annual pruning keeps it compact, or the silver-leaved branches can be fanned against a hot wall to grow to 5 or 6 feet. *Genista cinerea* of late June and *Spartium junceum* in July are other pea-flowered brooms, honey-sweet and golden.

Buddleia alternifolia, garland butterfly-bush, begins in late May when cascades of gray-green brighten to lavender garlands for two weeks. The mass of orange-eyed, lilac bloom looks particularly lovely next to yellow climbing roses, tumbling over fences and low walls. It spreads a warm scent of wild honey, piquant and summery. The orange-ball tree, *B. globosa,* is an oddity in northern gardens, like a

Philadelphus ✕ Burfordensis

perennial for us, erupting each spring to a great display of netted foliage. Through June countless little balls of orange open, calamondins in effect, wildly attractive to bees.

Then there is the unique dusty zenobia, *Zenobia pulverulenta,* of acid woodlands, worth finding and keeping. In early June, racemes of plump, waxen bells like blown-up lilies-of-the-valley nod along the bending stems. Their honeyed sweetness is perceptible long before you see the flowers among the simple leaves that are almost the color of rue. Southerners call this native plant honey-cup; its 3-foot mound is hardy into Massachusetts.

Zenobia pulverulenta

7

Fragrant Trees and Vines for May and June

Above the sweet abundance of lilacs, mock-oranges, and azaleas, a number of lovely trees now burst into bloom, compounding the sweetness of the early summer air. Late crabapples and magnolias continue the procession that began in April, and the most fragrant of vines—wisteria, clematis, and honeysuckle—in late May and June cover our lattices and arbors with flowers of nostalgic and entrancing perfume.

AMERICAN CRABAPPLES

American crabapples differ from European and Asiatic species in that flowers do not open until mid-May when the leaves are developed. These are long, elliptic, scallop-toothed, and twigs end in thorny points. If fruit sets, it is green, bitter, yet pleasantly aromatic. The trees are also alternate hosts for juniper rust, although some strains are resistant. Flowers and scent vary, too.

The graceful Southern crabapple, *Malus angustifolia,* spreads out branches laden with rose-pink bloom. It grows wild from New Jersey south. The fragrance borders on the violet bouquet of earlier kinds though hardly so pure. The more northern white and pink garland crabapple, *M. coronaria,* a welcome volunteer on our hill, is fragrant with the unexpected odor of some Tea-Noisette roses, neither rosy nor sweet, yet apparently pleasant to some noses.

Prairie crabapple, *M. ioensis,* seen most often in doubled forms, has this same aroma. The hanging rosettes of Bechtel's crab have the fermented breath of the Bourbon rose, 'Souvenir de la Malmaison', which is to say they smell of beer not roses. 'Prince Georges' is an old hybrid between the prairie and Southern crabapples, better than either; 'Charlotte' and 'Nieuwland' are more double.

LATER MAGNOLIAS

A number of American magnolia species grow throughout the eastern part of the country. Best are sweet-bay, *Magnolia virginiana,* and the great bull-bay, *M. grandiflora.* Sweet-bay or swamp magnolia grows naturally in wet areas from Massachusetts to Florida and west, but adapts itself to drier ground so long as that is acid. As we see the tree, trunks are seldom higher than 20 feet, usually several together. *M. virginiana* seedlings vary greatly; a few have flowers almost scentless, others verge on the unpleasant, but the best kind distills a blend of lily, gardenia and fruit—rich, stimulating, memorable —and thriving plants usually have the most perfumed flowers. By the end of May, small creamy flowers open; each lasts a day, and there is never a mass of bloom, but buds continue to open until August, delighting us for more than two months.

Bull-bay is possibly the most spectacular of all large-flowered evergreens. Great trees of it can be seen in almost every botanical garden of the temperate world for it began traveling abroad around 1732. It is a species of endless variation, in foliage, flower size, fragrance, and hardiness. Occasional trees grow around Long Island Sound and there are many in the Philadelphia area. Yet no one strain, so far as we know, has been selected for hardiness under northern conditions; most strains are named for some quality of foliage.

Toward May's end, great ivory balloons of buds open into saucer flowers with the feel of glacéed kid. Cupped the first day, they often measure up to 8 inches across, expanding overnight up to 12 inches; the recent 'Celestial' opens to a full 15 inches, an incredible sight against the whorls of glistening dark green leaves. Their typical scent is lemon, not the simple sweet-and-sour of lemon-verbena or lemon-geranium, but sharp citrus softened to perfume by a note of lily. Flowers continue to open into August.

In the South, bull-bay reaches 80 feet but in colder areas we are delighted with a shrubby 8 to 10 feet so long as the plant blooms. Espaliered against cornered walls of stone or brick, out of prevailing wind, bull-bay thrives and is more likely to survive bitter winters. In Washington, D. C., it is often so gracefully trained and in England we have seen pairs espaliered beyond the second stories of Georgian country houses, the gleaming foliage lovely against the pink brick.

Other fragrant American magnolias include the amazing *M. macrophylla,* with 30-inch paddle-shaped leaves and great flaring June flowers of varying sweetness; and *M. Fraseri* which diffuses a scent of limeade on opening. We warn you against *M. tripetala* for the narrow-petaled flowers have an absolute stench—but they keep it to themselves.

To complete this account, we mention here the late Oriental magnolias, more often shrubs than trees, that bloom in summer after their leaves have expanded. The mounding *M. Sieboldii* (*M. parviflora*) opens buds from late May until August. The round white petals spread to some 5 inches, centered by rose-red stamens· enclosing a pale green cone, their flavorsome bouquet of pineapple-orange-lily free for a short distance and delightful near the house in the shelter of a wall.

LOCUSTS, FRAGRANT AND OTHERWISE

Walking one day in the northwest area of Washington, D. C., we met for the first time the black locust, *Robinia Pseudo-Acacia,* and a lifelong friendship commenced. For long stretches of wooded areas, the piercing sweet scent of jonquil assailed us, yet no narcissus were in sight. The fragrance was pouring down from groves of tall, gaunt trees with ferny foliage now hung with 6-inch clusters of pure white flowers, shortened wisteria in effect.

From some points of view, the black locust is hardly a desirable tree. The outline is stark, the tree late to leaf, early to shed, brittle-branched, suckering, and subject to borers. Yet once the unpromising twigs sprout fans of maidenhair in late April, and in mid-May the fragrant panicles appear, we overlook all liabilities. The flowers exhale one of the most exquisite of flower scents, and when the air is moist and still, the perfume spreads over a great area, puzzling travelers along country roads who do not recognize this American tree that Europeans have appreciated for hundreds of years.

There are many forms of black locust with varietal names to match, but they are not necessarily good bloomers. The columnar 'Fastigiata' and chartreuse-tufted 'Friesia' flower regularly. One that we long for but cannot locate is perpetual black locust, *Robinia Pseudo-Acacia semperflorens*. Even better than a mass of bloom in May would be occasional flowers later, on a tree set near bedroom windows. Occasionally flowers of wild trees have a rank scent, perhaps too much jonquil. Black locust grows in any impoverished soil, and steep slopes are its delight. Although it has a reputation for suckering, we only wish that certain superb specimens we know of, did!

Pink-flowered locusts have become popular as street trees in the Midwest; possibly they are part clammy locust, *R. viscosa,* for the bloom lacks the extreme fragrance of the wild white. Decaisne locust, *R. Pseudo-Acacia Decaisneana,* and Idaho locust, *R. idahoensis,* have the mauve-pink color of scentless *R. viscosa,* as has Mr. H. Rohrbach's 'Pink Cascade', *R. ambigua bella rosea.* This is magnificent in bloom, actually having more flowers than leaves, far superior to pink wisteria. Though it attracts many bees, the flowers have no perceptible fragrance. The beautiful rose acacia, *R. hispida,* also lacks scent.

Black locust is often confused with honey locust, *Gleditsia triacanthos,* which sounds as though it should smell good but does not. It has great triangles of slender leaflets, long spines in clusters all over the wood, and hard round seeds; a honeylike substance in the long twisting pods explains the name, for country boys once chewed them for their good taste.

RUSSIAN-OLIVE

The silver-twigged Russian-olive, *Elaeagnus angustifolia* of Europe and the Caucasus, hangs out a multitude of tiny, yellow-lined silver bells that release an amazing fragrance. Though not an olive, old trees with their gnarled trunks, gray heads of slender leaves, and long-stemmed fruit do resemble the classic *Olea europaea;* to the Portuguese it is Tree of Paradise. Growing to a 15-foot tree, Russian-olive is used increasingly in public plantings where the broad silvered heads sway in every breeze like weeping willows. It will grow even in subsoil, and once established, drought is its way of life.

Russian-olive takes six or seven years to bloom; then one day in late May, patience is rewarded when you smell something different and trace it to the metallic nubbins hidden among the leaves. In later years the flowers are noticeable if you stand beneath the tree and look up, but from a distance, no. So they make themselves known with superb scent, a blend of grape-flavor and jonquil with a note of the exotic cestrum. Children find in it grape-lollipop.

The one native species, *E. commutata,* the silverberry of the Midwest, is a tall shrub that appears sprayed with aluminum paint. From May through June, racemes of quite conspicuous golden stars pour out a similar bouquet and in fall each star becomes a silver-dusted coral berry. Suckers soon make a 12-foot thicket. (We wish this desirable shrub could be made available to us by nurserymen.) Cherry elaeagnus, *E. multiflora* from Japan, makes a broad dense shrub with hidden May flowers betrayed by their scent; by the end of June branches sway under the weight of long-stemmed cherrylike fruits, gold-dusted red, delicious to taste.

FRINGE-TREE AND STORAX

The fringe-tree of southern mountains, *Chionanthus virginica,* is one of our most ornamental natives. More often a multiple-trunked shrub than a tree, the smooth gray branches delay leafing out until June, then let down at the same time scented panicles like strands of silk embroidery floss. Visitors almost think we have invented the tree, so rarely is it planted here. Southern gardeners have long appreciated their grandsir-greybush, old-man's-beard, snowflower, or grandaddy-greybeard, but fringe-tree seems to us the most appropriate. Only the staminate have scent, one of those uncomplicated odors that fill the air far around and delight everyone—the sweetness of white clover or the first cut of alfalfa or flowers of American elder or dry sweet woodruff, a scent as refreshing as a soft spring rain.

We have planted it to take full advantage of its two weeks of exquisite scent, and near lilacs, so that the front lawn and the house, too, with windows open, are enveloped in fragrance. In the corner of front steps and south guest-room window, this fringe-tree grows multiple-trunked to the top of the cottage, some 20 feet. We prune to keep a clear silhouette below and a bower of branches above that give shifting shade to house plants summering on the entrance terrace. Beneath the tree lilies-of-the-valley and blue periwinkle carpet the ground and yellow Mid-Century lilies, 'Joan Evans', follow fringe-tree bloom.

In the fern garden, among azaleas, clethra, and other wildlings, it appears beautifully appropriate overshadowing a low bench; far from the house, it scents another great area close to the brook. The large oblong leaves turn brilliant yellow in autumn, one more advantage of this very lovely tree.

The storax of the Old Testament, *Styrax officinalis*, and gum benzoin, *S. tonkinense*, are close relatives of the lovely *Styrax Obassia*, one of the hardiest of the genus. It reaches at least twenty feet here, and in mid-May long strands of broad white bells disperse a rich scent of vanilla and orange-blossom. The smaller and later Japanese snow-bell, *Styrax japonica*, its horizontal branches dripping with bloom, has no fragrance, but the shrubby *S. grandifolia* of our southern woodlands is strongly perfumed and worth seeking for milder gardens.

CHINESE AND JAPANESE WISTERIA

Perhaps the greatest glory of May is the wisteria. Indeed we cannot imagine spring without it and whenever we have moved to a new place, we have always arranged for a Chinese wisteria, *Wisteria sinensis*, right along with wallpaper and curtains. For one vine, a great arborlike structure was built out from the front of the garage, and along the whole east side of the cottage. Old and tremendous now, we gaze with rapture at the two-toned lavender cascade and never tire of its ineffable scent. This one has bloomed since the very first spring, when scarcely 3 feet high, and a few scattered clusters keep coming into fall. Every venerable vine of it we have ever smelled has had fragrance. It is one of those unique and indescribable odors,

99

with some honey and a hint of lilac in the winged and keeled bloom, but the rest is its own, a perfume graven in memory as wisteria.

Our white Chinese wisteria, *Wisteria sinensis alba,* preferred to climb into the nearby apple tree. It flowered near the top, a milky rain of fragile florets, deliciously spicy with cinnamon, different from the usual bouquet and coming a week later.

The impressive Japanese wisteria, *W. floribunda,* is something of a collector's item, requiring a special situation and special care for its shower of bloom. Strings of countless little flowers hang to a possible 3 to 4 feet, so for this vine a pergola must be proportionately higher unless we are expected to pass through the cascade. Japanese wisteria starts a week or two later than Chinese, when its foliage-fronds are well-developed and lay in a green thatch above the rain of bloom. The wide-spaced flowers are supposed to have excellent fragrance, yet those we have smelled have only a frail sweetness. As nothing ruins wisteria bloom faster than warm nights and hot wind, we prefer the earlier *W. sinensis* and forms that appear close to it. 'Naki-Noda' or 'Naga-Noda', as it grows in our area, has 13-inch clusters in early May, two-toned violet flowers of deeper color than *W. sinensis* and just as fragrant. *W. floribunda macrobotrys* opens mid-May with 15-inch clusters of pale lavender-gray that have the wedged look of *W. sinensis* and a magnificent perfume, typical wisteria but sugared and spiced, best of all the Japanese. Others may have better color but invariably less scent, nor are the natives, *W. frutescens* and *W. macrostachya,* worth sniffing. Nurseries grow wisterias in containers these days to show that plants do bloom. Nose your way among them to find the best one, assured it will flower forever.

CLEMATIS AND A MAY JASMINE

The clematis that concern us are not the large, summer-blooming beauties but the many small-flowered species that load the air with vanilla or almond scents. These are a prolific, adaptable lot, and you may find room for several in your fragrant garden. Earliest to open in mid-May is the energetic anemone clematis, *Clematis montana,* which can grasp its way to 30 feet or more. Since buds emerge from year-old wood, this must be pruned back in spring as with certain large-flowered clematis, but only enough to avoid undue tangling. Our worst winters (to 10 degrees F) have yet to harm the long strands, but in colder areas it loses all wood and is not worth growing, even though root-hardy.

The typical form is white but we prefer pink anemone clematis, *C. montana rubens,* which adorns one end of our long eastern arbor,

Clematis montana rubens

Jasminum ✕stephanense

Akebia quinata

meeting the purple wisteria halfway along. In nurseries we notice considerable variation in potted specimens: some are insipidly pale, others open deep rose and fade a good pink, with purple-stained leaves and stems. This is the kind to select. In full bloom a mature vine is magnificent and a joy to smell, but of what it smells is controversial— macaroons? boiling toffee? fresh-baked bread? To us, the scent is strong vanilla, coming through as milk chocolate. It spreads but is stronger in passing than close up, and quantity seems only to send it out farther, not to increase the intensity beyond bearing. Here is a sweetness some find cloying—we do not.

Similar to *C. montana* but evergreen is the lovely white *C. Armandii*, hardy to Baltimore and south Jersey. Flowers are somewhat larger, as in the pink 'Apple Blossom'. They appear in May, covering the glossy foliage with an avalanche of bloom that smells of honey and almond like the fall-blooming species.

Midsummer clematis are disappointing to smell. All those reputedly sweet—*C. orientalis*, 'Duchess of Edinburgh', *C. recta*, *C. heracleaefolia* and its var. *Davidiana*, 'Mrs. Robert Brydon', *C. crispa* —have only a hint of honey, nothing of the intensity of sweet autumn clematis. A late-summer climber we should like to have is primrose-colored and supposedly primrose-fragrant, *C. Rehderiana*, unobtainable unless imported; it once grew in the Spingarn collection in Dutchess County, New York, and was hardy there.

In August the creamy clouds of sweet autumn clematis, *C. paniculata*, bring the sweetness of a well-flavored vanilla layer cake to the arbor at the back door, and for weeks the kitchen is filled with scent. Toward the end of bloom it has a musty sweetness, and we enjoy that, too. *C. paniculata* is seen everywhere, much more than its American counterpart, *C. virginiana*, and *C. paniculata* seeds freely with variable results as to time of bloom, size of flower, quality of scent. One of our plants buds by August 10 and is gone when others are beginning. Another, out of a hedgerow, is very late, very white, wonderfully sweet of honeyed almond. It is like the bloom of English May, *Crataegus Oxyacantha*, yet individual, and to us a characteristic scent of autumn, along with the heady aroma of ripening Concords and Winesaps, a sign that summer is coming to a close.

But long before this, just as *C. montana* is finishing, *Jasminum ×stephanense* opens toward the end of May. It has soft leaves cut in the manner of poets jessamine and the wiry strands are wreathed with pale pink scented flowers. From which parent it has acquired hardiness is difficult to say, but ours has survived nine years of drought and fierce winters. The plant needs age to bloom, ours has only recently flowered. The strawberry stain on the flowers, their lovely form, and good jasmine perfume have been worth the wait.

INCOMPARABLE HONEYSUCKLE

Toward the end of June, our country world is filled with one of the most delectable of all scents, that of the Japanese honeysuckle, *Lonicera japonica Halliana.* This can be an utterly maddening vine, so invasive it would take over both our hill and woods if allowed, and strangle every tree and shrub there. In June, however, all is forgiven. It literally drenches our acres in perfume, permeating the whole atmosphere, and we revel in it.

In this country, honeysuckle has come to mean but one—this rampant Oriental. While the type has white flowers stained purple outside, Hall's opens white and turns soft buff-yellow. The perfume of these two is supreme among honeysuckles, a pure "fine quick scent" of light sweetness that never tires the nose, giving as much pleasure in the last inhalation as the first. For all its light quality, it is quite strong: even a single sprig in October guides us to it by scent alone. In *L. japonica chinensis,* purple-leaved, and var. *aureo-reticulata,* yellow-patterned, foliage is more impressive than bloom. Other climbing honeysuckles duplicate the scent of Hall's but have not its adaptability, and only one or two are readily found.

One species we long to try but cannot locate is the native *Lonicera flava,* yellow trumpet honeysuckle, that grows in the southern Appalachians and Ozarks and has proved hardy to lower New York. In the South, yellow honeysuckle can mean either this or the odorless flame-azalea, *Rhododendron calendulaceum,* which also opens in early June. Of many other loniceras, few have fragrance to merit the evocative common name. The native climbing trumpet honey-

Lonicera japonica Halliana

Lonicera thibetica

suckle, *L. sempervirens,* has none nor do such handsome shrubs as
L. Korolkowii, L. Morrowii, and *L. tatarica.* We have already praised
the very early *L. fragrantissima.* A large plant of Amur honeysuckle,
L. Maackii, in early June will perfume its immediate neighborhood.

Best of low, shrubby honeysuckles is *L. thibetica* which blooms through May and often later. The small lavender flowers have the creped texture as well as the changeling bouquet of *Daphne Mezereum* that varies from lilac to lily, on thin branches that arch gracefully to 4 feet. As for 'Goldflame', the gloriously perfumed, everblooming *L. Heckrottii,* this belongs in the night garden for it is scentless by day. But whether shrub or vine, the fragrant honeysuckles deserve more appreciation.

For centuries in Europe, lonicera has been called woodbine for its throttling way of binding a host shrub or tree. More than 400 years ago, the physician, William Bullein, observed, "Oh how swete and pleasant is Woodbinde, in woodes or arbours, after a tender soft rayne, and how friendly doe this herbe, if I maie so name it, imbrace the bodies, armes and branches of trees with his long winding Stalkes and tender leaves, opening or spreading forthe his swete Lillis, like ladies' fingers, emog the thornes or bushes."

8

Pinks, Peonies, and Iris

For the early summer garden, there are fragrant plants without number—perennial, biennial, and annual. Though none is free of scent outdoors, bouquets of them perfume our rooms. In borders, we always enjoy the pink and white gas-plant, *Dictamnus albus* (*D. Fraxinella*), with leaves redolent of burned orange peel. From May to July the columbines offer delicate sweetness, particularly *Aquilegia chrysantha* and *A. viridiflora,* and for years we have extolled the astilbe, also called spirea. From June to August, in sun or open shade these ferny plants with white to pink to red spires of bloom delight us. To Mrs. Wilder their scent suggested new-mown hay; to us they are like the autumn clematis when it takes on a musty sweetness. None of these, however, is emphasized in our plantings as are the spicy *Dianthus* whose fragrance is legendary, though it is rarely free, and peonies and iris chosen for fine scent.

CARNATIONS AND PINKS

The gilliflower of Normandy with its divine essence of cloves was the progenitor of all carnations. In the Middle Ages, flowers of *Dianthus Caryophyllus* were used to spice potables, and so the name, sops-in-wine. Today, clove fragrance in its purest form still favors only *Dianthus*—carnations, pinks, and a few sister species.

While there are many, all are not blessed with perfume. Scentless sorts were almost unknown in European gardens of the sixteenth and seventeenth centuries, those of Gerard and Parkinson, Clusius, Tusser, and Rea. They did not grow such rockery treasures as *Dianthus alpinus, D. callizonus, D. glacialis, D. neglectus, D. sylvestris,* the invasive *D. deltoides,* tiny *D. microlepis,* and lemon *D. Knappii* which have little or none of the family's pride. The biennial *D. chinensis,* supposedly sweet-smelling in the wild, is without odor as it grows in this country today in countless strains of annual pinks. Elizabethans would have regarded these as useless weeds. After the rose, the clove-gilliflower was their favorite—"Of all flowers (save the Damask Rose) they are the most pleasant to sight and smell."

CARNATIONS—*DIANTHUS CARYOPHYLLUS*

The original wildling from the rocky promontories of France had good scent but nothing compared to what came with doubleness. Semidoubles were common by 1597 and by 1600 there were so many gilliflowers that Gerard found them too numerous to describe, but was impressed by the Great Double Carnation with 3-inch flowers, and "a rather tender constitution." By 1650, distinction was drawn between the hardy, small-flowered, very fragrant clove gilliflowers—ancestors of our border carnations—and the tall, large-flowered carnations, forerunners of modern greenhouse types.

The early clove gilliflower grew to 18 to 24 inches from a loose tuft of narrow glaucous 6-inch leaves. Three to nine small flowers on slender laterals made up the wide-branched stems and opened from July to September. Petals were shallow-toothed and unbearded at the throat. Our border carnations are very like but flowers are larger and color selection wider.

For fragrance, any large-flowered carnation taller than 15 inches is impractical outside a greenhouse. Enfant de Nice, Chabaud, Malmaison, Teicher, Giant of Nice and Grenadin strains prove too big and time-consuming for border use. But 10- to 15-inch, well-proportioned, "domesticall"-size plants can be grown from seed with confidence that every flower will be sweet-scented, every plant hardy. These are all fine mixed-color strains with plants of slightly different types: Dwarf Vienna, Baby, Enfant de Nice Dwarf Bouquet, Clove Beauty, Tree Carnation, Fragrance, Camellia-flowered, Dwarf Grenadin. And they provide the greatest amount of perfume for the least effort of any hardy flower we know.

Some have extraordinary scent. A dwarf Vienna seedling here has 1-inch flowers of coral-red with a fragrance half auratum lily, half clove. Others vary subtly from pure clove, syrup-sweet or hot with other spice like nutmeg and cinnamon. We discard the few that turn out to be stingily endowed and this applies to any seed-grown carnation or pink. Marguerite carnations, also known as annual carnations, combine the quick growth and everblooming habit of *Dianthus chinensis* with the form and strong perfume of *D. Caryophyllus*.

GRASS PINK—*DIANTHUS PLUMARIUS*

Grass pink has been cultivated as long as clove gilliflower, but its humble height and small single flowers did not attract florists. "Pinks are of many sorts and of little esteem, they only serve to set the sides of borders in spacious gardens, and some of them for posies, mixed with the buds of Damask Roses. Most of them are single and there are some double flowers, the best, those which are called 'feathered Pinkies'." So John Rea castigated them in 1676. Gerard çalled the species *D. plumarius* for its deeply cut or fringed petals, and we hazard a guess that the name pink may have first belonged to Cheddar pink with its neatly pinked or "pynken" petals.

The original 10-inch plants, "with spices in their throats," grow on limestone throughout northern Europe, making dense mats of 3-inch needle-tipped leaves that spread into great gray-blue mats. Flowers open pale pink or rich rose, fading to white or pink, always with a reddened eye that does not occur in carnations. The old French name for them was *oeillet,* little eye. Each slender stem bears one to three flowers from late May through June. Modern strains vary in height from 5 to 15 inches, and are never so full-petaled that they burst their calyces, as do many carnations.

Laced pinks show a continuous border of the same color as the central zone; paisley-laced, few of which have survived, are more intricately patterned, and Highland pinks are well-marked. Today there is an Allwood strain that blooms beyond the original May-to-June period, continuing all summer. Bizarre petal markings have in no way depreciated scent; all these charming flowers are full of clove. Lacing occurs only in pinks, never in carnations, and differs from picotee types in that a hairline of white (or whatever the ground color) edges each petal, while in picotees, color is most intense at the edge.

Grass pink has other common names—Scotch pink, star pink, snow pink—and Latin names like *Dianthus fimbriatus* or *D. fragrans.* Mrs. Earle observed that "The white kinds always seem the most richly scented." She tells of the "slightly double country Pink known as Snow Pink . . . often used as edging for small borders . . . Last summer, on a heavily clouded night in June . . . borders of this Snow Pink shone out of the darkness with a phosphorescent light . . . like softly shining stars. It was a curious effect, almost wintry, even in midsummer. The scent was wafted down the garden path and along the country road like a concentrated essence, rather than a fleeting breath of flowers—'a running ribbon of perfumed snow'."

We have collected all the snow pinks offered. A treasure from Georgia has no name but "old white grass pink." The double, fringy, 1-inch flowers bloom over a long season and with a wealth of perfume. 'White Reserve' is also wonderfully sweet and blooms throughout the summer, on a plant skimpy to the point of invisibility. What we like best about a third ubiquitous white, 'Mrs. Sinkins', aside from fragrance, is Mrs. Wilder's description, "that fat and sweet-smelling dame . . . so beruffled that she more often than not manages to burst her 'impalement', thus quite losing countenance." She dates from 1868, and her 2-inch explosions of petals often masquerade for 'Her Majesty' and 'Snowbank'. Obtaining named varieties by mail has proved unsatisfactory—aside from three 'Mrs. Sinkins', 'Essex Witch' was the scentless 'Mrs. Dinah Weller', and collections of "fragrant doubles" have turned out to be weak-scented singles.

The best way to have an adequate supply of snow pinks, or of any pinks, is to grow them from seed. In warm soil, they germinate as fast as zinnias and seed is viable for seven years. Select the best offered, and results will be gorgeous. Mrs. Elston strain promises wonderful whites, Highland Hybrids have many markings, Spring Beauty is large-flowered; Mayflower, Double Dwarf and Little Jock are all low and early, in delightful pastels.

PERPETUAL PINKS—*DIANTHUS ×ALLWOODII*

More than fifty years ago, Montagu Allwood of England through selective breeding of carnations and pinks produced an everblooming hybrid. Plants took on the color patterns of either parent—the flakes, stripes, and picotee-edging of carnations, or the eyes and lacings of pinks—as well as their scent, intensified if anything. Being hybrids, all had more vigor than either parent and they did bloom from June until frost. He called them Perpetual Pinks and the strain was fixed. Plants are available by mail but they are easy from seed, producing a crop the first year if sown early. Allwood seed is offered as such and

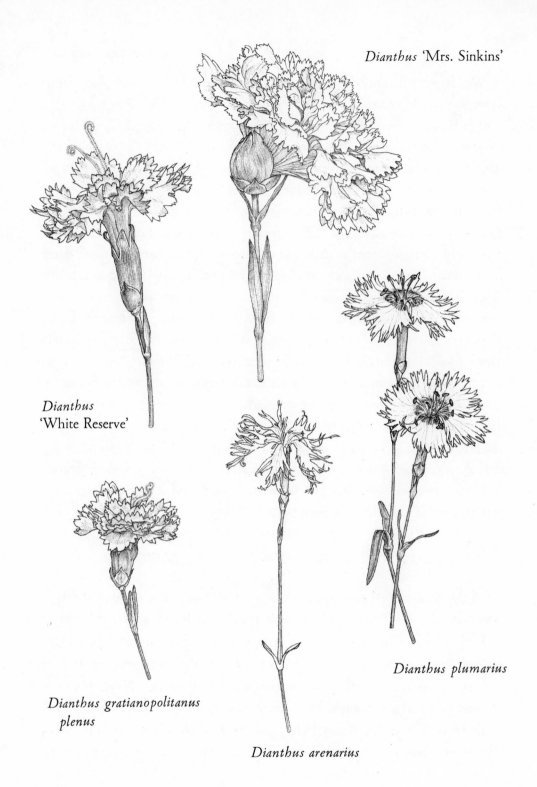

Dianthus 'Mrs. Sinkins'

Dianthus
'White Reserve'

Dianthus plumarius

*Dianthus gratianopolitanus
plenus*

Dianthus arenarius

we suspect that the mixtures—Clove Beauty, Fragrance, Camellia-Flowered—are also from the Allwood Nursery.

OTHER SPECIES DIANTHUS

There are many other species *Dianthus* for the fragrant garden. Sand pink, *D. arenarius,* is like a diminutive *D. plumarius* with deep-fringed flowers, white or pale pink, amazingly sweet for their size. They begin in early May continuing through summer, and grow best in something richer than sand.

Sweet-William, *Dianthus barbatus,* has been in gardens for centuries. London-tufts, it was called and the "homely cottage smell" appreciated. A black-red one with dark matching foliage is still listed and has the best scent of all, a blend of other spices, not the clove of dianthus. Sweet-William, hybridized with more fragrant species, has passed along its cluster heads, wide leaves and free blooming to many offspring. With *D.* ×*Allwoodii* it produced Sweet Wivelsfield, a strain of single-flowered, highly marked dianthus, quite fragrant. Probably from a cross with *D. plumarius* came *D.* ×*latifolius,* coarse-leaved with mildly sweet double flowers in the expected heads. Old hybrids like 'Beatrice' and 'Silvermine' are valued for their constant bloom. 'Napoleon III' may belong here, a cluster-head in brilliant cerise, with marvelous clovy aroma but a weak constitution.

Cheddar pink, *D. gratianopolitanus* (*D. caesius*), takes its name from the Cheddar Gorge of Somerset in southwest England. Plants offered here as Cheddar are usually grass pink; but double Cheddar, with small rose-pink flowers early in May above a blue-gray mat, has the species look with short spreading leaves, wider and without the rapier points of *D. plumarius.* The rosy petals have throat hairs but no eye, and edges are neatly dentate or pinked, never fringed. Flowers have the family bouquet in quantity, perceptible at a distance if plants are numerous. The miniature *D. arvernensis,* with penny-wide single flowers of raw magenta, is found in many plant markets in April.

Until flowers open, the green hump of leaves of spiny pink, *D. Noeanus,* (often grown as *Acanthophyllum spinosum*), resembles a hedgehog cactus more than a dianthus. The flower-stems as they begin to spindle in June are so thin that, when flowers open by mid-July, we might fail to see them but for their amazing perfume that blends clove with the honeyed sweetness of bedstraw, a combination that carries far on warm nights. This one craves desert conditions.

The accommodating superb pink, *Dianthus superbus,* differs in many ways. The plant comes from high meadows and woodland verges of Europe, China, and Japan. Here with us it thrives with some shade and richness, and the support of other plants for the weak stems. From a loose mat of light green leaves that hold fresh color through winter, thin branching stems rise to 2 feet by mid-July and bloom until frost. The white, cool pink, or rosy lavender flowers, intricately shredded and snipped, have clove sweetness, though not the "most fragrant sent, comforting to the spirits and senses afarre off," that Parkinson claimed. But fragrance varies from seed as do individual plants. Here they are long-lived because we cut back stems as they go past, saving seed of the prettier forms. One called 'White Lace' is as indispensable to the August border as nicotiana. The everblooming Rainbow Loveliness strain, half *D. superbus,* has feathered and eyed pastel flowers exceptionally clovy.

As for culture, all fragrant dianthus *must have lime*. Ground limestone can raise pH to a neutral 7.0 but regular applications are necessary. Even in naturally sweet soils, dianthus benefit from a mulch of limestone chips. Plants must also have full sun and good drainage; coarse sand lightens heavy soil and does not disintegrate. While *Dianthus plumarius* and many of the small species will thrive in poor soil so long as it is sweet, carnations and the perpetual pinks require a fat diet to keep up production. Compost is the best form of richness with doses of 5-10-10 fertilizer as alternative and wood-ashes for strong stems.

PEONIES OF PLEASANT SMELL

Peonies offer the nose a wide assortment of aromas from the rankly medicinal, through variations to pure Damask rose. The old-fashioned Memorial Day piney, *Paeonia officinalis,* has a strong rather unpleasant odor. Yet among the Herbaceous Hybrids are some that are surprisingly good to sniff, like 'Cardinal' and 'Massasoit'.

The majority of our peonies derive from the Chinese *Paeonia lactiflora* (*P. albiflora*) with crimson shoots and several-budded stems. Their flowering starts the end of May, is heaviest the first week of June, while late sorts wait until June fifteenth. The wild single blush peony is distinctly rose-scented, but few modern singles or Japanese types with crested centers share this quality. Even the fully double can be scentless or unpleasant. Yet there are dozens that delight us with a bouquet of peony and rose, and a few so roselike that with eyes shut, a peony and a Damask rose can hardly be distinguished. Edward Auten of Princeville, Illinois, has emphasized scent in his hybridizing and most of his double whites and several pinks have incredible perfume.

Here are a few peonies of excellent fragrance, especially enjoyable indoors, where *P. officinalis* is unbearable: the white 'Kelway's Glorious' and 'Baroness Schroeder'; the pink 'Mrs. Franklin Roosevelt', 'Georgiana Shaylor', 'Walter Faxon', and 'Myrtle Gentry'; the red 'Big Ben' and 'Phillippe Rivoire'.

Those with pronounced rose fragrance include early 'Laura Desert' and 'Old Siwash'; midseason, 'Dr. J. H. Neeley' and 'Flower Girl'; and late 'Siloam', 'Auten's Pride', and 'Eloise'. 'Belle Chinoise' and little 'Sistie' are hardly show flowers, yet pour out quantities of attar just as the old roses are passing. These are the most fragrant peonies of all.

The very early cherry-red single, *P. ×Smouthii,* often mistaken for fernleaf peony, has the odd scent we like to avoid, as do many of the species. The flamboyant Herbaceous Hybrids vie with Oriental poppies in visibility, season, and strange, unflowery odors, although there are exceptions.

The shrubby Japanese tree-peonies, descendants of the lovely *Paeonia suffruticosa* (*P. Moutan*), all have scent. The more perfumed seem to have a yeasty sweetness that shades from narcotic and repelling to something quite delightful. Visiting a named collection as buds open in mid-May is the one way to select. The Lutea Hybrids, crosses of *P. suffruticosa* with *P. lutea,* have intriguing odors, perhaps a bit strange to our occidental noses but appropriate to the exotic coloring of the blooms. Sweetest of the Saunders Hybrids is brilliant 'Roman Gold', while several old Lemoine beauties are outstanding—'Alice Harding', 'L'Esperance', 'Mine d'Or', 'Souvenir de Maxime Cornu' and its sport, 'Chromatella'. These hardy plants bloom through the last half of May.

IRIS

By the end of March the netted iris, *Iris reticulata,* opens reputedly with a strong violet scent which we do not perceive. Sweet violets opening at the same time smell nothing like netted iris, but you may want to plant a few kinds in a hot dry spot, and sniff for yourself. In June the few flowers of *I. graminea,* purple plum iris, appear, smelling of fresh apricots. *I. pumila atroviolacea,* the progenitor of modern dwarf bearded kinds, has but a modicum of scent. Equally disappointing are the Siberians, the Japanese, bulbous Dutch and English, yellow flag *I. Pseudacorus, I. fulva* of southern bogs, and the roof and crested iris.

Best to smell are the tall bearded iris, which stem from *I. mesopotamica, I. cypriana, I. pallida, I. germanica,* all quite fragrant. The perfume that we consider uniquely iris, distinctive, delicious, comes from the German iris, *I. germanica,* the two-toned purple flags that crowd banks and driveways of old country places the first of May, thus heralding the long iris season. The scent of the taller light blue *I. pallida* in its usually seen form, var. *dalmatica,* by

Iris, an intermediate
bearded form

Iris graminea

some is considered even better, but this often develops a rank quality in strongly scented modern blues like 'So Sweet' and 'Blue Valley', while old purple flag is consistently delicious.

These two support the claim that iris perfume belongs to the blues. A few superior newer hybrids are 'Blue Sapphire', 'Chivalry', 'Violet Harmony', 'Sapphire Sea', and our great favorite, 'Symphony', a light blue aristocrat of incredibly fine fragrance. And even if frost comes too early for its second display in October, 'Blue Surprise' is delectable for spring alone with a far-reaching fragrance and a long season. Older blues of *Iris pallida* fragrance that we enjoy include 'Great Lakes', 'Blue Rhythm', 'Jane Philips', and 'The Admiral'. 'Whisperwood', a taller purple flag is celery-scented; 'Black Forest' smells like pure *I. germanica* and fall-blooming 'Black Magic' is redolent of anise.

The zebra iris, *I. pallida variegata,* an old form still easy to find has the typical sweetness. *I. pallida odoratissima,* an iris antique of 1797, with small lilac-blue flowers of magnificent odor is a choice curiosity.

Of the thousands of other named clones almost every one has a characteristic odor. A few have none, many smell somewhat unpleasant, but the majority duplicate fruit aromas and other flower fragrances. In the "Alphabetical Iris Check List" of 1939, published by the American Iris Society, the scent of each clone is indicated, but the best way to find what you like is to visit an iris nursery at peak bloom. Be sure to consider the recent Lilliput Hybrids, some of which are surprisingly good to smell, like 'Pigmy Gold', 'Little Shadow', 'Happy Thought', and 'Lilliput'.

If your iris multiply beyond the scope of your garden, something delightful can be done with them. In August, remove all roots and leaves and pare, slice, and dry the rhizomes in full sun or bury in a pan of clean sand in a slow oven overnight. The resulting chips can be ground to coarse powder for orris, or added as is to dry potpourri for fixative. Their fragrance develops only after about two months and varies according to the scent of the flowers.

9

Just Roses

The rose is the flower symbol of our civilization and has been associated with the history of every people from the Indian Ocean to the Mediterranean Sea. Because rose petals held their scent yet released it readily to oil and water, it was for centuries the one flower perfume. Naturalists of Greece and Rome—Theophrastus, Herodotus, Pliny the Elder—wrote of two roses of great sweetness: a very double flower, even "one-hundred-leaved" or -petaled that may have been a primitive forerunner, now lost, of our *Rosa centifolia,* and the Rose of Praeneste that bloomed again in fall. This we still have in our Autumn Damask, and even today its perfume is unsurpassed.

In our own search for fragrant roses, we began with the Damask and others of ancient vintage for we could not resist the enthusiasm of the old garden journalists, Alice Morse Earle, for example: "The fragrance of the sweetest Roses—the Damask, the Cabbage, the York and Lancaster—is beyond any other flower scent, it is irresistible, enthralling; you cannot leave it. You can push aside a Syringa, a Honeysuckle, even a Mignonette, but there is a magic something which binds you irrevocably to the Rose. I have never doubted that the Rose has some compelling quality not shared by other flowers. I know not whether it comes from centuries of establishment as a race-symbol, or from some inherent witchery of the plant, but it certainly exists."

Through research and selection, our gardens now have heavily scented bloom in increasing quantity each year. The end of May and early June is a time of intoxication, a time to gaze, to note, compare, gather, to deeply enjoy these plants of fragrance, truly old yet ever young. Our emphasis is still on the old roses. Many catalogues praise the latest Hybrid Teas and Floribundas, but there are few nurseries in this country that specialize in these rarities. Yet they are easy to grow, the most fragrant are quite hardy, and they can outlive us all. As Mrs. Marion Page commented in the *American Rose Annual* 1928, "One comes back to these old-fashioned roses as one does to old music and old poetry. A garden needs old associations, old fragrances, as a home needs things that have been lived with."

MODERN ROSE FRAGRANCE

"Are modern roses less fragrant than the old kinds?" is a familiar question. Considering the sequence of rose development, we conclude that present-day roses can be just as fragrant, but in a different way. Quantity they have, yes, in the sense of strength; quality, not "old rose" but marvelous word-defying blends that to many noses are preferable.

When only European garden roses were available for combining— the types and forms of *R. gallica, R. centifolia, R. alba, R. damascena* —we can assume that their progeny were about as fragrant as the parents. With the introduction to cultivation of *R. chinensis* around

1759 came change. The earliest progenitors, Parson's Pink China ('Old Blush') and Slater's Crimson China (*R. chinensis semper-florens*), had little individual scent, nevertheless they contributed to their matings with European roses fragrances with an unexpected fruit note. The Bourbons, originally 'Quatre Saisons' × 'Old Blush', all have this trait. It was only when these and the once-blooming garden roses were rebred to *R. chinensis* that fragrance began to vary quantitatively. The once-blooming Hybrid Chinas of 1815-1835 were eventually crossed with Perpetual Damasks, and then came chaos. The resulting Hybrid Perpetuals from about 1840 on ranged from intensely sweet to entirely odorless, but so compelling was the beauty of these flowers that interest in fragrance became secondary. When the two Teas, Park's Yellow China and Hume's Blush China, with their Oriental bouquet of orange pekoe, were interbred they produced novel color blends of pink and yellow.

The four ancestor Chinas changed not only scent but form, contributing slender buds and a furled way of opening, resulting in the revolutionary "high-centered" bloom. The earliest Hybrid Teas were 'Victor Verdier' of 1852 and 'La France' of 1867, but they were not recognized as a class until 1893. After that came Pernet's yellow, and the hybrid deluge.

While present-day roses can be strongly sweet, not many of them are, according to introducers' descriptions. The *American Rose Annual,* from 1960 through 1964, gives a fair appraisal of the scent situation. Of a total of 765 introductions, twenty were regarded by their creators to have "very strong" or "rich" or "heavy" fragrance; 105 were "strong," "sweet," or "very fragrant"; then there were 223 simply "fragrant," or "moderately," and these were outnumbered by 264 of "slight" scent. From these last two groups came the majority of roses given high promotion and the follow-up that gave rise to the complaint that roses "don't smell the way they used to." Even so, although thousands of fragrant hybrids have undoubtedly gone to oblivion, there remains for rose enthusiasts an accumulation of deliciously scented modern Hybrid Teas.

Superb fragrance alone is not enough to ensure a ready market for the modern rose. It must have other qualities as good as those of competing varieties. Then with a superior plant, the new rose that boasts strong scent may become a personality, memorable even among dozens of other fine roses. Most modern roses that are claimed to be very fragrant still smell of tea, with often a fruit note. Think of all the species in their heredity, the back-crossings and interbreeding: if they have even an eighth Damask blood, that is a lot. In red and pink Hybrid Teas the rest is China-Tea influence, while in the yellows and blends, genes of Yellow Tea and *R. foetida* dominate. In other classes, *R. multiflora* plays an important part, so that, proportionately, chances for seedlings of little scent are far greater than before. Still, rose fragrance is a sometime thing. Occasionally a rose comes along with a heavy dose of Damask. Then we say, "it smells like a rose."

VARIATIONS IN SCENT

Scent enthusiasts have had fun comparing rose perfumes to the bouquets of fruits and other flowers—to raspberry, melon, banana, and quince; violet, jasmine, nasturtium, clover; apricot and peach, apple and lemon, mignonette, hyacinth, honey and clove. Detecting elements of these in your favorite roses is one of the amusements of gardening. Yet the experienced rosarian (who, by the way, does not smoke) admits that roses, particularly the complicated twentieth-century blends, can smell different at different times of day, with changes in weather, and when grown in various soils. Too many factors must be just right to make a list of similes practical.

Furthermore, rose oil is composed of more than a dozen compounds, in as many combinations and proportions as there are varieties of rose. Scent becomes apparent as these volatilize with warmth, each compound at its own rate of vaporization, the most volatile first. In the relative coolness of night, roses hold their petal-fragrance; even the wide-open Rugosas, so free of perfume in full sun, must be held to the nose for a good whiff in the evening. Then, our ability to detect or even to define particular odors varies, as does experience, the extent of nasal memory, and possibly nasal areas "blind" to certain substances.

While chemical components of many rose oils can be named with accuracy as Neville Miller, an expert on rose fragrance, has done so fascinatingly in the 1962 *American Rose Annual,* we feel that from the gardener's point of view the odors of the genus can be identified more easily by devising categories that reflect rose lineage. So the old roses and their early hybrids, representatives of which are still with us, form the basis for our comparisons. The analyses of complicated blends we leave to perfumers and chemists.

Since the many hybrids we describe are unquestionably good to smell, quantity is not so much our concern as quality and kind. Damask is, of course, elemental rose, and we use the words "Damask" and "rose" interchangeably. Throughout history the idea of rose fragrance has been realized in *Rosa damascena,* which today we know as the repeating *R. ×bifera.* Several alcohols compose rose attar—whatever their proportion, their rate of diffusion seems constant for the odor of roses that have it in large amount never varies in quality, although there are times when strength decreases.

Of course, it can be claimed that all sweet-scented roses have an attar, an expressible oil of some sort. However, only certain roses produce true Attar of Rose. *R. ×bifera* and closely related Damasks, *R. centifolia* and its sports, and the old Hybrid Provence Roses have it in greatest abundance. The type Rugosas are particularly rich, often spiced with clove, and have the advantage of blooming into fall. Then with a scent out of all proportion to their mere five petals, most American species are generously gifted with the fragrance of Mediterranean Damask. Mrs. Wilder delights us: "This true old Rose scent, the scent that has charmed humanity from time immemorial, is assuredly the most exquisite and refreshing of all floral odors—pure, transparent, incomparable—an odor into which we may, so to speak, burrow deeply without finding anything coarse or bitter, in which we may touch bottom without losing our sense of exquisite pleasure. And this is far from being the case with all fragrant flowers . . ."

Then there are fragrances genuinely rose yet altogether unlike rose attar. The Musk Rose, *R. moschata,* in any of its several forms, has a pollen-type perfume that carries in cool air; in a moderate climate the Musk Rose is one of the few roses perceivable at night. Fermented honey with a touch of clove is as close as we can come to interpreting its perfume. Modifications of it are found in Pemberton's Hybrid Musks.

Rosa chinensis in the form of Park's Yellow and Hume's Blush, both now lost, provided the pekoe bouquet of most modern roses. Tea merged with Musk and the hardier 'Old Blush' China gives the full range of Tea-Noisette perfumes, so strange and bewitching that they defy description. The tender Teas of the South are direct descendants of the first two and have the true Tea aroma in generous supply. The later Hybrid Teas, once *R. foetida* joined them, were infused with spice or fruit or both, perhaps on top of Damask, but just as often with no Damask at all.

Often denounced as scentless, *R. chinensis* 'Old Blush' has a mild odor of nectarine that comes through noticeably in its descendants, and it has also bequeathed a distinct aroma of pepper to foliage and to some flowers. Either scent mixed with Damask is sure indication of China genes.

The Austrian Roses, *R. foetida* and particularly the semidouble 'Persian Yellow', introduced a peculiar, unrosy emanation most unpleasant to some noses. Blended with Hybrid Perpetuals and early Hybrid Teas by the French genius, Pernet-Ducher, *R. foetida* gave rise to incredibly exotic fruit bouquets. Sometimes a particular kind is easy to identify—raspberry, melon, banana—but when the term fruitlike is used here, it refers to stone fruit, a melange of apricot, peach, and European plum, but most of all, the perfumed nectarine.

Another variation on the fruit theme frequently occurs as lemon, as the comparisons with lemon-verbena and rose-geranium indicate. Citrus scents combine deliciously with either Tea or Damask, and when all three are present in small amount, the odor, quite common, comes through as apple or even vaguely, "wild rose." (The odor of Eglantine is entirely different, a fragrance of foliage rather than flowers.)

The Blackberry Rose, *R. multiflora,* we include because it gave rise to countless Polyanthas and Floribundas that have come to dominate rose plantings. It has a characteristic scent, a warmness given off by the pollen that reminds us of an overheated iron skillet, and others of some sort of fruit. When crossed with European species, the scent of *R. multiflora* tends to disappear, coming to the fore only now and then; but its own dwarf form, *R. multiflora nana,* is well scented, and crosses with Musk and related Asiatic species pour out magnificent perfumes.

THE JUNE DAMASK ROSE

The scent by which we measure rose perfume, Parkinson's "most excellent sweet pleasant sent . . . neither heady nor too strong, nor stuffing nor unpleasant sweet, as many other flowers," is truly a wondrous odor that originates in a quite homely plant, *Rosa damascena,* June Damask Rose. Out of the haze of centuries, the one plant we can claim today to be species Damask is old 'York and Lancaster', *R. damascena versicolor*. For years Rosa Mundi was distributed here as this, but Rosa Mundi is the handsome striped form of another species, *R. gallica versicolor,* the "Red Damask" of colonial gardens. Actually, there is no pure Damask that is red or even rose-colored; Omar Khayyam's was poetic license.

'York and Lancaster' is stiff, gaunt, untouchable with prickles crowding the wood. Leaves are insipid green and flowers small, of indifferent form, the white petals variously stained pale pink. We much prefer its repeating counterpart, *R.* ×*bifera.*

The Damasks we admire are very old hybrids. At the same time that French plantsmen were experimenting with the Provins Rose, *R. gallica,* and producing hundreds of variations, a great number of hybrids appeared, blendings of *R. damascena, R. centifolia, R. alba,* and occasionally *R. gallica.* This group was called Hybrid Provence and includes roses more like Damask than any other. As a rule, the plants reach 4 to 7 feet, then bend beneath the weight of their very double, beautifully formed, and superbly fragrant flowers. 'Celsiana' is one of the few old semidoubles to survive an era that scorned all but the fullest flowers. The handsome center bud opens pure pink, 2½ inches wide, with petals so ruffled that the corona of stamens is often hidden; after a day or two, the color fades to white and the size swells to almost 4 inches. This color change led to many names—Rose Varin, Belle de Cels, Pallidior, La Coquette, Damascena Mutabilis—and ours came to us as the Snuffbox Rose. Shoots easily reach 8 to 9 feet, and look best laid along a gray fence.

'Kazanlik' is a rose cursed with confusion. It is not the form of Damask known as *trigintipetala* or thirty-petaled, nor is it in any way semidouble, as often claimed. This is the 'Kazanlik' of Edward Bunyard, a collector of old roses, so we call it that for want of better name. Buds come in typical clusters, so full that from the time of sprouting, the long, ferny sepals cannot meet above the petal mass. The flowers are at first flat as if sliced across, then reflex like some pink tissue ornament—a confection of a rose. The fragrance is unmistakable Damask. This has come to us as Rose of Hundred-Leaves, Blossvale Pink, and even *R. centifolia;* the Joseph J. Kern Nursery now lists it as *R. damascena trigintipetala.* In each case it is the very double 'Kazanlik'.

'Prolifera' is typical Hybrid Provence, a 6-foot bush that appears to be *R. centifolia* plus Damask, but *R. gallica* may be responsible for its deeper-than-pink coloring. If you want one enormous plant for an "instant" batch of rose petals for potpourri, get this. It is one of the earliest to open, about a week after the Rugosas. The

Rosa damascena 'Celsiana'

Rosa damascena 'Kazanlik'

stubby buds quickly expand into a carmine-rose mass of neon brightness and superb scent. There is no central pouf, just a pit from which emerges an aborted bud, or proliferation. This is not 'Prolifera de Redouté', which was pure *R. centifolia* with extremely foliate sepals, but probably 'Steeple Rose' of Mrs. F. L. Keay's famous Maryland garden.

Other old kinds to consider here are 'Leda', the milk-white Damask washed with cherry; 'La Ville de Bruxelles', Vibert's "damask with peculiar foliage" of fresh, rugose green and gross pink bloom; and the two sometimes Albas, 'Koenigen von Danemarck', tall and thorny with beautifully formed pale pink flowers, and 'Félicité Parmentier', a reflexed ball of flesh-pink petals in silk organza. These distinct rose personalities, richly sharing the Damask scent, are not quite so satisfying to us as the first three. But consider them surely, if you have the room.

AUTUMN DAMASK OR 'QUATRE SAISONS' ROSE

Supreme among all fragrant roses is the patriarchal Autumn Damask, *Rosa damascena bifera*. Virgil wrote of the Roses of Paestum, that "bear twice in the year" and Pliny of "the most esteemed" Rose of Praeneste, "that goes off the very latest of all." In the twelfth century, the Arabs brought it to Spain from the Middle East, and Spaniards carried it to the western hemisphere. Every land they settled—South America, the West Indies, Mexico, our own West Coast—came to know this old beauty by new names: the Alexandrian Rose, Mission Rose, Rose of Castile, Castilian. Much later, the French called it Quatre Saisons and the English, Rose of Four Seasons, or Monthly.

While England had the once-blooming Damask by mid-sixteenth century, the Autumn Damask must have remained a stranger until the late 1700's, when that famous rose historian, Miss Mary Lawrance, described three Roses of Four Seasons. Neither Gerard nor

129

Parkinson mention it, and Bacon could not very well have castigated Damasks as "fast flowers of their smells" had he known this one. The scent is supreme. Francis Lester, who loved this classic flower, described it as "divinely fragrant . . . the perfect example of a fragrance with the power to create visions that somehow seems to be the essence of all the romances of a thousand years."

To the modern rosarian, the flowers appear wholly "unimproved," a delicate pink semidouble with sometimes enough petals to have a button eye. The buds, three or seven, pointed and enclosed by slender winged sepals that extend far beyond, are on such short pedicels that the central flower cannot open wide. But this does not reduce the production of a perfume so amazing that it blinds us to the muddled flowers. William Paul appreciated the "old group of Autumnal Roses . . . which are more remarkable for the delicious fragrance of their flowers, than for their size or symmetry or form. How delightful it is to wander through a plantation of Damask Perpetuals on a still moist morning in autumn, when the flowers are just expanding! It is not necessary to pluck them to inhale the perfume they inherit, for the very air is laden with their fragrance." In recent years 'Quatre Saisons' has undergone much improvement: by wise bud selection, grafted plants have been produced that bloom all summer without other care than adequate water and annual fertilizing. Some will reach 5 feet or more, but relatively newer sorts seldom grow beyond 3 feet. 'Quatre Saisons Blanc Mousseux' or 'Perpetual White Moss' often appears as a sport on the pale pink 'Quatre Saisons'. The moss, unlike the sticky branched glands of *R. centifolia* moss, is a brush of green bristles, not aromatic.

Of the many Autumn Damasks once grown, American catalogues now list but four. 'Rose du Roi', the first Perpetual Damask to have a flower of high quality, was raised from seed of the Portland Rose. Plants offered here come from Wilhelm Kordes, and they are sumptuously beautiful. Fat buds come in corymbs of three or four, and the first to open is a marvel of design, some 3 inches across. Folded, flounced petals of bright red surround a neat pouf of rose-pink, the color of the petal reverses, and the outer petals enclosing all this are velvety maroon, resulting in a flower of three distinct colors. The scent is all that we expect of a red rose, incredibly rich and fine.

Listed simply as 'Four Seasons Rose' is a narrow plant with clear pink flowers completely double with pouf centers; these open all summer from the slender buds we so admire. 'Rose de Resht' has the crowded clusters, everblooming habit, and fragrance of 'Quatre Saisons', but not the leaves, which are mid-green with pointed leaflets. Bushing out to 2 feet or more, it fits easily into a border of herbs where its miniature cerise rosettes look lovely behind tumbling lavenders. Fragrance is fine and buds never stop forming. The very double 'Jacques Cartier' with button-eyed flowers of mottled pink has excellent fragrance, is strongly upright to 4 feet or more, and exceedingly thorny.

THE FRENCH ROSE

The Red Rose of Provins or French Rose, *Rosa gallica,* is an ancient inhabitant of gardens. Best known is the semidouble form, *R. gallica officinalis,* Apothecary Rose, whose oil and fruit as well as dried petals were once treasured medicants. Long confused with Damask, and even called Red Damask, it is still offered as *R. damascena.* Brought in by colonists, it came to be known here as Tulip Rose or Offley; if allowed to sucker, it will live forever. Own-root plants of true Gallicas average 3 feet, but we prefer grafted plants in the garden for these stay in place, grow taller and fill out handsomely.

Apothecary Rose, credited with "exquisite" fragrance, has only modest scent. However, we treasure it for the quality noted centuries ago by Parkinson, ". . . the sent hereof is . . . not comparable to the excellencie of the damaske Rose, yet this Rose being well dried and well kept, will hold both colour and sent longer than the damaske, bee it never so well kept." So the petals go into the potpourri,

Rosa centifolia 'Unique'

whether moist or dry, and are magically sweeter in death than in life. By the early 1800's there were more than a thousand named varieties of French Rose, and Josephine Bonaparte had them all. With doubling came increased scent, and the full-petaled old Gallicas are weighted with attar—as delicious for nose-diving as any. 'Belle Isis', 'Charles de Mills', 'Fanny Bias', and 'President de Seze' are among the few pure-scented Gallicas occasionally offered.

Rosa gallica officinalis has flowers of classic design, ruffled rose-red with golden stamens and a greenish pistil-pillow in the center. This is the flower that appears in borders of old illuminations, in heraldic figures, in Elizabethan embroideries. It is one rose that surely belongs in herb gardens. Rosa Mundi, a sport of var. *officinalis* and the ancestor of all streaked roses, opens palest pink, splashed, speckled, and lined with rose-red. The modified Damask scent is persistent, stronger when petals are dried. Two other "mad" Gallicas are worth a search. 'Camaieux' and 'Tricolore de Flandre' are handsome, full-petaled versions. The old semidouble Black Rose, 'Tuscany', and almost double 'Tuscany Superb', have amazing color but little fragrance.

Reportedly from Russia via Canada in 1906, the gay 'Alika' has old-rose fragrance in abundance. The 2½-inch semidouble flowers, bright cherry-red, come in clusters from beautifully foliate buds. Prickles, sepal behavior, and carpel arrangement indicate the presence of some American species; even the scent differs from that of Apothecary Rose, is stronger, sweeter.

THE CABBAGE ROSE

It was the Cabbage Rose, *Rosa centifolia,* and its various forms that served as models for several of Redouté's most beautiful engravings in *Les Roses* and also for those sumptuous bouquets painted by the seventeenth- and eighteenth-century Dutch masters. All Centifolias, including the Moss Rose, have a fragrance so distinctive that even with eyes shut, it is easy to tell a Cabbage Rose from a Damask or an Alba. Centifolias have rose attar in abundance, refined with a note of olive oil that is at once cosmetic, feminine, and soothing. "A delicious old-timey fragrance, like nothing else in rose perfume," as Mrs. Keays described it.

The plant is gaunt, throwing up 5-foot random canes that leaf out and bloom only near the tops, leaving the lower wood prickly bare. Grafted plants behave no better. To conceal the bareness, we plant Centifolias through the center of an old rose border with Gallicas and other lower, bushy growers along either side. In June these support the Centifolias when they bend beneath the weight of bloom that, on warm still days, so freights the air with scent that you can almost see it quiver with volatilization.

Old Cabbage Rose always has five large, oval leaflets that overlap the leaf stem and "are snipt about the edges," unlike any other rose leaves. Each cluster is made up of three or sometimes seven buds (three, one, three) as in the Damasks. Bloom, typically rose-pink, is globular and deep-hearted for a day or two, then saucered, as outer petals reflex a little. Recently the true Cabbage Rose has come to us as 'Red Provence' and 'Rose des Peintres', while in the past most plants sent out for it have been the Damask 'Kazanlik'.

As early as 1696, Old Cabbage began to sport to fascinating forms of identical fragrance. Crested Moss Rose, *R. centifolia cristata,* with its tricornered enclosure, prevents confusion with any other rose. Yet it is not a Moss. Instead the sepals have a ruching of wings, glanded but not mossy. The Lettuce Rose, *R. centifolia bullata,* has great puckered leaves, colorful as those of a Savoy cabbage, exactly as Redouté pictured them. 'Unique' (or 'Vierge de Clery'), the crystalline white Cabbage Rose that blooms a week or so later, at first threatens to be red, but the magnificent blooms open white and are as perfumed as any of the pinks.

Not introduced until 1856, 'La Noblesse' is typical Centifolia, yet with qualities of its own. Flowers are smaller than those of Pink Cabbage and hold their cupped, many-petaled form better. As other Cen-

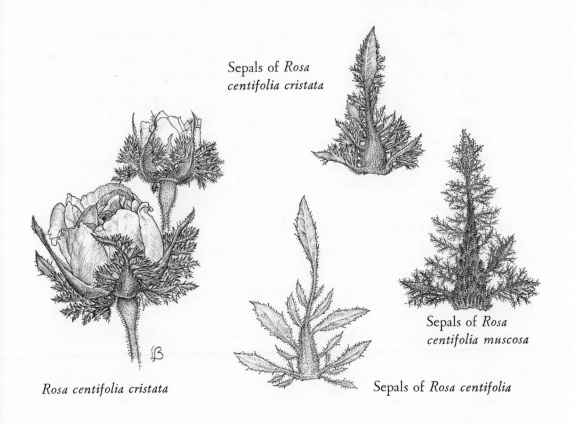

Sepals of *Rosa
centifolia cristata*

Sepals of *Rosa
centifolia muscosa*

Rosa centifolia cristata

Sepals of *Rosa centifolia*

tifolias go past, it blooms on a well-filled bush. 'Petite de Hollande',
with flowers and foliage half the size of voluptuous *R. centifolia,* gains
somehow in charm. The 4-foot plant fills out to a respectable bush
and by mid-May is loaded with dainty buds. The 2-inch pink flowers
are prettiest half open and release an amazing amount of fragrance.

THE MOSS ROSE

The most distinguished sport of the Cabbage Rose is the Moss
Rose, *R. centifolia muscosa,* the sepals thickened with a sticky nap
of ornate glands. Many of the old roses have simple glands, globules
of balsamic oil at the tips of short hairs, but in true Moss Rose, the
hairs divide and divide again, each twig capped with a glistening
red droplet. The slightest touch of buds or upper stems leaves aro-

135

matic resin on the fingers, un-roselike, yet the essential ingredient in the bouquet of Moss Rose. Mossiness tended to disappear in the hybrids and none has ever surpassed the beauty of a half-open bud of 'Old Pink Moss'. Hybrids of Moss and 'Quatre Saisons' have the Damask's pseudo-moss, green glandless appendages, while those of Moss and Gallica have stubby sepals and only a token roughness. 'Old Pink Moss' is usually listed now as 'Common Moss'. Our first plant came labeled 'Mousseux Ancien', which has a lovely sound. There are fewer buds than on the pink Cabbage, one to three on long stems but otherwise this is the same. The white form occurred spontaneously and picked up a new name with each sporting—'Shailer's White Moss', 'Clifton Moss', 'White Bath'—probably all alike. 'White Bath' has the same lovely buds and fragrance as its pink counterpart and the flower is irresistibly beautiful. It is not yet obtainable here; what passes for 'White Bath' seems to be 'Blanche Moreau'.

Next to 'White Bath' 'Comtesse de Murinais' is probably the most fragrant white Moss with scent definitely Damask. After a hot day when few roses smell as they did in the morning, the Comtesse holds her own with the ever-sweet Rugosas. The flower is small, flattened with button center, and pale pink quickly fading white. 'Mme. Louis Leveque' is a well-perfumed late Victorian, resembling a Hybrid Perpetual and bearing little moss. The great globular flowers have elegance and a classic quartered design. Pale pink, they mature with a haze of lavender. Fall bloom is likely on established plants. 'Gloire des Mousseux' has a certain coarseness but is well fringed with moss and the big rich pink flowers are full of fragrance, the suave Centifolia bouquet of a proper Moss. In sudden heat, buds sometimes fail to open. 'Violacée' has excellent scent, like that of the very double Gallicas from which it must have come. Buds are only a bit whiskered and open to 2-inch, pouf-centered flowers of intense ruby-red that soon blues to deep, sumptuous purple.

'Salet' is the best recurrent Moss; 'Mousseline', 'Deuil de Paul Fontaine' and 'Crimson Globe' leave much to be desired. As budded in American nurseries, the century-old 'Salet' makes a shapely 5-foot bush seldom without buds; these are more fern-and-lichened than mossy, and balsam-rich. The bloom is the rose-pink of 'Common Moss' and a hint of olive oil pervades the strong Damask perfume. You may have this under the name 'Old Pink Moss', but if the plant reblooms into September it is 'Salet'.

THE ALBAS

The aristocratic Albas, with subdued gray-green foliage of beech-leaf modeling and matte finish, make backdrops of rose tapestry in the garden just as they did in Renaissance paintings. Only a few type Albas remain, but there are hybrids that seem to belong here. Flowers are white, flesh, or pink, the wood light green and hardy, the buds long and heavily winged. Alba perfume is Damask but light, refined, with not quite the depth and richness found in *Rosa* ×*bifera* or the Rugosas; it has been compared to hyacinth but none of ours have that scent.

Centuries-old 'Maiden's Blush' will always be treasured. The first flower of each cluster has the shape of an informal peony, stamens tucked deep among crisp, crumpled petals of pale glowing pink, surrounded by light green, leafy buds. 'Maxima' is similar, pure white, but without the strength of scent. In Europe the form, *Rosa alba semiplena,* is so fragrant it has been used as a source of attar; here the true *R. alba* is a handsome semidouble, with little odor.

Differing in various ways are others. 'Celestial' has semidouble bloom, coral-pink amid blue-green foliage, on a stocky, 5-foot bush. 'Chloris', with thornless canes 10 feet long, displays two-toned pink buds the size and shape of 'Rosenelfe', marvelously sweet. On 'Mme. Legras de St. Germain', extremely double flowers open faint yellow and age translucent white. 'Mme. Hardy', with jade-eyed ivory rondels and foliate buds has great beauty but little scent, while 'Mme. Plantier', a white seldom given credit for fragrance, opens pouffed blooms in great cascades over a long period and their Damask scent is gratifyingly sweet.

THE RUGOSAS AND HYBRIDS

If your garden is small and your fragrant ambitions large, plant one of the Rugosas. Today, as they are budded and grown in our nurseries, Rugosas never stop blooming. Their scent is heavenly, strong Damask with a sugar-sweetness that makes us think of pink Jordan almonds and the rose-water confections of the Near East; often there is a hint of cinnamon or clove. Unlike many rose perfumes, this is constant and, while time of day has little effect on the volatilization of Rugosa attar, it diffuses farther on cool moist air. After a summer rain even a few open flowers make themselves known yards away in our meadow. And June on Martha's Vineyard is full of the fragrance of Rugosas that have naturalized among the dunes, their white or rose-red flowers nestled in mounds of rich green, poignantly beautiful in that setting of sand, sea, and sky.

Rugosa leaves are rich, glistening green, deep-netted beneath, while their stems bristle with fierce thorns, downy when young. In England and California, plants grow to 6 feet but here in the East a rounded 4 to 5 feet is their limit. To establish them along your own bit of seacoast, set the graft of budded plants well below the surface and the Rugosa tops will take over within a year or two, but these will not bloom so dependably as plants on understock.

The best garden forms are counterparts of *R. rugosa* but have flowers semidouble and double, or if single, of unusual color. Of course, the double forms are longer-lasting and more fragrant, so if you plan to make potpourri—for which Rugosa bloom is superb—select one of these, and in the course of a summer, you can gather from a mature plant all the petals you need to begin a moist base. Rugosas are among our earliest roses and every mid-May the race is on to see which will open first.

Lonicera japonica Halliana with *Rosa rugosa* 'Delicata'

The single flowers of 'Frau Dagmar Hastrup' are translucent pink shaded deeper at the edges, and with centers of tufted cream stamens. The plant makes a thin spreading mound seldom over 3 feet high. 'Belle Poitevine' and 'Delicata' seem alike but 'Delicata' has more lavender in its pink and fewer petals. 'Belle Poitevine' makes a well rounded bush green to the ground. It blends well with blues and is a fine source of petals. 'Delicata' is more upright, to 5 feet, needs white, rose or light yellow nearby to emphasize the blue in its cool pink, which harmonizes well with purple roses. 'Blanc Double de Coubert', the beloved paper-white favorite, has flowers a bit more than semidouble with a few petals capping the centers, and the scent, in Mrs. Spry's words, "the apotheosis of the white rose."

Rugosa 'Magnifica' is a semidouble dark crimson with a purple cast, but not truly purple in the way of Gallicas. The plant becomes large and rounded in a few years and thick clusters of flowers never cease coming. In them the cinnamon scent is most apparent. 'Hansa' is everblooming and can survive even sub-zero winters. The fully double flowers, like bombe peonies, are a magenta of fluorescent brilliance and have incredible sweetness. In the garden, the raw color looks better with the pure yellow of a climber like 'Golden Glow', or next to a strong violet clematis like 'William Kennett', which is also early-flowering.

We grow these handsome thorny shrubs just inside a rail fence where their rounded contours offer spots of bright color all summer. Or one or two can be placed in the corners of a dooryard garden where the lower branches bend to the ground. Most Rugosas are the right height, too, to set beneath first-floor windows on south walls where their fragrance makes more bearable the hot evenings of July and August.

No matter how far removed from the species, somehow the hybrids are pricklier than *R. rugosa* itself. Flowers may be quite large but stems are short and bending. Except for the three scentless Grootendorsts, all have a high degree of fragrance. Our first blooms only in May to June. 'Agnes' has light buff semidouble flowers, redolent of Damask and *R. foetida,* which is one parent. The buds are especially lovely, studded along drooping side shoots very early in the season. Bushes reach 7 feet even with the canniest pruning.

140

'Conrad Ferdinand Meyer' is a tremendous, formidably thorny plant, reaching 12 feet with no effort at all. Shoots must be arched down and fastened to encourage bloom from every node. Flowers come singly or in small clusters on short stems, so prickly they cannot be handled without gloves, but what flowers! Double, cupped, heavy-textured, pure pink, with a fragrance that is beyond belief, a peppered blend of Damask and spice. Only superb scent justifies coping with such a plant. The delicate blush-white 'Nova Zembla' is its sport. Both bloom freely at the beginning and end of summer, with occasional flowers in between.

'Sarah Van Fleet' is only slightly less vigorous, with ultimate size a broad 7 to 8 feet. Slender buds open to semidouble saucers of a deeper pink, week after hot dry week, the scent almost as bewitching as that of 'Conrad Ferdinand Meyer'.

More than sixty years ago 'Rose à Parfum de l'Hay' was bred especially for fragrance from roses known to produce quantities of attar: Damask, Rugosa, and old Hybrid Perpetual 'General Jacqueminot'. The ruffled rose-red flowers have as much scent as any when about three-quarters open but lose it when full-blown. Fragrance depends somewhat on weather, and cool nights certainly help. Thick clusters of buds top exceedingly thorny new growth while singles come from older wood, June to October.

Three old hybrids, the offspring of Rugosa and Hybrid Teas, are 'Golden Dream' ('Goldener Traum'), 'Dr. Eckener', and its sport, 'Golden King'. All have fierce thorns on long, thick canes, but the flowers are lovely, fragrant, and recurrent. As with others that are more climber than shrub, shoots bloom best when fastened horizontally along a low fence. Each has large, semidouble ruffled flowers somewhat like 'Mme. Gregoire Staechelin'. 'Dr. Eckener' opens gold-flushed orange-red, ages to salmon; 'Golden King' begins lemon yellow, paling almost to white in hot weather; 'Golden Dream' is amber yellow flushed apricot, aging to cream. These smell heavenly and very like Rugosas with a faint note of orris added. Thirty years ago they were hailed as the only truly recurrent yellow climbers, with flowers of Hybrid Tea quality and pronounced "old-rose" fragrance. In those days a Damask-scented yellow rose was a rarity and, in fact, still is.

For gardens in very cold areas two perfumed reds are worth considering. 'Amélie Gravereaux', with quite double cupped flowers of vivid rose-red, is regarded as the only hardy red rose likely to bloom more than once a season. 'Ruskin' ('John Ruskin'), rich crimson, repeats even better.

AMERICAN SPECIES

Many of the wild roses of this continent share with the old European species and with *R. rugosa* of Japan the true attar-of-rose perfume. Every June we rediscover them, amazed that these simple flowers contain so much scent. Plants sucker vigorously into dense patches of varying height, their reddened stems and brilliant fruit showy in hedgerows and along woodland verges in winter.

The low and bristly *Rosa nitida* is unmistakable; in mid-June small circlets of deep bright pink nestle among the slender, shining leaflets. *R. virginiana* also has glossy leaves, wider and larger, and thick corymbs of long-sepaled buds at every twig tip from late June into July. Single pink flowers open a few at a time and can scent a room if brought indoors. Even more perfumed is 'Rose d'Amour', *R. virginiana plena,* with lovely scrolled buds which sometimes refuse to open, and small two-toned rose-pink blooms that recall 'Rosenelfe'. The Carolina rose is often confused with the Virginia, and indeed many forms could be either. *R. carolina* has narrow, dull, wedged leaves, and soft pink flowers solitary or in pairs. The diminutive *R. carolina plena* has no scent at all.

Over the plains of the Midwest and up to Canada grows the delightful dwarf prairie rose, *R. arkansana,* low in stature but flamboyant in bloom with heavy clusters of larger than 2-inch blooms and later,

Rosa virginiana plena

Rosa arkansana
'Woodrow'

Rosa arkansana 'J. W. Fargo'

great scarlet fruits. Flowers vary from flesh-pink to cherry-rose, and after the first flush in June occasionally appear even into September. 'J. W. Fargo' is a semidouble form, pure pink, strongly perfumed; 'Woodrow' is the baby of our wild roses, with almost full rosettes on red, 10-inch twigs. As *R. arkansana* progresses to doubling, flower width decreases, the receptacles widen, and height is stunted. We encourage 'Woodrow' to ramble through the rock garden where its tiny gray-green leaves and dainty flowers poke through, but never invade, mats of dianthus, phlox, and antennaria.

Recurrent blooming is more pronounced in *R. californica,* denizen of low moist areas near the Pacific Coast. The small, pale pink, clustered flowers appear above downy leaves through most of summer and are wondrously sweet. Finding true stock is difficult, and what currently passes for *R. californica plena* is something else, possibly 'Banshee'. Four or five forms of this old hybrid have suckered around farmsteads in the colder parts of North America, and have often been mistaken for the Alba, 'Maiden's Blush'. It mystified Edward Bunyard, yet he did not hesitate to proclaim its fragrance, "... the flowers were remarkable for the Eau de Cologne scent, and will delight all lovers of scented Roses, being 'sui generis' in this." Flowers are indeed sweet, with perfume as compelling as that of Rugosas or 'Quatre Saisons'; buds brought inside open to pink perfection and pour out scent. Smooth light green leaves, long thready sepals, and autumn color indicate a merging of some American species, most likely *R. virginiana,* with perhaps Damask—genetically plausible. 'Banshee' flowers in June only.

THE CHINA ROSE AND HYBRIDS

China Roses, circa 1800, were the first genuine monthly roses. Previously, three or four Autumn Damasks might rebloom in fall, but these—our present 'Old Blush', and *R. chinensis semperflorens,* dark red and dwarf, send up one set of buds after another until frost. As a group the Chinas are considered scentless, yet the few we grow have distinctive fragrances, not powerful, but of the sort readily transmitted to seedlings, so that China heritage can often be detected by sniffing. The tousled semidouble flowers of 'Old Blush' have a bouquet of nectarines, faint but definite, a perfume that comes through in such beauties as the Oger group and 'Zéphirine Drouhin'. Petals fade in reverse, flushing from light to deep, a trait peculiar to the Chinas; perfumed 'Archduke Charles' goes from pink to crimson, while in the sweet-scented 'Mutabilis', pale yellow ages to glowing ember-red, a sequence repeated in the Floribunda 'Masquerade'. They are surprisingly hardy. More restrained than 'Old Blush', with little globular flowers of formal perfection, is the delightful 'Hermosa' of 1840, as prolific as any Floribunda, one hundred and twenty years younger and certainly more fragrant. Flowers never seem to expand but hold their shape even when old and dry.

The fascinating 'Gruss an Teplitz' is more than half China, and certainly the plant behaves like a China, with its steady display of bright crimson flowers, few hooked prickles, and tapered foliage. Blooms are many-petaled yet semidouble, shapeless perhaps and inclined to nod on the slender pedicels, but the perfume is strong, an entrancing blend of clove, damask, and pepper. Just one flower half-open scents a small room. The plant can be relied upon to reach 6 feet or up to 10 feet in a protected corner. Even when many-caned and old, the bush is not thick and looks best with cousin Bourbons beyond a wide border of perennials.

Smallest of Chinas is "Miss Lawrance's Rose," *R. chinensis minima*, and its modern derivatives with beautifully proportioned flowers on dwarf plants, but there is little fragrance. The exception is 'Sweet Fairy' (not to be confused with the scentless Polyantha 'The Fairy'). On a spreading foot-high bush buds open constantly to roll-petaled miniatures of 'Hermosa' in pale pink that fades a fragile lavender. The odor is amazing, the peppered Damask of 'Reine des Violettes', incredible in anything so tiny. A dozen other miniature hybrids can

Rosa chinensis minima 'Sweet Fairy'

be called scented, with blends of Tea and spice that reveal their involved parentage: 'Baby Bunting', 'Baby Ophelia', 'Bit O'Sunshine', 'Bobolink', 'Candleflame', 'Centennial Miss', 'Cinderella', 'Jackie', 'Perky', 'Pink Heather', 'Sunbeam', 'Yellow Doll'.

We should like to see the old designation, Hybrid China, used again since many puzzling old roses seem to belong here. In 1871, Parkman described Hybrid Chinas as "the offspring of intermarriage of the French (Gallica) and other June roses with the Chinese Rose and its hybrids. It has, however, none of the ever-blooming qualities which distinguish the China Roses." Instead, they flower profusely for four to six weeks in every possible color of roses, with fragrance not the least diminished by the China genes. Hundreds of hybrids were

146

produced from 1815 to 1835. Plants are characterized by long limber canes, often thornless, and smooth, pointed leaves, gray-toned or dark glossy green. Many roses considered Gallicas belong here.

'Alice Vena' has been grown for generations in colder areas, the original name mispronounced or lost. Globular black-red buds expand to small flowers of intense maroon, so precisely imbricate they resemble double anemones. Petal reverses are dull rose, and the two colors age to sooty purple and mauve. The dusky, heavy-scented 'Alice Vena' cascades from a dense 4-foot bush and is in every way superior to other old purples like 'Cardinal de Richelieu', 'Hippolyte', and what passes now for 'Lévêque' ('The Bishop').

'Du Maitre d'Ecole', when half-open, looks like a Hybrid Perpetual with its dark cupped center, curled petals, and 5-inch size. The light crimson flowers reveal antique form as they age, however, with tucked-in centers, a green eye, and flounced petals that lighten to rose-pink. The fragrance is pronounced Damask, and the big bush is weighted to the ground with a tremendous June crop. 'Fantin Latour' is quite handsome, a thick, button-eyed pale pink in upright clusters of Centifolia arrangement. Curiously weak-scented in its first season, this later developed the superb Centifolia perfume and is now a potpourri dependable.

THE BOURBONS

In the early nineteenth century few roses flowered in fall. Then an accidental pairing of pink Autumn Damask and 'Old Blush' China occurred on Reunion Island, L'Isle de Bourbon, which is due east of Madagascar. There the two roses were used in hedgerows. The plant that combined the characters of both roses reached French nurserymen by 1822 and they took advantage of its abundant fall bloom and quantities of seed to produce dozens of varieties, all recurrent. These became the Bourbons, *R.* ×*borboniana,* the most refined of all nineteenth-century roses. The few we now have, with their dearth of prickles, smooth pointed leaves, and vigorous growth, exhibit far more of China heritage than Damask. In some, the tight bud-clustering remains, and in all the Damask scent is modified in pleasant ways. 'Old Blush' imparted a bouquet of nectarine to some, of pepper to others that adds to their distinction. All have proved hardier here than Hybrid Teas. As a group they bloom best when bent over and fastened horizontally.

Even among Bourbons, 'Reine des Violettes' is unusual. Many old roses are purple or smell as sweet, but this Queen of the Violets has fragrant foliage as well. In April, this and apple-scented Eglantine are the first roses to perfume the garden. Hot sun on young leaves spreads a warm peppery scent for yards around and this persists through summer. The green shoots are supple, thornless, and long enough to bend along fences. We encounter pepper again in the flowers, that with Damask is one of the most intriguing perfumes among roses. Petal reverses make for a two-toned effect, at first magenta then shading to deep smoky lavender; scalloped and rolled petals enclose a perfect pouffed center. Some flowers occur singly, others in tight clusters of three or four, the gray-green leaves close beneath.

Globular roses that hold their cupped form, never opening wide or reflexing, were high fashion in the late nineteenth century. Two delightful varieties came from the French nurseryman, Pierre Oger —the rose-pink 'La Reine Victoria' in 1872, and then its sport 'Mme. Pierre Oger'. These two are the epitome of globular perfection and resemble the shell flowers made by Victorian ladies. Neither fades in the usual way but flushes deeper at petal edges until a week-old flower glows flame-rose as though lit from within. This intensifying of color is characteristic of China Roses but never so fascinating as in these dowager Bourbons. Individual blooms are only 1 to 2 inches across and they have the typical fragrance of Damask with a suggestion of fruit, not overpowering but in perfect proportion.

'Zéphirine Drouhin', almost a century old, has a surprisingly modern appearance. Singly or in small clusters, the shapely buds unfold to few-petaled flowers whose centers never show. The color is a stunning begonia-rose in fine contrast to the handsome copper-red of new foliage. Bloom begins in late May and continues through summer, if some of the newly emerging canes are cut back. Its scent is the Bourbon bouquet of Damask and nectarine that competes with 'Crimson Glory' in strength. The great canes, 10 to 12 feet long by the end of summer, are thornless and a delight to handle. What modern climber can match this!

By the end of the nineteenth century, 'Mme. Isaac Pereire' had become a favorite. Considered one of the most fragrant of all roses, it provided pounds of petals for the potpourris then so popular. The sumptuous 4-inch flowers, deeply quartered, are a light velvety crimson. Bushes grow to 6 feet and some canes reach higher; bending them down encourages bloom. In the sport, 'Mme. Ernst Calvat', the foliage is plum-toned when new and the flowers a rich pink like huge Cabbage Roses. The scent of either is heavily Damask with a hint of the China bouquet, apparent yards away, a treasure in the fall garden. We have come to prefer the beautifully formed 'Mme. Calvat' to the more tender 'Reichspräsident von Hindenburg' whose blooms are marvelously fragrant but coarse, on stubby stems.

HYBRID PERPETUALS

In the nineteenth century the culmination of rose-breeding came with the Hybrid Perpetuals, the flowers the size and shape of 'Peace', from pale pink to darkest red. At first Hybrid Chinas crossed with Damask Perpetuals produced a class with stubby-stemmed Damask flowers and fragrance. Then with more China blood, stems grew longer, blooms became roll-petaled and deep-centered, and scent often disappeared.

Enough very fragrant ones remain to show how magnificent these roses can be, with perfumes to match their dimensions. Usually wood is thick and upright to 5 feet and more, and vast amounts of food and water are required to produce the great blooms in quantity after June. Many can be trained as moderate climbers. Even one plant superbly cultivated is a revelation to scoffers at the old roses. Most famous is 'General Jacqueminot' of 1852 with a perfume never to be forgotten; unfortunately it rarely repeats.

These are easy to find, quite fragrant, dependably recurrent:

PINK, PALE TO DARK ROSE-PINK

'Arrillaga' 1929

'Baronne Prevost' 1842

'Georg Arends' 1910

'Heinrich Munch' 1911

'Heinrich Schultheis' 1882

'Marchioness of Londonderry' 1893

'Marchioness of Lorne' 1889

'Mrs. John Laing' 1887

ROSE-RED, LIGHT CRIMSON, CERISE

'Alfred Colomb' 1865

'American Beauty' 1886

'Captain Hayward' 1893

'Marie Baumann' 1863

'Marshall P. Wilder' 1884

'Merry England' 1897

'Mme. Victor Verdier' 1863

'Ulrich Brunner' 1881

CRIMSON, BRILLIANT TO BLACKISH

'Black Prince' 1866

'Henry Nevard' 1924

'Jubilee' 1897

'John Keynes' 1865

'Louis van Houtte' 1869

'Prince Camille de Rohan' 1861

THE SWEETBRIER

Sweetbrier, *Rosa Eglanteria* (*R. rubiginosa*), is still the first rose to scent the air of spring. Just as hyacinths are passing and narcissus are coming in, the infant leaves fill the air with an out-of-season aroma of apple, for they bristle with oil-laden glands beneath and around the edges. It is the bouquet of applesauce before sweetening, a pungent

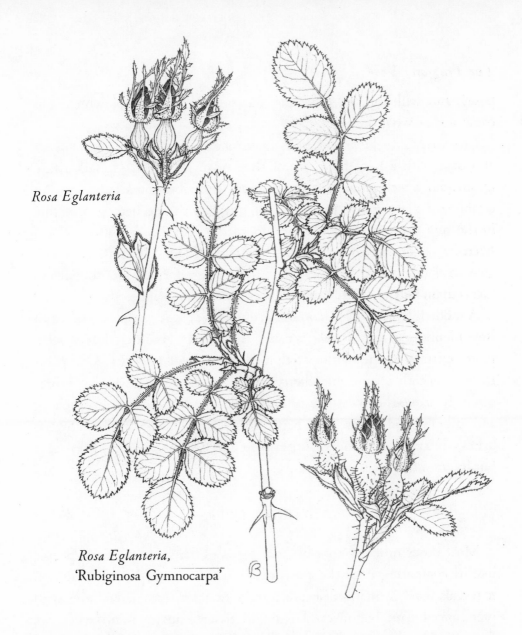

Rosa Eglanteria

Rosa Eglanteria,
'Rubiginosa Gymnocarpa'

goodness unlike that of any other fruit or rose. This pleasing scent is diffused whenever the atmosphere is cool and moist in early morning or evening, but most pervasively after a shower when it can be detected yards away. In summer drought, leaves must be bruised to release the scent. In *Planting and Rural Adornment,* London, 1796, an anonymous plantsman suggests, "for nosegays, also, there is nothing more proper than sprigs of Sweetbrier, when divested of its prickles; for they not only have a good look as a fine green in the center of a posey, but will improve its odour, let the other flowers of which it is composed be what they will."

Late in May, clusters of buds open one or two single pink flowers at a time with a faint fragrance of their own. As every one sets a hip, in autumn a well-grown Eglantine rivals the viburnums for color. An established plant grows to 10 feet or more, with the fiercest armature in the rose garden. We have the big coarse Penzance Hybrids—'Meg Merriles', 'Lord Penzance', 'Amy Robsart', 'Flora McIvor'—but their gain in floral interest has been lost in foliage odor; we do not recommend them for they smell more of black currant than apple.

A modern hybrid, *R. Eglanteria (rubiginosa)* × *R. gymnocarpa,* from Roy Hennessey, is valuable because the small gland-rich leaves seem more resistant to the blackspot that plagues the old species. Our plant thrives beneath a venerable cherry, with 15-foot canes flowering incongruously above the lower cherry branches. The leaf scent is far-reaching and pippin-good, even into September. Two recent Hybrid Sweetbriers, 'Fritz Nobis' and 'Sparrieshoop', have foliage with little scent but fragrant flowers of great beauty.

AUSTRIAN BRIERS

Most noses find the odor of *Rosa foetida* offensive, but some people like it, comparing it to the clean smell of linseed oil. In mild dilution it reveals itself in many delectably fragrant roses, especially those with pronounced fruit bouquets. To us, all that comes to mind when we do sniff the glittering Austrian Copper once-a-May, to check if our tastes are changing, is stinkbug.

The one Hybrid Foetida with acceptable scent is Pernet's historic cross, 'Soleil d'Or'. This has a genuine perfume, a blend of Damask and fruit, as surprising as it is delicious. The plant retains the briery look in its small rounded leaves and long red canes with short-stemmed flowers strung their length, and needs careful blackspot protection. Once established, it will bud again in fall. June bloom is quite double, not well formed, about 2 inches wide, but the flowers later are shapely and larger with pouf center and good quartering. Orange yellow petals, brushed lightly with orange-red, give the effect of a pure orange flower.

SCOTCH BRIERS

Rosa spinosissima, found throughout the mountains of Europe, in Iceland, and in parts of Asia, has been called the Scotch Rose because of the efforts of two Scots around 1800 to make the little wildling garden-worthy. Before then it had been called Pimpernel or Burnet Rose, but the colorful results of the Browns' selecting became known as the Scotch Briers. The type flower is single white and, as Gertrude Jekyll noted, "The wild Burnet-rose has very little smell; but the Scotch Briars, its garden relatives, have quite a powerful fragrance, a pale flesh-pink kind, whose flowers are very round and globe-like, being sweetest of all." Dr. Skinner's diminutive white double, 'Beauty of Dropmore', failed to open well here, but even so gave forth an amazing perfume of rose-geranium; the lemon note was a surprise and we regretted losing it to two dreadfully dry summers. Graham Thomas has the delectable 'Double White', with "a scent as fresh and sweet as lily-of-the-valley." Scotch Roses sucker wildly, are covered with slender prickles, have small leaflets and black fruit; grafted plants are preferred.

Best of all is a treasure of 1838, 'Stanwell Perpetual', a mixture of Scotch Brier and Autumn Damask. The shrub most resembles the Scotch Brier, with its small gray-green leaves and heavily prickled, deep red wood. Grafted, it forms a loose, presentable bush, 3- to 4-feet high and wide. In early May, this old hybrid has quantities of semidouble flowers that open blush and fade white; even the fragrance of this initial crop is undistinguished. Then something most unusual occurs. Strong red canes shoot up from the base; new buds develop, larger than those of May, borne singly amid a ruching of leaves.

153

Rosa spinosissima 'Stanwell Perpetual'

These open to delicate pink, fully double flowers with pouffed centers. Most pleasing of all, this second blooming of 'Stanwell Perpetual' has marvelous fragrance, an intoxicating blend of lemon, lavender, and Damask, comparable only to the double white Scotch Rose we knew, a perfume to be enjoyed again and again. Years ago a favorite mixture for sachets was this very combination of rose petals, lavender buds, and leaves of rose-geranium or lemon-verbena; they were called Grandmother's Sweet Bags.

Less scented is the spectacular American hybrid, 'Harison's Yellow'. Countless flowers of purest lemon-yellow festoon the long spiny

154

branches in early May; these have a warm, yeasty aroma with a nip of the *R. foetida* fume. Later hybrids from Wilhelm Kordes merged *R. spinosissima* with Hybrid Teas. The semidouble amber 'Frühlingsgold', single strawberry-stained cream 'Frühlingsmorgen', and the double creamed apricot 'Frühlingsduft' are best, their light fragrances blending tea and spice with, oddly, a suggestion of *R. foetida*.

The Scotch ancestry of 'Golden Wings' is in no way apparent. It is more a Hybrid Tea that reaches shrub proportions. Single flowers open to 4 inches of soft yellow, paling to ivory before dropping. The scent of 'Golden Wings' is mouth-watering, different from the fruit bouquet of many Hybrid Teas, a spicy aroma that makes us think of Kieffer pears bubbling in cloves and syrup.

THE MUSK ROSE

Parkinson was first to observe that the odor of *Rosa moschata* came from the anthers, "the chiefest sent . . . consisteth not in the leaves (petals) but in the threads of the flowers." It is a perfume shed by pollen, a breath of mead or some exotic honey that spreads over great areas even during the cool of evening. The Musk of Gerard and Parkinson, that flowered "not untill the end of Summer, and in Autumne", with "small darke greene leaves" that were "smooth and shining" seems lost to us now. The name, musk, was derived from a supposed similarity, but in very low dilution, to a highly odoriferous gland of the little musk deer. The old French name, Muscadelles, suggests the flowers may have had the bouquet of muscat wine in-the-making. In any case, this ancient full-blooming Musk Rose was the parent of the American hybrid 'Champney's Pink Cluster', and the subsequent Noisettes and Tea-Noisettes, tender but superbly beautiful.

Many great climbing species roses of China and India share this antheroid aroma, but these are plants for estates and parks in warmer climates than ours. The species presently offered as Musk is the massive Himalayan *Rosa Brunonii* of 1820; through May and June

Rosa moschata 'Nastarana'

the golden-eyed flowers dispel a rich ferment of honey and grape far beyond sight of them. In England, 'La Mortola' offers more open clusters with larger flowers, while in California, *R. Brunonii* has given rise to 'Musketeer', 'McCoy's Double', and 'Arabian Nights', all handsome and fragrant, but tender. 'Wind Chimes' with dainty rose-pink stars is everblooming and much hardier.

For us whose winters are medium-harsh, there are several hardier possibilities. The little everblooming 'Nastarana' may go by the wrong name but it has the look of pure species. Pemberton's Hybrid Musks give us a dozen or more powerfully scented variations. A very old sort, a hybrid, is *Rosa ×Dupontii* 'Snow Bush' with large single flowers flushed pink and a fragrance to recall 'Girona'. Hardiest here is the white *R. Heleniae*—which brings the warm Musk scent to southern Canada; 'Patricia Macoun', its handsome hybrid, has glossy foliage almost hidden in June by a profusion of semidouble flowers, definitely fragrant.

To the student of rose history, 'Nastarana' is of rare interest, for it recalls the old descriptions of the true Musk of Gerard and Parkinson, except that their plant reached 10 to 12 feet and did not bloom until August. Old engravings of *R. moschata,* particularly Andrews', might be of this very rose. 'Nastarana' may be to Gerard's Musk what the Polyantha nanas and 'Katharina Zeimet' are to *R. multiflora.* Even in warmer climates, it reaches only 3 feet, and needs winter protection in ours. Bloom invariably begins by June first and continues until frost. The semidouble white flowers open from pointed pink buds, and the scent lies in the golden stamens. It has *R. multiflora*'s hot nose-searing quality combined with a strong suggestion of clove.

PEMBERTON'S HYBRID MUSKS

The term Hybrid Musk has been applied to a group of shrubs and moderate climbers that appear to have little connection with the

Musk Rose, of whatever species. The few roses that deserve the designation came from the hand of the Rev. Joseph Pemberton of England, who, in his *Roses* of 1920, described "the original parent, *R. moschata*" as a 6-foot shrub with soft, light green leaves and red-bronze wood, both pubescent. His creations, whether 4 feet high or 10 feet long grow like everbearing raspberries, blooming in summer on laterals, but in fall in great subdivided corymbs at the ends of shoots rising from the base. Whether single, semi- or fully double, all share a remarkable fragrance that, as Mrs. Wilder observed, is "curiously un-rose-like".

No Damask scent can be detected, nor is there much of the fruit bouquet derived from China and Austrian Brier. Pemberton's Musks and the early Noisettes release their scent freely at almost any daylight hour, but particularly when heated by the sun. On a summer breeze the perfume is intoxicating, sometimes perceptible yards away. It is a blending of the hot honeyed scent of *R. multiflora,* some clove, and the orris of Tea Rose in varying amounts; it can even verge on the fermented odor of 'Souvenir de la Malmaison'.

Some Musks do quite well in half shade and look lovely climbing through the lower branches of small trees. The flowers come in ice-cream colors, soft pastels that age to cream or white and harmonize well with other shrubs. Modern derivations, those since 1930, are far removed from the Pemberton ideal, and almost scentless varieties like 'Eva', 'Hamburg', 'Wilhelm', hardly deserve inclusion in this distinguished class. True Hybrid Musks are indispensable for the fragrant garden, especially in fall, but do allow plants at least two summers to build up wood before judging their qualities of scent and bloom.

'Kathleen', beloved of Will Tillotson and many others, has the look of a species: no distracting hints of *R. multiflora* or Tea mar its elegant simplicity. The not-very-thorny canes grow to 12 feet, and are surprisingly hardy. Foliage is softly hairy, red-stained when new, slightly rugose. The quantities of flowers—single and wedge-petaled, opening blush to warm white—have the quick-curling stamens of all near-Musks, and a pervasive scent that is our standard of comparison for these. 'Kathleen' thrives in high shade as well as full sun, and looks at home even in a thin woodland of American wildlings.

'Cornelia' might be a Rambler, with its 6-foot arching canes, copper-washed foliage, and large clusters of small, semidouble flowers that open coral and fade pale salmon. These drape beautifully along a fence or pile up in a quite hardy mound. In full bloom 'Cornelia' will perfume not one garden but an entire neighborhood. *R. multiflora* scent dominates the strange hot sweetness.

'Penelope' and 'Felicia' share the salmon and cream coloring of their parent 'Ophelia'. The plant of 'Penelope' is thick and upright to 5 to 6 feet; the flowers, semidouble saucers of powerfully fragrant shrimp-pink, are followed in late fall by round hips of the same tint. 'Felicia' is fully double, smaller, and blends the fragrance of Tea and Musk roses in everchanging proportions. Stems are sparse-leaved and almost thornless, usually to 4 feet. The perfume of 'Pax' is a heavy meld of Tea and Musk; the plant cannot survive our winters without protection. Flowers, so generously produced, are largest of any in this group, semidouble beauties of amber-eyed cream that open from slender scrolled buds of soft yellow, on stems long enough for picking. 'Pax' throws out 6- to 8-foot canes and lights the night with moons of heavenly scent. 'Danae' has smaller flowers of similar coloring with more petals.

'Daphne' resembles *R. multiflora* with tiny winged buds, broad clusters, close-ribbed leaves, and red-bead hips that last all winter, but most of all in the flowers, 1-inch fluffs of lavender-pink that pale to white. The scent is *R. multiflora,* nothing else, and the plant grows upright to 5 feet, filling out to a huge bush. The extremely double white flowers of 'Prosperity' have only faint fragrance.

'Vanity' is most unusual: imagine a large-flowered Polyantha like 'Else Poulsen' elasticized 6 or 7 feet, and you have the effect. Several of the sparse-leaved plants set close together make one great bush, or one plant can grow through another leafier rose. In fall, great airy pyramids of slender stems display wide-set seven-petaled flowers, the bright rose of *R. gallica officinalis*. Their perfume is close to what we call rose, a delicious blend of Damask and warm Musk unique in this group.

'Buff Beauty', younger than Pemberton's latest, is vintage Musk. Copper-toned new growth greens to deep olive, to contrast beautifully with 2-inch fluffs of orange-sherbet. Of all our roses, this was the one Neville Miller liked best—an intoxicating blend of mulled Tea and Musk that is superb.

THE BLACKBERRY ROSE

Rosa multiflora has unmanageable, invasive habits and the only form admissable to the garden is the thornless *R. multiflora japonica* which in June is a cascading mass of tiny white flowers that look like blackberry bloom. The scent has a curious quality. When an iron skillet is overheated, we get that feel of *R. multiflora* lightly coupled with the wild sweetness of buckwheat honey. Together, they give an impression of warmth, a scent of summer that recalls sweet alyssum in hot sun. This comes from the stamens and disappears with doubling of petals. Variations of *R. multiflora* usually share its elemental scent. The southern 'Picayune' has it and the Baby Roses, Polyantha nanas, sold only as seed, are quite sweet-smelling and everblooming as well.

R. multiflora seldom bequeaths fragrance to its hybrids but there are two excellent exceptions dating from 1881 and 1883, when *R. multiflora* was combined with the Tea Rose. 'Cécile Brunner', the original Sweetheart Rose, has the heady bouquet of the Hybrid Musks. It is an exquisite salmon-centered cream-pink that blooms all summer, singly or in loose clusters. In our climate the bushes need protection and seldom overreach 2 feet, but farther south 5 feet is usual. The more vigorous climbing form grows 15 feet or more in a season and produces countless June flowers, just as dainty and fragrant, with a second crop in late fall. In 1925 occurred another sport, 'Rita Sammons', like a rose-pink 'Cécile Brunner', with reddened foliage, extra vigor, and even more perfume. This is the form we prefer for it is as hardy as the miniature Chinas. The other choice hybrid, 'Perle d'Or', has been called Yellow Sweetheart but is really an even-toned cream-orange, with outer petals reflexing to an informal flower. In scent and foliage, it seems far removed from the coarse *R. multiflora,* and its fragrance is closer to Tea than that of 'Cécile Brunner'.

ROSA WICHURAIANA AND THE CLIMBERS

The Memorial Rose, *R. Wichuraiana,* is ideally a creeper, the limber canes rooting where they touch ground and weaving a close mat of small gleaming leaves that in July or August are calicoed with 1-inch white stars. They have a light, pleasing fragrance somewhat like white clover and usually called "wild rose". However, scents of native "wild roses" are quite different.

Many of our loveliest hardy Climbers stem from *R. Wichuraiana* and have stronger perfumes, suave blends of Tea rose and unripe apples or spice, sometimes apparent at considerable distance. Scented hybrids include the Walsh varieties like 'Evangeline' and 'Nokomis', and European 'Albertine', 'Albéric Barbier', 'Sanders' White Rambler', and 'May Queen', all occasionally offered by specialists here.

Then there are excellent kinds as 'Climbing American Beauty', 'City of York', 'Dr. W. Van Fleet' and its sport 'New Dawn' (but lightly scented), and 'Golden Climber'. Those farther removed from the species and quite fragrant compose a very long list indeed, some of them more shrub than climber:

'Autumn Bouquet'	'Golden Glow'
'Copper Glow'	'Hon. Lady Lindsay'
'Dream Girl'	'Katie'
'Easlea's Golden Rambler'	'Morning Dawn'

'Rhode Island Yellow' (formerly   'Ruth Alexander'
    #84)   'White Dawn'

Other scented climbers of mixed heritage cannot be overlooked:

'Blossomtime'   'Nymphenburg'
'Dr. J. H. Nicholas'   'Thor'
'Ghislaine de Féligonde'   'Viking Queen'
'Mme. Grégoire Staechelin'

TEA AND TEA-NOISETTE ROSES

The original Tea-scented China, *Rosa ✕odorata,* lives now only in Redouté's graceful renditions and in a few early hybrids, but its scent is carried by the tender Teas of the South and in many hardier Hybrid Teas. The basic aroma is of dried tea, for the leaves of *Thea sinensis* have little odor when fresh. It may also vary to clove and spice or to a fruit bouquet, as do blends of tea leaves; often a fermented sweetness predominates, particularly after Tea joined Noisette to produce the great yellow-flowered climbers. But in the Teas the attar of European roses is missing, and early nineteenth-century gardeners must have found the fragrance curiously un-roselike. Now we accept the tea or fruit scent as simply other manifestations of rose, and many noses prefer their oriental delicacy.

In mild climates, true Tea Roses bloom for twelve months. They need a long hot summer to harden wood, and a short winter that stays above 10 degrees F. A few seem hardier—particularly with the protection of a wall—as 'Safrano', its apricot-cream flowers semidouble and prettiest in bud having a delicious spicy-tea bouquet; the fragrant 'Lady Hillingdon', with more petals in the same tint; and 'Gloire de Dijon', with a deep, full-petaled bloom of salmon-buff and strong tea aroma.

Excellent varieties for warmer areas than ours include the pale pink 'Catherine Mermet' and the pink sport 'Bridesmaid'; the rose-washed pink 'Maman Cochet' of exquisite bud and the blush-white sport

'White Maman Cochet'; pink 'Duchesse de Brabant' of unusual cupped form; salmon 'Comtesse Riza du Parc'; pink-tipped lemon 'Marie van Houtte'; the diminutive yellow 'Souvenir de Pierre Notting'; glowing salmon-red 'Mme. Lombard'; and long budded amber-orange 'Souvenir de Mme. Boullet'. Another, the antique cream-white 'Devoniensis', raised from the Yellow Tea, has egg-shaped buds and quartered classic blooms with far more fragrance than the old species. Back-crosses of Teas with 'Old Blush', like the delectable 'La Belle Suzanne' and 'General Schablikine', smell more of fruit than flowers, and are somewhat less tender.

Hybrids of Yellow Tea and Noisette appeared by 1830. 'Lamarque', heavy-headed and lemon-white with pronounced Musk ferment, came first and now covers whole houses in the deep South. The pouf-centered, salmon-buff May-to-October blooms of 'Jaune Desprez' were a sensation in 1838 and have hardly been equalled since; their fragrance, devoid of tea, has the mango blend of orange, pineapple, and banana found in some magnolias and occasionally in Hybrid Teas but unexpected in such an old rose. Later mixings tended more and more to heavy golden flowers, tea-scented. 'Chromatella', 'Solfaterre', and 'Céline Forestier' led to the resplendent 'Maréchal Niel' of 1864, whose great ruffled bells of unfading lemon became a tradition in Southern gardens and the showpiece of conservatories in the North. All are still grown, but 'Maréchal Niel' is most fragrant, with a memorable, intense, tea bouquet.

"Mme. Alfred Carrière' of 1879 exhales a mild mingling of Damask, fruit, and tea from cupped white flowers at first flushed pink. Two favorites seem midway between Tea and Bourbon and survive our winters with a minimum of protection. 'Sombreuil' reaches some 7 feet and blooms continuously, opening great creamy saucers of quilled petals that dispel a variation of tea with the odor of Scotch-brand Magic Mending Tape! To a few noses this is the preferred rose perfume, but most find it strange. 'Souvenir de la Malmaison' disappointed Gertrude Jekyll with its "heavy smell of decidedly bad quality" and

Mrs. Keays explained this as "Some find it 'beery' which is perhaps only another way of finding it refreshing." But the writer, George Stevens, considered it "just about the sweetest of all old roses," which is how many regard it today. We find the scent devoid of Damask with a soft fermented sweetness like that of Bechtel's crabapple. The flowers are perfection, flesh pink and white, and the bush form seems never to stop flowering. The climber rests through the heat of summer to produce a second crop of superb bloom in September. Neither is very hardy, but the bush form is easier to bring through bitter winters.

HYBRID TEAS—BUSH AND CLIMBING

Among the Hybrid Teas—Tea Rose married to Hybrid Perpetual —can be found almost every kind and quantity of rose perfume in flowers that come not only in June but until November. Many older varieties have superb scent and are still being propagated. The introduction of 'Peace' in 1945 was a rose milestone, the date conveniently separating these elegant older Hybrid Teas from those of today. Their dates of introduction indicate their staying power:

'Angels Mateu' '34	'Margaret Ann Baxter' '28
'Christopher Stone' '35	'Mme. Butterfly' '18
'Crimson Glory' '35	'Mrs. Charles Bell' '17
'Eternal Youth' '37	'Neige Parfum' '39
'Etoile de Hollande' '19	'Ophelia' '12
'Girona' '36	'Polly' '27
'Golden Dawn' '29	'Portadown Fragrance' '31
'Heart's Desire' '40	'Radiance' '08
'Hector Deane' '38	'Red Radiance' '08
'Ibiza' '38	'Shot Silk' '24
'La France' 1867	'Snowbird' '35

'Snow White' '38
'Sterling' '33
'The Doctor' '36

'Warrawee' '33
'Will Rogers' '37

There are a few unavailable Hybrid Teas exceedingly good to smell, with other good qualities, too, that we mention with the hope that they might again be found worth propagating.

'Eulalia' '34
'Fantasia' '42
'Frau E. Weigand' '28
'Mme. Jules Bouché' '11
'Night' '30

'Rose of Freedom' '48
'Tom Breneman' '49
'Velsheda' '37
'Volcano' '50

Of course, our lists of most-scented Hybrid Teas are not all-inclusive, but if you select from these, you will be sure to have beautiful roses of delightful fragrance that will grow well in most sections of the country. These are First Choice introductions since 1945, many with the handsome husky plants we have come to expect of the new breeds, and all easy to find.

'Chrysler Imperial' '52
'Curly Pink' '49
'Mirandy' '45
'Mister Lincoln' '64
'Mme. Louis Laperrière' '51
'Pink Perfume' '46
'Royal Highness' '62
'Rubaiyat' '46

'San Fernando' '48
'Silver Lining' '59
'Sterling Silver' '56
'Suzon Lotthé' '50
'Sutter's Gold' '47
'Symphonie' '50
'Tiffany' '54

Second Choice are special favorites of some growers, all fragrant, faulty in various ways but far too good to overlook:

'Angel Wings' '58

'Applause' '49

'Betty Uprichard' '22

'Charles Mallerin' '47

'Condesa de Sástago' '33

'Confidence' '51

'Dame Edith Helen' '26

'Emily' '49

'Ena Harkness' '46

'Fred Edmunds' '43

'Golden Rapture' '33

'Good News' '42

'Helen Hayes' '56

'Helen Traubel' '51

'June Bride' '57

'Konrad Adenauer' '54

'La Jolla' '54

'McGredy's Ivory' '30

'Mojave' '54

'Orange Ruffles' '52

'Pink Fragrance' '56

'Pink Princess' '39

'Sweet Sixteen' '43

'William Harvey' '48

In recent introductions it is obvious that there is a new concern for fragrance, which certainly delights us. In this regard, these roses merit close attention: 'Dave Davis', 'Eiffel Tower', 'Lavender Charm', 'Lemon Glow', 'Granada', 'Oklahoma', 'Sabine', 'South Seas', 'Sweet Afton', and 'Mexicana'.

The climbing sport of any Hybrid Tea with fragrance will have flowers just as perfumed as those of the bush. We list so few here because many do not bloom enough to justify the space and care they require; others began tall and have no dwarf form. These are sumptuously scented but preferably for gardens warmer than ours. (Climbing is indicated by Cl.)

Cl. 'Christopher Stone' '42

Cl. 'Columbia' '23

Cl. 'Crimson Glory' '46

'Ednah Thomas' '31

'Gold Rush' '40

'Guinée' '37

Cl. 'La France' 1893

'Mercedes Gallart' '32

'Reichspräsident von Hindenburg' '33

'Ruth' (Alexander) '37

Cl. 'Shot Silk' '31

'Souvenir de Claudius Denoyel' '20

Cl. 'Snowbird' '49

Cl. 'Sutter's Gold' '54

Floribundas were never bred for scent, only for color and lots of it, but perfume has asserted itself as a sort of afterthought. All of these are fragrant and available:

'Dr. Faust' '57	'Masquerade' '49
'Fashion' '47	'Nadine' '62
'Geranium Red' '47	'Pink Chiffon' '57
'Happy' '54	'Pinocchio' '41
'Iceberg' '58	'Spartan' '55
'Kathleen Ferrier' '52	'Vogue' '47
'Little Darling' '56	'White Ma Perkins' '62
'Magenta' '54	'World's Fair' '38
'Ma Perkins' '52	

A FEW MORE POSSIBILITIES

White Banksia Rose, *Rosa Banksiae albo-plena,* is a magnificent climber that in spring is hidden beneath a snow of half-inch pompons, delicately violet-scented; it is thornless and tender.

The Macartney Rose from China, *Rosa bracteata,* grown in the South for more than 160 years, opens throughout summer large, pure white flowers that smell of lemon. The hardier hybrid 'Mermaid' has simply a "wild rose" perfume, but has kept the glossy foliage and pairs of stiletto thorns.

Cinnamon Rose, *Rosa cinnamomea plena,* though long a garden plant, is not worth seeking for fragrance alone; the rather shapeless little flowers have only a mild scent that with drying takes on a cinnamon quality.

Father Hugo's Rose, *Rosa Hugonis,* charms us in early May with golden garlands of bloom, both gay and sweet-scented.

Cherokee Rose, *Rosa laevigata,* another Chinese climber naturalized in the lower South, produces thick-petaled white bloom in May with a fragrance that recalls gardenia. Hybrids like the pink 'Anemone' and rose-red 'Ramona' have even greater beauty but less vigor and perfume.

Lilium candidum

10

Fragrant Lilies,
Old and New

The lily and the rose have been the flowers of June from time immemorial, and as the Damask was the rose of antiquity, *Lilium candidum* was surely the lily. When sixteenth- and seventeenth-century plantsmen were making up their compendiums, this was the one species worth writing about, for the marvelous ones of the Orient have come into cultivation only in the last 150 years.

While rose attar (or its substitutes) is possibly the one ingredient used in some amount in every perfume, there seems to have been no essence of lilies until recently in Bermuda, where capturing the fragrance of Easter lilies has become a thriving business. However, some perfumes and toiletries do suggest a lily aroma even though they are not so labeled. Just as gardenia perfumes are not made up to full strength so, perhaps, lily has been considered too much of a good thing in captivity. Mrs. Wilder found lily odors "languorous and decadent . . . in all of them despite the sweetness something brooding and sultry

169

that is enervating and unwholesome." It is true that in the confines of a room, they can be reminiscent of church ceremonies and funerals, but we have learned to separate scent from association and so enjoy their fragrances free of distraction.

For us lilies seem to separate themselves into the five distinct perfumes of *Lilium candidum, L. longiflorum, L. auratum, L. speciosum,* and *L. regale.* These are well worth growing for their great beauty and to imprint their scent distinctions on the memory over several seasons. Minor species duplicate these or dispel some combination of them or have odors of their own.

THE MADONNA LILY

Until the western Renaissance, then, only the pure white Madonna lily, *Lilium candidum,* was painted by artists and praised by poets. In the late fifteenth century Bartholomaeus Anglicus noted that "nothing is more gracious than the Lily in fairness of colour, in sweetness of smell, and in effect of working and virtue." He might have added, "nor more puzzling to please," but perhaps he had no difficulty growing this native of the hot hills of the Aegean. Other gardeners have, but we can report success by a method described in Constance Spry's *Garden Notebook:* "A friend told me that she had taken out a trench and filled it entirely with wood ashes and planted her lily bulbs which had already been attacked by botrytis in this medium. She assures me that they recovered completely and grew in a most satisfactory way."

When we burned down an old chicken house to a sumptuous mess of corncob ash, rusted nails, and charcoal, we found we had a comparable medium, and set each bulb into a bucket-size hole of it. No soil, sand, peat, or lime was added, just a top camouflage of soil that barely covered bulb tips. Leaf rosettes were quick to appear and came unharmed through every vicissitude of winter. No mottling of botrytis marred the leafy stems that began to furl in April, nor has botrytis appeared even after seven years. Each bulb has produced five or six more, each stem has carried up to twelve buds, occasionally fifteen. These lilies need a companion plant to conceal their ripening stems and Mrs. Francis King suggested clary, *Salvia Sclarea;* in the fragrant garden this is a more apt associate than the usual scentless delphinium that tends to upstage lilies.

Madonna lilies reputedly thrive in English cottage gardens perhaps because wood ashes are worked into the soil. These are rich in calcium that sweetens soils and in potash that forms strong stems and disease-resistant foliage, and *L. candidum* is among the few lilies that thrive in sweet soils. If your soil is acid and you have no ashes from fireplace, barbecue pit, or burned wooden refuse, use limestone chips and sand, with as little soil next the bulbs as possible. Set them with the tip only an inch or two below the surface, and do not protect the rosettes, which are winterproof, but draw a mulch carefully beneath the basal leaves to keep roots cool in summer. And, of course, plant in a sunny place.

Buds of Madonna lily begin to open mid-June with the late roses and from first to last fill the air with a unique perfume. It has a cosmetic quality like violet sachet or mild baby powder, unlike the fragrance of any other lily. A few other flowers have a scent similar in quality—August-lily (*Hosta plantaginea*), St. Bruno's lily (*Paradisea Liliastrum*) and the shrub *Viburnum setigerum*. Both flower and root of Madonna lily were once made into pomades to remove wrinkles, whiten the complexion, and "do a-way the spottys."

Madonna lily's one hybrid, *Lilium* ×*testaceum,* is called the Nankeen lily because of the color, a creamy apricot somewhat like the "melon" of modern day-lilies, flowers downfacing and recurved, with much of Madonna's perfume. Culture is similar, with lime, full sun, and shallow planting essential.

THE EASTER LILY

Perhaps the snowy *L. longiflorum* exhales the loveliest fragrance of the genus. In March and April, when greenhouses are rich with the combined sweetness of hyacinths and lilies, we revel in wandering up and down the narrow aisles, breathing the perfumed air. At the spring flower shows, it is usually Easter lilies that with hyacinths perfume whole floors of other plants.

Ace and Croft are low forms, never above 2 feet and excellent for forcing under glass. Estate is the one tall kind to either force or grow in the garden for flowering. Easter-gift bulbs planted outdoors in the garden after frost danger often bloom again by midsummer. Set bulbs in individual pockets of peat and sand and top-dress annually with 5-10-10 fertilizer. They are hardy enough but first shoots may be ruined by late spring frost, so be prepared to cover them as you do early-set tomatoes. The Tetraploid Longiflorums are a fine virus-resistant strain, with big, thick-petaled flowers, rich fragrance, close-set leaves, and built-in hardiness on sturdy 15- to 18-inch stems. This stockiness permits planting in foreground clumps; as the leaves keep their verdure until frost, no cover-up is needed. In our garden, one group centers a ring of favorite fragrances with the roses 'Stanwell Perpetual' and 'Rose de Resht' on either side, tender-toned clary sage 'Vatican' beyond, and plants of snow pinks and lavender 'Provence' in front.

THE FORMOSA LILY

The slender white species with Easter-lily fragrance seen in September borders is *Lilium formosanum*. This is quick and easy to flower from seed and even tiny bulbs will produce a bloom or two. Formosa lily requires a strongly acid soil and, because it is so virus-prone, a location far from other lilies. Forms include the dwarf July-flowering var. *Pricei,* intermediate 3-foot 'Wallace' of August, and very late, 5-foot 'Wilson' that may last until the end of October. In proper soil these are hardy and long-lived. Narrow leaves, willowy stems, and a head of only three to four narrow, out-facing trumpets give these a wild graceful air that makes them look at home among low species rhododendrons and ferns.

THE GOLDBAND LILY

To many familiar with the genus, the goldband lily, *Lilium auratum,* of Japan, is most magnificent of all. The great flaring white chalices brushed yellow along the midribs have the soul-stirring quality of the Chinese tree peony and, like that noble plant, look best planted in solitary splendor. American-grown bulbs develop graceful candelabra heads, are virus-free, and more likely than imported bulbs to live long in your garden and increase slowly to clumps.

Lilium auratum scent, distinctly different from other lily bouquets, is found in many other flowers—poets narcissus, nicotiana, musk-hyacinth, evening stock. Just a few lilies freight the air for yards around, and a gentle breeze carries the scent far beyond the garden. This is the lily odor Mrs. Wilder found "strong, unctuous . . . unpleasant", but we cannot agree. Reactions differ, of course, for here is a perfume to love or loathe.

Dry heat and strong wind finish off flowers of goldband lily in a matter of days, yet in a protected location of high shade a twelve-budded head of *L. auratum* can give pleasure for three weeks. Because in Japan goldband grows in volcanic ash, we took Elizabeth Lawrence's suggestion to set bulbs deep in pockets of coal ashes with rich soil beneath and beyond. They have done exceedingly well, increasing slowly to three stems per bulb, each many-budded. The form *platyphyllum* has proved even more adaptable. Flowering time varies from bulb to bulb: ours open the last week in July, but others can delay until September and are particularly desirable then when cooler nights prolong their garden reign.

THE AURATUM HYBRIDS

In the past twenty years there have been amazing developments in lilies, particularly from the merging of *L. auratum* with *L. speciosum*. In 1869 the Bostonian, Francis Parkman, made the first recorded cross of the two species and the many hybrids are called Parkmannis. From Jan de Graaff of Oregon and others come the Auratum Hybrids, remarkable for their huge flowers, broad recurving petals, and tremendous vigor. The pink and deep rose of *L. speciosum* may be superimposed on the white and gold of *L. auratum* as in the Imperial Crimsons strain; others are almost red as 'Empress of India', or heavily spotted, as Imperial Silver strains or even pure white, like a superior form of *L. auratum* alone, as 'Empress of Japan' and Imperial Gold strain. Best of all, the exotic pungence of goldband takes on much of the sugar-sweetness of *L. speciosum,* an incredibly delicious blend that is perceptible long before you come upon the flowers. More like *L. speciosum* are the Jamborees and the Potomac Hybrids. De Graaff's Jamboree strain has tremendous branching heads of three dozen or more buds on slender forking pedicels, with 7-inch flowers in the white-edged ruby of *L. speciosum rubrum* Red Champion strain.

The Potomac Hybrids were developed in Beltsville, Maryland, from the same cross of *L. auratum* and *L. speciosum*. If the rubrum lily (*L. speciosum rubrum*) has slowly disappeared from your garden, try the Potomac Hybrids. Flowers have the same rose-and-white coloring of old *L. speciosum* 'Punctatum' with petals recurving into a ruffled turkscap; the head is loosely branched with sometimes two dozen buds, and bloom continues for four weeks. With its delicate coloring and airy arrangement, we find this looks delightful towering over the various grays of lavender, artemisia, caryopteris, and rue, while the larger Jubilee lilies are more in scale with butterfly-bush, summer phlox, and echinops. Both strains flower from the end of July through most of August, reach 6 feet in full sun, and have remarkable fragrance—if possible, an improvement over that of either parent. Neither seems to need staking though stems tilt if unsupported. A generous pocket of rich soil is enough to get them started, with thick mulch and annual fertilizing thereafter.

Lilium speciosum rubrum of Japan, best known as rubrum lily, has graced gardens since 1832. Along country roads plants lean over weathered rail fences or sway above masses of old lavender-pink, white, and calicoed phlox like swarms of rosy butterflies. The scent does not carry far but is very sweet, somewhat like that of white petunias or heliotrope. Mrs. Wilder called it "mawkish," but we find its mildness indispensable to August's melange. *L. speciosum* bulbs must have acid soil and some protection in winter. They grow well in the small enclosed city gardens of Philadelphia, and along the Jersey coast where a barrier cuts off wind nothing could be lovelier. Several variants are available: the early-flowering, dainty pink-and-white 'Punctatum'; the cherry-pink, spotted var. *rubrum;* Red Champion strain, almost rose-red within white borders and extremely healthy; wonderfully fragrant 'White Champion', the best white, totally unspotted but green-eyed with crystalline papillae in the throat, slightly less hardy, and opening August into September—it is exquisite in open woodland among ferns, thalictrum, and fringed bleeding-hearts.

THE REGAL HYBRIDS

At home in the northern valleys of China, the regal lily, *Lilium regale,* was for decades the one lily easy to grow, even blooming from seed in two years so that whole rows were possible. Regal scent is powerful, the fragrance drowning out all others, a strong, spicy emanation with a hint of cinnamon, almost too much of a good thing. This one we never cut for indoors, but in the garden the far-spreading scent is better on dilution, announcing itself before you are aware the first bloom has opened. By July the slender-leaved stems rise to 5 feet or more, topped by flat-headed clusters of out-facing trumpets, waxen white stained rosy-brown in bud. The chief hazard is spring frosts; one year a 28-degree night in late May ruined the 8-inch brushes of leaves to the extent that the bulbs never recovered.

Today there are so many regal-like hybrids of superior hardiness, vigor, and bloom—all in July—that the old species has fallen from popularity: few of the new ones have memorable fragrance, but considering the strength of scent of *L. regale,* that is an advantage. The Shelburne Hybrids developed from *L. regale* have been superseded by Champlain Hybrids in soft pinks and yellow as well as thick white. The very hardy Sentinel strain from Oregon, while not derived from *L. regale,* gives the same large, pure white trumpets on superb many-budded stalks that reach 5 feet; Pink Perfection strain grows taller, with pyramids of splendid wine-rose stained trumpets that mature to pink.

Species resembling *L. regale—L. Sargentiae, L. sulphureum,* and *L. leucanthum centifolium,* each with the half-open trumpets of *L. regale* and similar scent—were combined to give us the shallow-bowled Olympic Hybrids whose great white flowers open in July. The original species, variously crossed with the scentless orange-yellow turkscap, *L. Henryi,* with 8-foot stems, supreme hardiness, and tolerance of sweet soil, produced the historic Aurelian Hybrids. These come in luscious pastels —coral-pink, sulphurous and citron yellows, creamy apricot, tawny gold, cool cerise, and many bi-toned effects due to deep staining on the exteriors. They average 5 to 6 feet with heads of several tiers of buds, most opening during July. The countless clones and strains are beyond the scope of our work, but many are perfumed, some moderately, others heavily so.

HYBRIDS OF *LILIUM RUBELLUM* AND *LILIUM JAPONICUM*

Two lovely species of pure pink have good scent like *L. regale* but more gentle, non-pervasive. The 12- to 15-inch *L. rubellum* blooms in late May with out-facing, rose-veined, somewhat flaring flowers, an ideal companion for ferns. *L. rubellum* has been crossed with Parkmanni hybrids (*L. auratum* × *L. speciosum*) with exquisite results:

the 4-foot, pink and white Atomic Hybrids bloom in late May; the Exotic Hybrids, having less of *L. rubellum,* open in late June. Both have *L. auratum* perfume in quantity.

The mildly spiced, pink to almost white *L. japonicum* is taller, to 3 feet. The wide-leaved form, var. *platyfolium,* is as lovely but more vigorous, making itself at home in our thin woodlands. Hybridizing *L. japonicum* with *L. auratum* and the Parkmannis has produced several exciting strains which have such fragrance, beauty, and vitality that they are surely destined to become garden treasures. Strains named Pink Cloud, Pink Diamond, Pink Glory, and Cameo have large broad-petaled flowers in radiant rose-pink, almost salmon, each with its own strongly marked character. They open in August and have the far-reaching scent of *L. auratum* with a delicious extra spiciness that makes them truly special.

OTHER SPECIES, EXOTIC AND NATIVE

Many other species have the grace of perfume and may fit into your garden scheme. The turkscap group, with every color to be found in lilies, has no one outstanding scent but includes every degree from the rank-smelling purple *L. Martagon* to scentless *L. tigrinum* to the delightfully sweet *L. lankongense.* Others with characteristic fragrances include the golden-orange *L. Hansonii;* miniature *L. pumilum* in brilliant enameled hues; lavender-pink *L. cernuum;* creamy, rose-stippled *L. taliense;* and the pure yellow *L. monadelphum.* We avoid the Backhouse Hybrids which reveal their *L. Martagon* blood in a strange effusion of Clorox, except for the lovely white var. *album,* which seems to have escaped the family curse for it has a small pleasing bouquet of its own. Strangest of lilies is the avocado-and-eggplant-colored *L. nepalense* that smells oddly sweet like the better Oriental tree peonies.

Native species of the West Coast have pronounced perfume but are hard to grow along the Atlantic seaboard. Mountain plants, they need plentiful moisture yet steep drainage, the mould of needled evergreens, and summers less extreme than ours. To those in quest of scent they are most tempting. The honey-sweet, changeable pink *L. Kelloggii* has the turkscap flowers of *L. cernuum*. Lightly scented of clove and *L. auratum*, *L. Washingtonianum* is pure white, flushing with age to deep magenta. Often confused with this because it also turns color, the Mount Hood or ruby lily has better form and much stronger perfume. It is even claimed to be the most fragrant of all lilies.

Distinctly different is the sweet, pure yellow lemon lily, *L. Parryi*. Its best qualities have been incorporated into hybrids that are easier to please, like fragrant 'Buttercup'. This is vivid yellow and cinnamon-spotted on 5-foot stems in July, an excellent example of the general superiority of modern hybrids over their wild parents.

GIANT LILY

The most heavily scented of all, a 10-foot giant from the Himalayas, is no longer considered a member of the *Lilium* genus. Although flowers are liliform, leaves are broad and somewhat heart-shaped, and so it is now classified as *Cardiocrinum giganteum*, not *Lilium giganteum*. The large bulbs are triennial and demand the richness that spells rot for all true lilies. The great tubular white flowers produce fragrance in alarming quantity, a combination of honeysuckle and martynia that is too sweet close by. But its stature and quality of remote stillness—the snowy peak of Fujiyama caught in a flower—preclude our being overpowered, and who would dare to confine such a bloom in the house?

11

On Every Summer Breeze

In July and August "the high Midsummer pomps come on," ancient honey-scented lindens pour forth their evening enchantment, wild grape and clethra scent the woodland, and in the shrubbery the butterfly-bushes warrant their name. Now phlox and day-lilies put on their finest show, and the "gold-dusted snapdragon" and sweet-peas "on tiptoe for a flight" brighten garden and vase. Shifting shadows on the lawn invite repose under ash and sweet-gum branches.

TREE OF SUMMER

There is only one great fragrant summer-flowering tree, but having this we hardly need another. The majestic linden or lime, *Tilia,* growing to 100 feet or more, has famously adorned the drives and avenues of Europe, as *Unter den Linden* in Berlin. And stately old specimens are found in almost every European park, also in plantings around English cathedrals. We remember these particularly at Ely, where one moon-lit July evening the flowers freely scented the air making that beautiful place even more exquisitely lovely.

Lindens must be quite old to bloom, at least 15 years. The several species, different in leaf character, share the same strange manner of flowering. Short green ribbons, really bracts, hang beneath the twigs, and complicated clusters of buds emerge midway from them. The flowers are simple five-petaled affairs full of stamens, and so many are produced in mature trees that the branches have a layered effect of alternating dark green and palest citron. For several weeks in late June and July, depending on species, these diffuse a wonderful clear grape-flower sweetness, not the almondine honey of the May tree or autumn clematis. The scent carries over great areas, farthest on a warm still day, and attracts swarms of bees, which make the trees sound alive by day and by night they litter the ground in stupor.

The European species are best, making our basswood, *Tilia ameri-cana,* look somewhat coarse and unrefined. Littleleaf linden, *T. cor-data,* has the small obliquely heart-shaped leaves of the group on a dense, slow-growing tree. Bigleaf linden, *T. platyphyllos,* has sported to several forms; best is var. *laciniata.* This flowers in early June and has the simple sweetness of watermelon, close to the fragrance of white clove and fringe-tree.

On the Continent, the most widely planted linden is *T.* ×*europaea.* Cool nights there encourage flowering throughout July, filling days and evenings with entrancing fragrance. The flowers, gathered and dried, are used for a tea, *tisane de tilleul,* that you can easily make, too.

Two lindens are particularly lovely and simple to distinguish. The golden linden, *T.* ×*euchlora,* has glossy bright green leaves and new yellow growth that gives the drooping branches a late afternoon glow. The flowers come by mid-July, the largest and most colorful of all the limes, pale yellow and in vast quantities, smelling deliciously of honey and grape-flower. Pendent silver linden, *T. petiolaris,* makes a tremendous upright tree with long thin branchlets hanging straight to the ground. In the slightest breeze, the broad dull leaves, white-napped beneath, twist on long petioles in the way of poplars. Flowers, more hidden than in other lindens, are of marvelous odor, honey and grape-flower close by, but mock-orange when diffused at a distance. To sit near the trunk of a great tree in the dim cave of shifting foliage and flowers is as intoxicating to us as the nectar is to the bees. Of staunchly upright habit, the white linden, *T. tomentosa,* has similar felted leaves and small green flowers that are merely honeyed.

SUMMER VINES, HARDY AND TENDER

Our wild grape vines offer fragrance in two seasons. In June when we take the brook path on the higher bank, we are always arrested

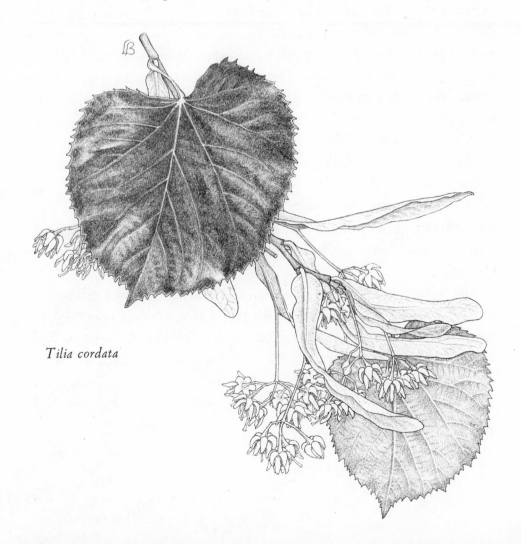

Tilia cordata

by an exquisite fragrance that seems to come from invisible flowers until we remember that this is blossom time for the wild riverbank grape, *Vitis riparia,* with wiry tendrils fastening the vine over the azaleas and spice bushes there. Searching among the rich green, deeply lobed leaves, we find the staminate flowers, mere wisps of stem green that combine honeysuckle and jonquil with the bouquet of sun-warmed September grapes. As Mrs. Wilder wrote, "indescribably gentle yet searching . . . Someone has called the Box the most memory stirring of all fragrances, but to us, in this country, I think it is the scent of the Wild Grape that has power to disarm us and leave us unprotected from memory's shrewd attack." Obviously Mrs. Wilder loved it, but Thoreau did not.

Vitis riparia's small black fruit is worthless. The grapes that fill September with musky sweetness—Concord, Niagra, and Delaware—are derived from coarse-leaved *V. Labrusca* whose flowers have no odor. The flowers of a more southern species, *V. vulpina,* frost grape, with leaves much like Boston-ivy, are equally delightful. Wild grapes are among the most ornamental of vines, as many a painter and sculptor has recognized. Where heavy vines can be supported on strong arbors or pergolas, they offer handsome screening as well as fragrance—but not in areas of Japanese beetle infestation.

There are freely fragrant honeysuckles for summer, too, both of them forms of *Lonicera Periclymenum.* The Dutch honeysuckle, var. *belgica,* with cream-brushed rose flowers extends June bloom into August, and the autumn honeysuckle, var. *serotina,* starting in July, opens its scented purple tubes until checked by frost. This is found as 'Winchester'.

The silver-lace vine, *Polygonum Aubertii,* a very fast grower if planted in rich soil in full sun, with power beyond 30 feet, is one of our scented reliables for big coverage. For spring-summer fragrance and bloom, we have grown it in a southern location with *Clematis montana* over and up a back-door arbor to cover a low roof. Now in a western spot, it is working more slowly to conceal a black-shingled roof that spreads out unbeautifully below our study windows. The scent, honey-almond, so freely dispensed by the 8-inch panicles is like that of autumn clematis, and most enjoyable through the open up-stairs windows.

A tender potted vine, passion-flower, *Passiflora,* now brings color and fragrance to porches and arbors. It may be grown in a cool green-house for late winter flowers that continue to appear through the summer, or stored through winter in a frostfree place and moved outside as the weather warms up.

Passion-flowers of wonderfully intricate design often have pronounced scent as well as egg- or cucumber-shaped fruit of excellent flavor. *Passiflora ✕alato-caerulea (P. ✕Pfordtii)*, easiest to find, inherits fragrance from *P. alata.* The faint mauve, purple-haloed flowers smelling like a fresh-cut orange begin to expand in April. Giant granadilla, *P. quadrangularis,* belongs in greenhouses or tropical gardens. The clambering oval-leaved vines are studded with 4-inch flowers of alternating white sepals and magenta petals, a thick corona of violet and white, and a lovely fragrance. Each flower develops into a long thick fruit as delicious as honeydew melon. Less rampant is *P. trifasciata,* the purplish leaves imprinted with a gray birdsfoot and the 2-inch pale yellow flowers softly perfumed.

Many passifloras are native in our South. Hardiest is maypop, *P. incarnata,* with 2-inch flowers similar to those of the larger *P. ✕alato-caerulea,* of sweet scent and a favorite of bees. The 10-foot vine, herbaceous here, sprouts afresh in May to bloom from July Fourth until frost. Fat fruits turning ripe at the first frost are a special treat.

SUMMERTIME SHRUBS

As the initial burst of honeysuckle is subsiding, and before lindens are in flower, common privet, *Ligustrum vulgare,* contributes to the air of June and July a certain distinction that is not unpleasant if perceived far away. Close by, it has a truly "stuffing" sweetness, just too much of a fine thing. It is even sickening to some noses (and stomachs). Yet, diffused, it has won our grudging appreciation for its power to charge the atmosphere of warm nights along back roads. We noticed this particularly on Nantucket Island where a lot of privet grows. Perhaps it was the mingling with salt sea air that made it so agreeable there.

Better for home plantings is the dainty Regel's privet, *Ligustrum obtusifolium Regelianum,* with horizontal fan branches that carry stubby clusters of tiny stars in June. The scent is somehow innocent of common privet's rank syrupiness, more like that of littleleaf lilac, gently sweet. The exceedingly handsome evergreens, *L. japonicum* and *L. lucidum,* hardy here when shaded in winter, and seen everywhere in the South, are no improvement on the scent of *L. vulgare.*

The American elder, *Sambucus canadensis,* is most adaptable, growing in almost every state. It blooms in June and July with a pure sweet scent, which we must wander down the fern path to catch for it does not spread. Our bushes grow large and thick, suckering widely in the moist ground. To keep them from taking over less vigorous plants, we often have to thin them out and on occasion cut them to the ground. Planted in full sun and drier soil, a specimen can be kept to a square yard with the help of a sharp narrow spade. In Europe, flowers of elder have an unsavory reputation, and no wonder: they are *S. nigra,* and smell as bad as the worst viburnums.

Elderberries are considered coarse shrubs with their large divided leaves and thick graceless stems, but we like the contrast of lacy flower heads against tropical green foliage, and believe a place can be found for one or two (two for better pollination) in most gardens of fragrance. The fruit is so generally liked that hybridizers have worked to improve the plants. Reaching about 10 feet when grown wet, 'Maxima' produces great platters of white flowers with fruits proportionate; 'Adams', seldom over 6 feet, gives generous clusters of very large shining black berries. Birds relish them, so to save them for pies, jelly, or wine, cover the ripening crop with nylon net, the inexpensive 2-yard-wide kind.

Summersweet, *Clethra alnifolia,* is our other woods' favorite. Up and down the Atlantic Coast, the air of late July and August carries the perfume, and here it delightfully scents summer days and evenings on the terrace. The spreading upright bushes grow wherever there is moisture and good light, sending up small candles of creamy flowers. They have so strong a sweetness, almost like heliotrope, that the fragrance spreads thousands of feet, even out to sea on westerly morning breezes. Sailor's-delight was accordingly one old name; another, sweet pepperbush, alludes to the long-lasting seed capsules that resemble strings of peppercorns. Because the sugary quality is never cloying, clethra is also pleasant near the house in high shade and acid, woodsy soil.

There is a pink clethra, *C. alnifolia rosea,* also fragrant, but less adaptable than the wild white summersweet. Other clethras are cultivated: *C. tomentosa* in the lower South is like a woolly *C. alnifolia,* blooming at the end of August, very sweet; *C. arborea* from Madeira is a small evergreen tree, grown in California and here in greenhouses— it has long racemes of good fragrance. *C. barbinervis,* considered better looking, has no scent at all.

Somewhat like sweet pepperbush in appearance and blooming at the same time, is sweetspire, *Itea virginica,* which grows best in swampy ground or along streams. Mounded thickets send up slender, fluffy white racemes, sweetly fragrant. This turns a splendid, vibrant red in fall.

SOME SUMMER BLUES

From mid-July until frost, the buddleias bring color as well as honeyed fragrance to the garden. The butterfly-bush most of us know is *Buddleia Davidii.* The old form grows to a great loose vase of stems, 10 feet high or more, flaunting horizontal panicles of lavender. Improved forms have long fat panicles, just as fragrant, of bright colors on short bushes that associate well with border plants. Even though

Clethra alnifolia

Vitex Agnus-castus

branches may live over winter, plants look better if cut back to a foot in April. Then they sprout anew into a compact 4 to 5 feet. Do place these near paths or fences where they can be reached with nets, for young collectors are as inevitably lured to butterflies as these are to buddleias.

Here is a sequence of buddleias, from light to dark: 'Charming', cool pink; 'Fascinating', lavender-rose; 'Fortune', lilac; 'Empire Blue', lavender-blue; 'Isle de France', rich violet, a tall older sort; 'Black Knight', the darkest, deep violet, best against a light background; 'Purple Prince', red-toned purple with broad-based clusters; and 'Flaming Violet', dark, pure magenta. 'White Profusion' makes a different type of bush—leaves are small, slender, the branching close so that by August the plant is a 4-foot mass of small, graceful trusses; untrimmed, enough wood survives to let the plant reach 7 feet.

For fragrant spires of blue at the end of summer, we grow three half-hardy shrubs. Each is strangely redolent of garden sage. They share a need for full sun, sandy soil, good drainage, and a protected location. The chaste-tree, *Vitex Agnus-castus,* if it loses no wood over winter, reaches 7 to 10 feet, branching irregularly in spite of its opposite bud arrangement. Through all of August into September, flowers open thick tapered spikes of fringed blue above hands of five or seven slender fingers. Since the plant is too tender to withstand harsh winds and winters, set it against a sun-heated wall with the August pinks of phlox, roses, and lycoris. Bluebeard, as we know it, is *Caryopteris* ×*clandonensis.* 'Blue Mist' has broad clusters of medium blue on a broad plant, while 'Heavenly Blue', ultramarine, grows more upright.

Sweet-scented oleander, *Nerium indicum,* hardy along the Atlantic Coast only as far as Norfolk, is a favorite Southern shrub or small tree, perhaps to 8 feet. Its ancient Chinese name translates to "mixed bamboo and peach," alluding to the bamboolike foliage and the peach-blossom flowers, rose-pink or white. The fragrance is a sweet blend of almond and vanilla, with sometimes a note of clove, incredibly free. In cities where the oleanders are a matter of local pride—Athens in

187

Greece, towns of southern Italy, here in New Orleans and Galveston —the flowers are admired for perfume as much as for their luscious color and exquisite form. In Galveston, known as Oleander City, some sixty varieties grace the streets and scent the air, for oleanders withstand drought, and bloom for months on end.

Nerium indicum is often confused with tall, coarse-leaved *N. Oleander,* the true oleander of the Mediterranean, large flowered but scentless. The fragrant *N. indicum,* always with spindle leaves in threes, comes from Persia and India and appears in centuries-old miniature paintings of those countries. In the North, oleanders are handled as tub plants and wintered indoors in cold but frostfree quarters—north window or greenhouse. They commence to bloom as soon as they can be safely put outdoors in the sun. These are a few clones of *N. indicum,* all fragrant: 'Double Yellow' or cream, in quantities on a compact plant, early summer; 'Dr. Golfin', single deep red in May and June, hardy in Norfolk; 'Mrs. Isadore Dyers', double rose-pink, everblooming, exceptionally fragrant; 'Mrs. Magnolia Willis Sealy', everblooming double white; 'Mrs. Roeding', double salmon-pink; and 'Sealy Pink', single, very old, everblooming.

BULB PLANTS FOR JULY AND AUGUST

For August there is the hardy amaryllis, *Lycoris squamigera,* with the strange habit of producing spring-to-July foliage that dies down before the delicate lilac-pink, lilylike flowers open on 2- to 3-foot stalks. They are fun, but only a pale imitation of the September scent and color of tender *Amaryllis Belladonna.*

Then there are a number of fragrant-flowering tender bulbs. These must be planted out each spring and lifted each fall for safe wintering indoors. *Gladiolus Murieliae (Acidanthera Murieliae),* known as the sweet-scented gladiolus, offers a soft, fresh, pleasing scent, not free except in a vase indoors. Plants grow some 2 feet high and soon form strong clumps. Even when set out in late April, buds do not break between the tall, swordlike leaves until August, to open at last in September. Bird-in-flight flowers spread 2 ½ inches, pure white with deep crimson heart in loose racemes that were made for cutting. Their fragrance is mild lily and clove, often more pronounced at a distance, as it catches your nose in passing. A stem or two adds much grace to the rotund flowers of autumn.

There are also the tender gladiolus hybrids. Their odors, derived from such wildlings as *Gladiolus tristis, G. carinatus, G. grandis,* and *G. caryophyllaceus* may be of clove, coconut, or plum and honey as in freesias, or truly delicious mixtures of these; hardy *G. byzantinus* and *G. segetum* have no odor. Flowers, 3 to 4 inches across, are quite ruffled, and all these have fragrance: white 'Sachet' and 'Sweet Cream'; semidouble 'Yellow Rose'; salmon 'This-Is-It'; 'Pink Fragrance'; deep pink 'Cologne' and 'Sweetie'; 'Red Sachet'; and maroon 'Dark Fragrance'.

Milla biflora, Mexican-star, to be grown like gladiolus, is set out in late April. The tiny bulbs give no inkling of the flower profusion to come, nor are the few slender leaves promising. By July the first cluster of five or more buds appears on a long stem. The flowers are crisp, sky-facing wheels, more than 2 inches across and the perfume modified auratum lily. Each lasts several days while stems continue to emerge until frost. (If the bulbs offered are quite inexpensive, you will receive hardy *Brodiaea uniflora* [*Milla uniflora*] with pale blue flower of slight scent above garlicky foliage in May—a great disappointment.)

The fragrance of freesias is a bouquet of very good honey and ripened plum, and a few sprigs can scent a winter room. Freesias are usually grown in a cool greenhouse to bloom through the late winter months, but now corms are treated to open through August and September if planted outdoors in late April. Flowers smaller than forced blooms but in the same gay colors have far more fragrance. The orange and yellows have most scent, whites and pinks are almost as good, but violets and reds are nearly scentless. Whether you grow freesias indoors or out, plant the netted corms on arrival and grow cool while roots develop (about 45 degrees F). Later they need full sun and steady support for the thin, heavy-headed stems.

The fragrance of the South American spider-lily, *Hymenocallis calathina (Ismene calathina)*, close up is strong and disturbing, like paperwhite narcissus, but more pleasing from a distance. Large bulbs may send up one or two bud clusters later; flowers of the first shoot last two weeks, while the polished strap leaves are handsome until frost. The large white flowers resemble a trumpet lily with the petals torn off, forming a six-lobed cup, hence the lovely name of chalice-lily. 'Advance' is a superior form of the wild *H. calathina,* and 'Olympia' has very large flowers; 'Sulphur Queen' and 'Festalis' are interesting hybrids. Wait to plant until soil has warmed up in late May or June; then buds will shoot up with astonishing speed. Plant in rich soil and sun and store warm over winter like tuberoses.

The little *Pancratium maritimum* is the Mediterranean version of *Hymenocallis calathina,* erupting from hot sandy soil in midsummer to bloom at less than 12 inches. With a deep trumpet instead of a cup, twelve-toothed, paper-thin, and backed by long slender segments, the flowers look very like snowy, oversize Campernelle jonquils, and smell sweetly of vanilla and jasmine.

SUMMER PHLOX

Phlox, an American genus, with countless species from mountains, prairies and woodlands, includes the August-blooming *Phlox paniculata* that brings a unique scent to the late summer garden. No perennial, no fragrance, so typifies the month of August as does summer phlox. The old wild forms have the most pronounced odor, the small-flowered whites and calicoes, rosy lavender and magenta. We shall always remember a sunny city garden, just a square plot, jammed with clumps of these and lavender bergamot, *Monarda fistulosa,* while over them swung the spotted pink turkscaps of rubrum lilies. Here was August

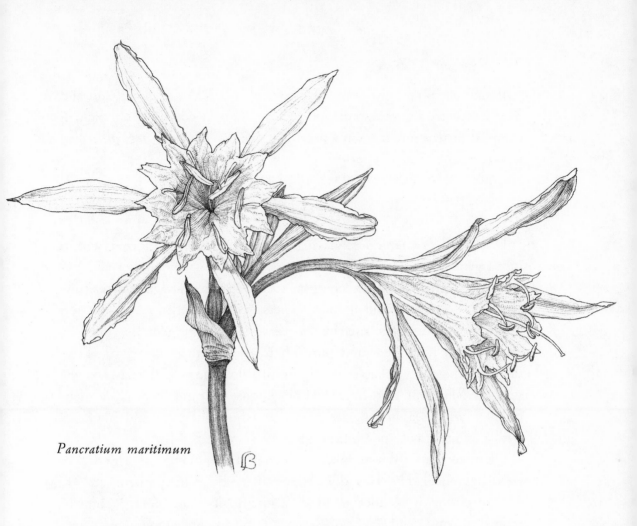

Pancratium maritimum

in essence, the mecca of every bee and butterfly for miles around. The fragrance has an indefinable reaching quality, a bit like clethra yet not so syrupy, a light musty sweetness that belongs to phlox alone.

Summer phlox, which blooms intermittently even to October, comes in many warm colors—scarlet, coral-orange, salmon, pale pink to cherry-red, claret—even in good lavenders and purple but the whites are still best for fragrance. 'Apollo' ('World Peace') is tallest, late flowering; 'White Admiral' makes great heads at 3 feet, branching freely; 'Princess' and 'Snowball' are newer pure whites; 'Prime Minister', old but still charming, is calicoed with a red eye; while 'Everest' is centered with lavender. Many other kinds grow in nurseries where you can enjoy test-smelling each one.

If summer phlox grows well for you, plant a lot of it in full sun and in places with a good circulation of air. Phlox needs deep soil rich in compost or dry manure with peatmoss worked in, and then *plenty of water.*

DAY-LILIES

Day-lilies, *Hemerocallis,* have been marvelously hybridized within just a generation's span. Twenty years ago only a few species and hybrids were grown, and the one that took over woods-edge and roadside had little to recommend it to gardeners except cheerful color and iron persistence. This was ancient *Hemerocallis fulva,* odorless, but the source of all pink, red, and purplish tones in present-day sorts. Day-lilies are the most reliable of all summer-flowering perennials. A few start in May but mid-June to mid-August, summer's peak, is definitely day-lily season for wise gardeners who want color and fragrance with a minimum of upkeep through the hot weeks.

Of more than a dozen species, all from Europe and the Orient, six have fragrance. The two that bloom first on 18-inch plants are *H. Dumortieri* with slender pointed segments in pure orange, brown-stained in bud, and *H. Middendorffii,* broad-petaled, orange-yellow. With only a few buds per stem, their season is short but they have what we regard as typical day-lily perfume, a nose-tingling blend of jasmine and honeysuckle, mild but definite. Their many early hybrids are by no means so good to smell.

Two others are also early, in light yellow. *H. minor,* with low grassy foliage and a few 2-inch trumpets on each unbranched stem, has scent in proportion to its size, small but there. The renowned lemon-lily, *H. flava,* has been grown in American gardens possibly longer than *H. fulva.* Custard-lily and yellow-tuberose are other revealing old names for the richly perfumed *H. flava.* Lemon refers only to color; the scent has the violet-sachet quality of Madonna lily and August-lily, *Hosta plantaginea.* Even today there appear to be no derivatives that duplicate or improve on its outstanding qualities. Once grown in great beds and borders, *H. flava* remains the one species easy to find in nurseries. It reaches 30 inches and suckers with almost as much vigor as *H. fulva*. The lovely flaring flowers begin to open the last week of May, in time to accompany the like-hued 'Harison's Yellow' rose and the lavender-pink Rugosa rose 'Delicata'.

Two July-flowering species, both vivid yellow and clump-forming, are *H. Thunbergii* and *H. citrina*. *H. Thunbergii* is day-blooming, with small flowers on tall stems amid very long slender leaves; in full bloom it reaches 4 feet and was once a common sight among phlox and bergamot in country gardens, adding to these a mild sweetness of its own. *H. citrina* on the other hand opens long tubes in early evening that are limp rags by morning. But they have excellent perfume, the jasmine-honeysuckle sort of early oranges. At one time *H. citrina*'s topsy-turvy hours were regarded as a trait to be bred out. Instead has come a race of night-lilies that grace our gardens in the evening with fresh wide-open flowers and these last until the next set opens. All of our best yellows and creams have come from these two species. These are the pale ones we favor, and we plant only the extended or night-blooming hybrids. By evening when we have time to look at our flowers, the day-bloomers are a sorry sight.

Over the years we have encountered many hemerocallis of faint odor or none at all, a few blessed with strong scent, and some with a fragrance that is really free. In order of bloom, these are some of our more fragrant favorites, old and new; all are either extended day-bloomers or nocturnal.

Early, opening from May 15 to May 31: Aside from the species, the best early golden-yellow is still old 'Judge Orr'. We have found nothing to compare with it for excellent perfume in early June. Even the far more prolific Terry varieties, 'Sooner Gold', 'Lime Sprite', and 'Spring Gold', are only mildly sweet as they grow here.

Early midseason, opening from June 15 to June 30: 'Crown of Gold' is very old, as these go, and hard to locate now, but its slender-parted, golden flowers have superb scent, on a par with 'Judge Orr' and others. 'Wisp', a Russell introduction of the 1940's, tubular, thick-substanced, the acidulous yellow of tansy, has a fragrance so strong that it is apparent several feet away. 'Goldeni', again old, is quite fragrant and makes a large clump of light orange bloom into August. 'Fond Caress' is wide-petaled cream-yellow, with gracefully bending stems and the delightful Tea-Noisette scent of certain roses, unexpected and pleasing in a day-lily. This one must have full sun.

Midseason, opening from July 1 to July 15: 'Hyperion', now forty years old, we still have, of course; with enough water it is magnificent, with 42-inch stems of flaring lemon trumpets, chartreuse-eyed, of unquestionable fragrance. 'Vespers' is our choice for replacing the venerable 'Hyperion', particularly in close quarters. This smooth thick-petaled lemon day-lily grows in our affections. It stays put, performs well even in neglect, and at peak of bloom, with last evening's flowers still presentable and tonight's fresh open, it is a glorious mass of light yellow. The fragrance is pronounced, as fine as that of 'Hyperion', in a classic weather-resistant bloom. One season a clump of 'Vespers' had twenty-eight stems, some with up to four new flowers a night. We tried to watch them open, between seven and eight P.M., but their movement is imperceptibly slow and steady.

Many old Stout varieties with good scent open in July. 'Patricia' had a flower to compare with today's best, but only seven buds per stem. 'Sonny' and 'Princess' took too long to establish. 'Ophir' is still about but flowers have a forever half-open aspect that is annoying. 'Vesta' is the only Stout variety we now grow, a lovely pure orange on 2-foot stems, powerfully sweet.

'Midwest Majesty', never described as fragrant in any catalogue we have seen, seems to us the most fragrant day-lily of any season. It is a handsome deep yellow on staunch 4-foot stalks; the 7-inch flowers open early, last well past nine P.M. and are worth many sniffs. 'Hesperus' could be its twin in form and color, but is taller with more flowers—once we counted sixty-eight buds on one stem—and slightly less scented. The newer 'Elizabeth Payne', a 5-inch fragrant, ruffled canary yellow, fresh at the end of the hottest day, is lovely for foregrounds, being 24 inches high.

Late midseason, opening July 15 to July 30: 'Kenwood' is the last of our sweet ones to open, flowering all through August and mingling beautifully with the lavender panicles of *Buddleia* 'Empire Blue'. Very fragrant pale yellow flowers, excellent at night, open on stems of various lengths so that bloom is not massed at one level.

The best way to locate other perfumed kinds is to visit the nurseries of specialists and smell for yourself. There are many more than these few but most are scentless. Day-lilies are so desirable for mass planting that fragrance has been less important than substance and branching. Day-lilies stand much abuse, but for good bloom, they need deep watering in times of drought. Also, they must be fertilized once a year and kept clean of old foliage. October is an excellent time for doing both since flower buds form in February or March and food is then available to them if it has been scratched in deep and the clumps mulched. Varieties that sucker widely can search for fresh soil and food, but the slow growers deteriorate if uncared for, and most fragrant varieties are of this kind.

ANNUALS OF FINE SCENT

Two of the most fragrant annuals are sweet-peas and mignonette. The perfume of sweet-peas is one of the loveliest, comparable in purity to honeysuckle, appleblossoms, and grape-flowers. The small-flowered, magenta species, *Lathyrus odoratus,* still grows in Sicily and Spain, but except for its powerful scent—honeyed, almost cloying—is hardly recognizable as the parent of today's frilled and silken beauties. In England, these are more noteworthy for color and size, but American strains all seem good to smell, though strength varies. A few firms offer mixtures of the most scented and, at present, this seems the best way to get perfumed sweet-peas. Among their rainbow colors, best are the luscious light pastels; strong deep colors seem to lose odor as they gain brilliance.

In recent years hybridizers have produced sweet-peas that bloom with average culture. Tough strains like Cuthbertson's Floribunda, or Burpee's Galaxy and Giant Late Heat-Resistant, or Zvolanek's Plenti-flora are less dependent on a long cool season. These produce quantities of bloom through June and July with five or more gorgeous flowers per long stem. 'Bijou', a spreading 1-foot mound, and 'Knee-Hi', a self-supporting 30-inch bush, both with long stems of large flowers in the full color range, are the pastels most perfumed. The tiny Cupid or Little Sweetheart strain has both scent and color, but is too low to have cutting stems.

Recalling that sweet-peas were the very first seeds we planted as children, and in unprepared soil at the foundation line of the house and with strings to support the *flowering* vines, we now pass over the complicated directions for show flowers and provide only basic culture: March sowing in fairly rich soil (or in late fall farther south), full sun, steady moisture, and lime in the soil—the same requirements as for garden peas. Turkey-wire or waxed twine netting supports the sprout-ing vines with privet clippings set along the base to prevent wind dam-age. Devotees insist sweet-peas be grown alone for largest flowers, long-est stems (and, we add, most care), but there is no reason they may not mount into thin shrubs or climbing roses where their August demise is out of sight. A thick mulch of straw from April on keeps soil evenly moist and cool, even through rainless weeks. (Perennial pea, *Lathy-rus latifolius*—white, rose, or carmine—has no odor, nor has the flam-ing scarlet runner-bean, *Phaseolus coccineus.*)

The broad bean of Europe, *Vicia faba,* now in our vegetable cata-logues, has the same needs as sweet-peas but grows without tendrils to a bush. This is F. A. Hampton's famous beanfield flower, a little purple-eyed white pease blossom that in quantity produces an inde-finable sensation, an effusion more of feeling than scent. It combines honey and auratum lily in an aroma that drifts over hundreds of feet.

By late summer, stalks are hung with huge pods of flat beans, surprisingly sweet and tender.

Shaggy little mignonette, that humble Egyptian weed whose perfume won the hearts of Frenchmen in the reign of Louis XV, still survives to enchant us. The foliage of *Reseda odorata* is weedy and thin, the branches sprawling, the flowers unimpressive, mostly rust-orange stamens against thready chartreuse petals. But this plant of small beauty has great scent, the refinement of sweet-pea and grape-flower with a hint of ripe nectarine that carries over the garden as the sun draws it out. Strength seems to depend on lime in the soil and steady moisture but plants may vary, too. As the many hardy volunteers appear, allow only the most fragrant plants to form seed. Strains with longer flower plumes in subtle, tawny tones do not seem to have lost much odor; the Machet strain is excellent, particularly Red Goliath and Red Monarch, and Allen's Defiance is remarkable, too. April sowing outdoors gives all-summer bloom, while pot-grown plants grace the cold winter greenhouse much longer.

HONEYED AND SUGAR-SWEET SCENT

Even without scent, sweet alyssum, *Lobularia maritima,* would be indispensable to many gardens. (We remember a friendship that started on a long Western train journey, when we discovered that our new acquaintance was also devoted to what both of us knew as Dreer's No. 1101, the sweet alyssum of that fine old firm.) And we recall how we were assailed and overwhelmed by the fragrance in Hamburg when we passed through the gates of the *Planten un Blomen* show where sweet alyssum was freely used in beds and in broad drifting borders.

Floes of white sweet alyssum edge the summer garden, spreading out like six-minute frosting. The violet kinds are especially vivid in fall, making velvet cushions on gray flagstone or a handsome foil for single yellow chrysanthemums. All smell warmly of honeycomb, noticeable at some distance on a sunny day, and especially appreciated in Novem-

197

ber when the tiny frost-hardy flowers are among the last in the garden. The double white sweet alyssum often edges benches in the cool greenhouse, the bloom like miniscule double stock or roses and with the same good honeyed scent; this needs more moisture and fertility than the vigorous singles, which may also be grown indoors in winter.

Two other honey-rich annuals are indispensable for cutting, the pincushioned *Scabiosa atropurpurea*—soft blue, salmon, cream, and blackest red—and sweet-sultan, *Centaurea moschata,* with 2-inch powderpuffs of bloom and such a rich meadiness that they can be oppressive indoors. Lime in the soil produces 3- to 4-foot bushes massed with splendid bloom—white, pink and rose, light purple, violet, and, most fragrant of all, the lemon-yellow *C. suaveolens.*

As for the warmly sweet, really biennial pansies, we often buy baskets of well-started plants in spring, sniffing as we select. Often they prove perennial, particularly the whites and yellows. Then sweet-scented bloom continues even after light frost if plants are watered with liquid plant food when set out, given another dose about a month later, cut back when they get straggly in the hot weeks, and fed again for August and later bloom. Their scent is hardly as free as that of a mass of petunias but still adds something to the garden air.

The long-beaked seedpods are the flower-arranger's reason for growing the strange native *Proboscidea Jussieui* (*Martynia louisiana*), yet the flowers can qualify for the fragrant garden. The upright speckled purple racemes have the most cloyingly sweet odor we have ever experienced, hardly a perfume, on a par with certain crinums; think twice before making room for this determined self-sower.

Hardly choice but quite undemanding is the upright *Silene Armeria* that smells exactly like fresh raspberries and is the color of raspberry ice. The 18-inch drifts are bright border-fillers from June into September.

Some snapdragons can be overly sweet—sugar without any alleviating flower note—but many are grand to sniff. With their ability to survive light frost, and their bold, bright, base-branching spires, they are among our favorite annuals. Occasional plants near the house have survived snowbound winters to become perennial.

The true wallflower, *Cheiranthus Cheiri,* is annual or biennial here. A wild flower of Europe, it is at home in the limestone walls and quarries of England where it cascades in fragrant gold and crimson tangles from May until September. Where winters are not too severe, nor summer too hot, wallflowers bloom the year round, and at least six months of winter bloom is possible in wall-sheltered spots from North Carolina south. Doubles are seldom seen, yet these are longest blooming and more fragrant than singles. Early Wonder and Fair Lady are strains of doubles in an assortment of delicate pastels and the usual brass, copper, and iron-rust shades. In view of our mean winters, we have given up outside wallflowers, and instead often sow seeds in midsummer for stocky little flowering plants at Christmastime. Seeds sprout quickly, and it takes five months to bloom. A lean mix of sand, garden soil, and ground limestone plus bonemeal keeps plants to window size. We do not bring them in until mid-November since they are safe outside as long as sweet alyssum blooms. Of course, they require a cold window with southern exposure; a 50-degree F greenhouse is ideal.

A winter annual that shares the wallflower bouquet of clove and lily is Siberian wallflower, actually a California wildling, *Erysimum asperum* (*Cheiranthus Allionii*). Fall-seeded plants commence to bud in March and open brilliant orange from April to June. 'Apricot Delight' is as sweet, and easier to please.

ASTRINGENT NOTES

In summer we find the sharper aromatic scents of marigolds, Dahlberg daisies, and nasturtiums a pleasant contrast to the many flowers of sweet scents, particularly in mixed bouquets. Though some cannot abide it, we like the sour refreshing pungence of marigold foliage and are not among those craving "improved" plants with scentless leaves. True the flowers have only a mild sweetness, but marigolds are not grown for this. The little Signet type, *Tagetes tenuifolia pumila* (*T. signata*), with stars of lemon, gold, or orange over ferny mounds, are the real powerhouses of marigold aroma; the foliage is sharp, good enough to add to summer salads, and the spritely flowers have a certain herbal sweetness.

Another tiny yellow composite that reseeds here is the dainty Dahlberg daisy, *Thymophylla tenuiloba*. Thready, light green foliage mounds 8 to 9 inches, supporting golden pennies on good picking stems. Leaves and flowers are heavily aromatic with a sour, cucumber pungence that brings a new scent to midsummer rock gardens or paving.

Nasturtiums, another of our childhood's earliest successes, will always be dear to us for their easy, vivid flamboyance—cream, gold, enameled orange, burning mahogany—and their peppered bouquet like that of certain old roses, not so sweet but just as enjoyable. *Tropaeolum majus* thrives in poor soil in full sun. The Fragrant Giants strain includes large single exceptionally spicy flowers in all colors on strong vines. The Gleam strain is bushy with semidouble flowers, some with outstanding scent as 'Moongleam', 'Golden Gleam', and 'Indian Chief'. Nasturtiums have succulent foliage, smooth, thin, with peltate leaves on grasping petioles; every part is edible including the flowers; young seeds, fat wrinkled triplets, taste better than capers, pickled.

12

A Midsummer Night's Garden

Dear to us, and to many others who are more likely to work than sit or stroll in the garden in the daytime, are the evening hours when we linger along the brook paths, stop by a bench, or relax on the screened terrace. In dusk and darkness the demands of the garden are mercifully concealed; now we can enjoy pale flowers so luminous in the evening, and breathe in the delectable bouquet of many night-fragrant plants, the "vespertine flowers" that we may not even see in the shadows.

EVENING-SCENTED LILIES

Surely lilies, especially the white ones, are the most beautiful of all flowers at night, and their pervasive drifts of fragrance most appreciated then. Nor is it necessary to grow a multitude. Planted nearby, just a few of the free-fragrant kinds will scent the air in sequence from mid-

Hosta plantaginea

June into October. First, there is the Madonna lily, *Lilium candidum,* in June; late in the month the Easter lily, *L. longiflorum;* early in July comes *L. auratum,* the goldband lily with hybrids like 'Empress of Japan' coming a little later, sometimes not until September. In July, *L. regale* with a powerful spicy scent takes over; and the Formosas (*L. formosanum*) bloom from September into October.

On warm summer evenings hybrid day-lilies—not true lilies, of course—come into their own around patios and along paths. We select the extended day-blooming or the nocturnal kinds in light yellow and cream for this evening enjoyment. Their pale boldness shows up dramatically at night and their scent, though not freely given, does add to the elixir in the warm air. Planted among ferns along the woods paths, they are beautiful in the gloom, and we bend to smell them as we walk down toward the brook.

Of the many plaintain-lilies of August, only *Hosta plantaginea* has strong fragrance. Above gleaming, lush green leaves appear compact heads of buds, pearls set in a spiral of pale bracts. The lowest is first to open, a great long finger that flares to a pure white lily, the stem elongating as each trumpet follows, a fresh one every evening. They look like Madonna lilies and smell like them, too, that strange sachet perfume that belongs to few other plants, but always white-flowered and liliform. At least half a day's sun and rich cool coil are required. Country gardeners often edge walks and porches with the big clumps. The hybrids, even 'Honeybells', have less fragrance.

NIGHT-FRAGRANT PERENNIALS

There are many other perennials to enjoy in the evening garden, as garden-heliotrope, the white or rose *Valeriana officinalis;* the continuing perpetual pinks, *Dianthus plumarius,* and the two pinks that do not start until July, the spiny pink, *D. Noeanus,* and the superb pink, both 'White Lace' and the Rainbow Loveliness strain. And the summer *Phlox paniculata* is always warmly sweet through summer nights, particularly the white kinds.

The white or purple yard-high sweet-rocket *Hesperis matronalis* blooms in May and June. The cruciform flowers remain crisply open all day and have good odor close up, recalling the bouquet of *Daphne Mezereum*. Toward evening the scent spills over the borders in a light diffusion that lasts the night. Once you have it, sweet-rocket self-sows forever. Removing spent stems ensures another season's bloom from a huge clump; uncared for, the plant is biennial. In England can be found double forms with even more perfume, the plants prolonged from year to year by cuttings grown in rich sweet soil.

All the evening-primroses do not flower at night; the golden *Oenothera fruticosa* and *O. missouriensis* work by day and are scentless. But for a rock garden in a hot, dry place there are three with tap-rooted rosettes that resemble dandelions—until they begin spreading sideways. Toward sundown, *O. acaulis, O. trichocalyx,* and *O. caespitosa* dramatically open chalices of silken white around a floss of quivering stamens. Theirs is a true perfume, a blend of lemon and jasmine, strongest in the last, the gumbo-lily of the Dakotas. Our candidate for the twilight garden is a form of the towering wayside weed, *O. biennis*. This is like *O. Lamarckiana,* with sticky buds on bright red stems that pop softly at sundown as if the 2½-inch pale yellow enameled rounds would carry sunlight into dusk. For several yards around, they float a soft perfume of lily and lemon. Plants volunteer in the border, where, tall and coarse, they seem inconspicuous among low shrubs. Quicker to flower and branching at a good height is an annual from Chile, *O. odorata,* the flowers as large and sweet, red-washed by morning.

ANNUALS OF NIGHT SCENT

In the case of the small evening-scented annuals, it is easy to gain a wide experience, for different kinds can be tried each year, always with the hope that they will not prove equally appealing and so hopelessly crowd the night garden. Some must be grown from seed; others are easy to buy in spring in baskets or plant bands. We always obtain some of our hybrid petunias this way, preferably upright single and double whites for visibility and fragrance. These are descendants of *Petunia axillaris* (formerly *P. nyctaginiflora* or "night-blooming"). Mrs. Wilder noted that "the white Petunia whose day scent falls short of being agreeable, gives forth a refined and delicious perfume after sunset." To us, it is a soft refined scent, rather like nicotiana, but sugar-sweet.

The evening stock, *Mathiola bicornis,* by day has a sad appearance, when flowers droop and petals fold in, like hands hiding treasure. Then as light wanes, the flowers expand to broad-petaled crosses of pale lilac, and the treasure is released, a rich fragrance, far-reaching, blending lily with honey. If you mind the daytime sag, sow the seed in out-of-the-way places, even beneath roses. In our rock garden the low rosettes look exactly right and the parched sweet soil there seems to increase the perfume while keeping plants compact.

The handsome ten-weeks stocks, *M. incana annua,* were also once called gilliflowers for they too have "spices in their throats." At Byron's home, Newstead Abbey in Nottingham, we saw them in a great formal garden, veritable pinnacles of splendor. They were used as bedding plants with enormous separate blocks of white, lavender, purple, and pink. The impact of color and fragrance was terrific, particularly to Americans accustomed to less dramatic bedding plants. What beauty they had, what ineffable distillations they gave forth. Never will we forget the English stocks, and in a night garden here, they can be as enchanting.

By day the blend of clove and lily in stocks does not hide the undercurrent of cabbage, a trait shared with wallflowers, but by night this disappears beneath an explosion of perfume. For a wealth of bloom, grow branching kinds like 'Beauty of Nice' and the dwarf ten-weeks sorts. Sown indoors in March, these will bloom through summer, while the compact seven-weeks kind, started in September, makes a cool sunny window delightful in winter. Colors range from white, pink, buff, and lavender, to carmine and violet, and most flowers are double.

The wild Peruvian four-o'clock, *Mirabilis Jalapa,* a perennial in old Southern gardens, here is quick from seed. It blooms even sooner if the tuber is dug in fall, stored like a dahlia, and replanted in May. Each year the bush grows larger and eventually needs support. The small petunia-shaped flowers on bright days do not open until late afternoon, when they unfurl and release a refreshing bouquet of lemon. Grown in half a day's sun, their working hours are longer. The cherry-red kind is most fragrant, but select from your own mixed seedlings and avoid odorless modern "improvements." In four-o'clocks the aroma is simple and free, a pleasant contrast to the strong perfumes of many other nocturnals.

NICOTIANA AND DATURA

The most familiar of evening-scented annuals is the jasmine-tobacco, *Nicotiana alata grandiflora.* In a patio in a bay of the house, it alone will perfume the night for four months or more. So it is planted in the little front gardens of London's Cheyne Walk along the Thames Embankment, doubtless an inspiration to the writers and artists who have lived there—Carlyle, Whistler, and Rosetti, among others. Sow it only once; volunteers come up forever after and seedlings are huskier if they are left to bloom where they appear. By July first, flowering begins; by August candelabras rise to 5 feet, their framework invisible when the white stars gleam forth in the night. In the morning they are unsightly, umbrellas blown inside out, but as soon as the sun sets, the drooping tubes stiffen, expand and reflex, remaining open as long as sun does not touch them. In light shade, on dull days, or brought indoors, flowers never close but fade naturally.

The scent they project can actually be felt; the essence rises like a spurt of cool gas from the center cavity. Some have it honeyed or sugar-sweet, but to us it is a heavy emanation of auratum lily. During the three weeks reign of the goldband lily, the comparison is easy to make, and together lily and flowering tobacco dominate the August dark. *N. alata* paired with the odorless, rose-flowered *N. Forgetiana* gives many shades of mauve in the Sandeae Hybrids; in the Sensation strain flowers remain open through the day. These have some lily perfume though hardly up to *N. alata.*

Two recent novelty nicotianas are excellent. 'White Bedder', a 20-inch telescoped version of the tall white with flowers as large but closer together, is rich-scented and open all day, too; it makes a superb winter-blooming plant for a cool window, but is chary of its fragrance then. 'Lime Sherbet' is similar, with scented flowers of a luscious creamy chartreuse. The genus *Nicotiana* contains many other species, almost all American, night-blooming, fragrant.

The common tobacco, *Nicotiana Tabacum,* a giant annual with diurnal reddish flowers is sweet-scented, but otherwise we go along with King James, who declared more than 300 years ago that smoking the dry leaves was "a custom . . . hateful to the nose, harmful to the brain, dangerous to the lungs and in the black stinking fume thereof nearest resembling the horrible Stygian smoke of the pit that is bottomless." Certainly smoking does dim the sensitivity of the olfactory nerves essential to the enjoyment of fragrance. Other scented species include *N. longiflora, N. suaveolens,* and *N. sylvestris.*

The well-scented daturas are glamourous relatives of horrible Jimsonweed, *Datura Stramonium.* The handful of species in cultivation have an old reputation for fragrance, but only two or three merit praise. We spent a few summers sorting out the kinds offered and believe we now have them straight. Angels-trumpet or wedding-bells of Mexico and our Southwest is *Datura meteloides.* There it blooms most of the year, common along roadsides, a nuisance on grazing land, but to gardeners a beloved thing and the patio plant supreme. Tender it is, never sprouting until June first and withering with the first cold, but the root is perennial and it has survived two winters here.

The entire plant is covered with gray nap. Buds sprout like candles in every axil, to unfurl one evening to splendid white trumpets open to the sky and perfumed with—of all things—lemon. The leaves *may* be described as scented, but they hold the stench of Jimson-weed; untouched, they keep it secret. By the end of summer, one plant will have reached 3 feet with a spread up to 5, with fertilizer even to 12 feet! A mound studded with full moons is radiant enough to light the darkest nights. The tubes open at a slow but perceptible rate, enchanting to watch. Later large thorny pods are packed with hardy seeds which come up in odd corners each summer.

D. Metel (also called *D. fastuosa* and *D. chlorantha*) is different, weedy, thin-leaved, smooth, rank. A tender annual, it never reseeds here. Upright trumpets of novel colors—yellow, blue, even red—fail to distract us from their dreadful breath of Jimson-weed. Best for scent but a chore to handle are the true angels-trumpets, the treelike *D. arborea* and *D. suaveolens*. The first in its double form must be grown as a potted plant; but *D. suaveolens* is easy from seed, blooming the second year. *D. arborea* reaches 8 feet with pure white flowers that hang like flaring bells. *D. suaveolens* bears great 12-inch downcast flowers on a plant 12 to 15 feet tall. Both are unsightly in daytime but by evening the great, snowy flowers unfurl, pouring out a plethora of auratum-lily scent, too much close by but delightful at a little distance. Up north these daturas are grown in tubs and wintered in basement or conservatory; trained to tree-form rather than pinched to shrubbiness, plants are free to display their imposing flowers.

TENDER PLANTS AND BULBS

In early summer, our large specimens from windows and plant room are set outside in filtered sunlight to continue their scented blooming. Then *Sansevieria trifasciata* is most likely to put forth fragrant sprays, and two night-blooming geraniums, *Pelargonium gibbosum* and *P. ×rutaceum* may reward our patient cultivation with maroon or chartreuse flowers of penetrating sweetness. At the edge of the terrace, the big poets jessamine begins.

208

Often miscalled jasmine because the flowers are supposed to have a similar perfume is *Cestrum,* a group of coarse subtropical shrubs. The two that interest us are night-blooming and smell alike, and one plant of either is enough. To us their incredibly free and distinctive odor has none of the flower-fruit bouquet of true jasmine but resembles orange blossoms (which are not orange-y); a similar scent comes from *Sansevieria parva.* Some noses cannot bear a whiff of it, others find it compellingly pleasant in greenhouse or garden; few can endure an evening of cestrum close by. Both species produce powerfully scented constellations of tiny stars on slender tubes. Hardly noticeable by day, drooping with pinched tips, they come alive at nightfall, petals reflex and perfume pours out. *Cestrum nocturnum,* the cream-white night-jessamine, may reach 8 feet in captivity; the pale chartreuse *C. Parqui,* willow-leaved jessamine, has smaller foliage on possibly 5-foot stems. Prune plants to control their bulk. Well-watered and fed, they bloom in repeated bursts throughout the year.

Several species of South African *Gladiolus* survive winters even in very cold gardens if they are heavily mulched. Usually grown in a cold greenhouse for March flowers, the very hardy evening gladiolus, *G. tristis* (the word means *sad* but has been applied to many evening flowers), in our gardens in Zone 6 opens graceful, 3-inch flowers of palest citron in May. As soon as light fades, they dispel a fragrance of sweetened coconut and clove that carries far; in a room, one stem of three or four flowers is quite enough!

Two so-called lilies, the amaryllid *Crinum* or swamp-lily, and the ginger- or butterfly-lily, *Hedychium coronarium,* are Southern garden plants of intense fragrance. Crinum bulbs spout a fountain of serried, straplike leaves often 6 feet long, and broad umbels of trumpets that droop by day but flare by night with a degree of fragrance. With plenty of manure and water, they send up stem after stem of lovely bloom over a long summer period. Two that have survived five winters here, heavily mulched, are *C.* ×*Powellii* and the hybrid 'Cecil Houdeyshel', but these have proved disappointing. Hardy enough to try here in shade is *C. Moorei,* with slender pink flowers that are vanilla-scented. Tender, of but medium height and cloying sweetness—bubbling caramel with too much vanilla—are *Crinum giganteum* and its hybrid, the broad-petaled, white cupped Christopher lily; the native *C. americanum,* their opposite in form, with narrow, flaccid petals, shares the candy sweetness. *C. Kunthianum* has the best scent of the milk-and-wine type. In these white lilies, ribbed with watered crimson, the saccharine quality gives way to a pleasing blend of lily and spice.

The tuberous-rooted ginger-lilies, *Hedychium,* put forth leaves like the cannas but on corn stalks topped by broad-bracted spikes. Toward the end of summer, these send forth strange flowers with flaring fila-ments, day-sweet but really marvelous by night. Best is garland-lily, *Hedychium coronarium,* a lei flower of Hawaii, with successive crowns of pure white aprons that have a smooth, alluring sweetness, a syrup of orange and honeysuckle that lingers even in wilting. *H. Gardneri-anum* and *H. flavum* are perfumed yellow versions. All reach 4 to 6 feet and, well mulched, are hardy to coastal Virginia. As they need rich soil and quantities of water, try them in a wooden water-lily bucket or plastic pail near a tap and in full sun. Good drainage is not important. Roots are stored like cannas over winter.

Despite the extra in-and-out trouble the tender bulbs require, there are some we always grow, as the glorious Mexican tuberose, *Polianthes tuberosa* "with her silvery light." Tubers are started indoors in April in 5-inch pots of rich soil and planted outside by June for August and September bloom. Indoors we grow them as warm as African-violets and outside give them the sunniest location. The single 'Early Mexi-can', with six-parted stars on inch-long tubes at the top of 2- to 3-foot stems, begins in July and continues until frost. These are favorites of Southern gardeners because of their relative hardiness there and intense perfume. In September or October, 'Double Pearl' opens ivory rosettes from rose-stippled buds on 2-foot stems. The fragrance the tuberose diffuses, particularly at night, is unique, a curious scent suggesting or-ange blossoms or hyacinth, both of which can be oppressive and strange, not sweet in the way of heliotrope or honeysuckle. But to some noses, it is enchanting, and late summer evenings are incomplete without the stars of tuberose casting their spell over the garden.

NIGHT-BLOOMING CACTI

Of the many fragrant *Cacti,* most interesting to us are the nocturnals that occur like comets in the night with a season of mere hours in a span of 365 days. Because the flowers are short-lived, most of them have strong scent to assure fertilization, but a few of the most spectacular—*Hylocereus undatus, Selenicereus Macdonaldiae* and *S. pteranthus*—produce no detectable scent. The plant commonly called night-blooming cereus is not a cereus, but *Epiphyllum oxypetalum;* many a gathering of neighbors has sat vigil on an August evening as the annual drama of the rosy buds began. Fully expanded, flowers have a medicinal, peonylike odor. Many in this list have lovelier flowers and far sweeter perfume. Those starred are on the lists of cactus specialists; the others are worth asking about.

*Arthrocereus microsphaericus
 Conophytum* species
 Echinopsis turbinata
Epiphyllum anguliger
*   *oxypetalum*
*   *pumilum*
*   *Cooperi*
*   *crenatum*
           Pittieri
 Eriocereus Martinii
 Hylocereus costaricensus
           guatemalensis

 Hylocerous polyrhizus
Nyctocereus serpintinus
Peniocereus Greggii

 Selenicereus Boeckmannii
*   *grandiflorus*
           hamatus
           vaupeli
 Trichocereus Bridgesii
*   *candicans*
           Pachanoi
           Schickendantzii

EVENING-SCENTED SHRUBS AND VINES

How we wish that fifty years or so ago a far-sighted ancestor had planted a linden tree near the house, so that now, great in size and dripping with bloom it might dominate our midsummer evenings. Mindful of the future, we now set out small specimens of *Tilia ×eu-chlora* and *T. petiolaris,* which we hope our grandchildren will bless us for.

In the night-stillness the scent of summersweet, *Clethra alnifolia,* that we are also aware of through the day, drifts up from the fern garden pouring forth clouds of refreshing scent. We sit quiet to enjoy it all through the evening. The latest of the fragrant mock-oranges, as 'Belle Etoile' and 'Silver Showers' continue into July and are lovely in the evening.

The everblooming night-scented honeysuckle *Lonicera Heckrottii* 'Goldflame' can be safely introduced to the garden while Hall's honey-suckle, fragrant in a different way, is almost too invasive. 'Goldflame' is an elegant sight as rondels of rose-coated cream emerge in tiers at twig tips from May until frost. By day, flowers are scentless but, as soon as the sun sets, waves of breath-catching perfume pour through the night, the far-reaching odor of auratum lily with orange and jas-mine, an opulent blend. Sprigs brought inside sweeten a room for sev-eral nights as buds open and clusters lengthen. The vine looks lovely on a fence between climbing roses, hanging over a low wall, or covering a post from ground up with elegant flowers. Once it is established, long thick shoots emerge to twine haphazardly to 8 or so feet, but most of the growth branches to twigs and bloom, with never a tend-ency to strangle. With 'Goldflame' we must be on the watch by mid-May for black aphids that may ruin flowers until July; after that they seem immune. When we spray the roses that last time before they open, we cover 'Goldflame' as well.

The riverbank-grape, *Vitis riparia,* sends its musky scent across the

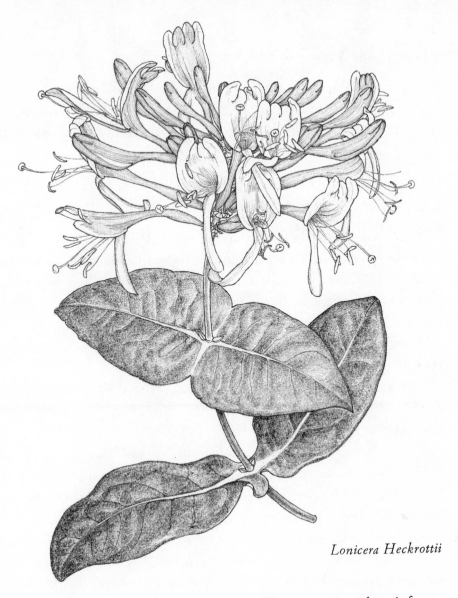

Lonicera Heckrottii

brook to the terrace, and the late-season *Clematis paniculata* informs the air of the southern arbor. Wisteria opens a few sweet panicles but its full glory is passed by June.

The annual moonflower, *Calonyction aculeatum* (*Ipomoea Bona-Nox*), is indeed a star performer for the night garden. Buds due to open reveal themselves by day on lengthening petioles, poised tips loosened. Then between seven and eight o'clock, they unfurl in short jerks to glorious rounds of white marked by pale green centers of bud pleats, and they perfume the night with a delicate but far-reaching version of

213

auratum lily. We place them inconspicuously, for by sun-up they are limp rags. The vine can go to 30 feet in two months but confined to an 8-foot trellis, growth will spread over the top and bloom heavily there.

NIGHT MISCELLANY

Many wildings have the nocturnal habit. Particularly lovely are two from the West, easily grown from seed sown before winter. *Mentzelia Lindleyi* (*Bartonia aurea*) has 2-inch flowers of burnished gold beneath a great boss of stamens like a St. John's-wort. *M. decapetala,* evening-star, opens splendid ivory aureoles around amber filaments, more than 4 inches wide. Both expand as night falls, releasing a strong sweet perfume that lingers until dawn.

The sand-verbena, *Abronia umbellata,* is a thrifty trailer for seashore gardens. Broad bright-rose clusters stay open all day, but are honey-sweet only at night.

Schizopetalon Walkeri, an easy annual, is low enough for the rock garden where scent is scarce in summer. The deep-fringed white flowers resemble a four-petaled pink and offer at night a refreshing aroma of almond, like plum blossoms in spring.

Saponaria officinalis came from Europe with the colonists. The masses of pale pink bloom are pretty along the roadside where it flaunts a simple sweetness on hot August nights. The double bouncing-Bet is more fragrant but too invasive.

13

Aromatic Herbal Scents

It is the sophisticated searcher for fragrance, the gardener long attentive to the odors of flowers and leaves, who finds so fascinating the remarkable variables among herbs with their scented leaves, seeds, and roots. In the herbs sensations of smell and taste are brought together so that we are not always certain to which sense they appeal the more.

On the whole, herbs are not free of fragrance; we think of only a handful that boldly announce their presence. However, when the hot summer sun beams down upon the herb garden, volatile oils are readily released in heady aromatic blends whose emphasis of mint, lemon, lavender, or basil changes with the gentle movement of the air, the vapors delightful indeed, but defiant of analysis. Except for this sunny release, we agree with Oliver Goldsmith, as we pinch a leaf of rose-geranium or mint that

. . . aromatic plants bestow
No spicy fragrance while they grow,

But crush'd or trodden to the ground,
Diffuse their balmy sweets around.

Among the herbs unmistakably in attendance are sweet basil, the piercing pennyroyal that clarifies the air on humid summer mornings after rain, lavender and wormwood, pine-redolent rosemary, pleasantly pungent rue, and valerian, a light airy wildling with a vanilla-touched flower perfume, now establishing itself in open woods across the brook. These are free as Damask roses with their scents and each is definite and different from the rest.

SCENT OF SUMMER

A characteristic air of summer seems to us to be contained in certain plants, and particularly in sweet basil, *Ocimum Basilicum*. Gerard claimed that "The smell is good for the heart . . . and maketh a man merry and glad." After a noontime shower, the symmetrical bushes release waves of scent that are carried in the moist air for yards around. Even frozen plants diffuse this summery scent, and the dried leaves contribute to any potpourri. Yet they carry no menthol, no balsam, no peppery quality. Repeated sniffings suggest first clove, then celery-seed, even the smell of tomato foliages, an association we make use of by adding dried basil to tomato dishes.

The basils are a delightful group of annuals, willing from seed, handsome at all times. The 2-foot type produces insignificant white flowers in August. Bush basil is its 1-foot counterpart, and least-basil is smaller still. These two are just as spicy as the big one and make charming pot plants for a cool winter window. Curly basil and lemon basil are nice variations. Each green size is duplicated in purple, with leaves equally sweet, bronzed-blue and gleaming. Even the flowers of the purple basils are worthwhile, lavender-pink in pleasing contrast to the dark leaves.

In the hot sun, the misty yellow panicles of true bedstraw, *Galium verum,* throw off a warm honeyed scent distinctly their own and notice-

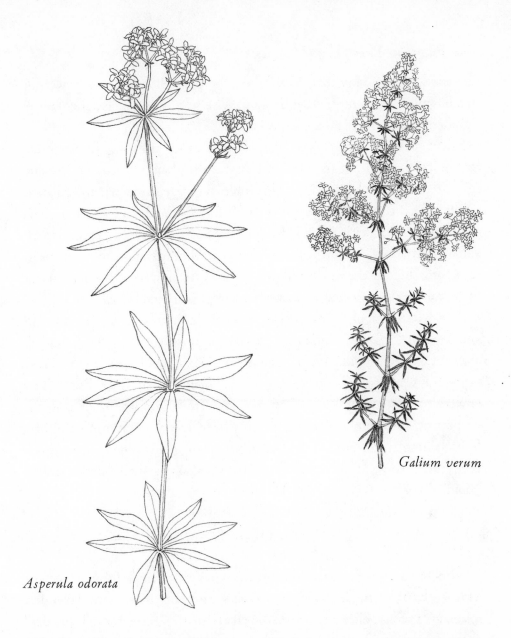

Galium verum

Asperula odorata

able several yards away. We cut small pieces to use as bouquet fillers
for the scentless summer zinnias and larkspur and also to dry for the
Christmas crêche. This perennial herb, which blooms from July into
October, has the fragile grace of water-milfoil but it is far from delicate
for it develops a formidable root system that digs in to stay, as we
discovered when unwittingly we introduced it to the Apple-Tree Garden. In three years the small original became a 2-foot nucleus that

217

feathered out in May to 3 feet. Then the plant flopped, the flowering tips having to turn up toward the sun. The scent was lovely, the flowers a golden haze—the plant a usurper!

Sweet woodruff, *Asperula odorata,* is another strewing herb to dry for the crèche and the rose jar, and to steep fresh in a bottle of Moselle for our version of May wine. The fragrance is released when you pick a few pieces, the cool sweetness of fresh hay or newly cut grass, a scent that strengthens with drying. Sweet woodruff is a pretty perennial, invaluable as a low ground cover in shade or beneath old-fashioned roses. It blooms before the end of April, the white flowers constellations of little stars, well displayed against whorls of grass-green leaves.

The true marigold, Mary-gold, is not the Mexican annual but old and revered *Calendula officinalis,* Shakespeare's "winking Mary-buds," and our pot-marigold. We detect no bitter pungency in their leaves; rather, a warm green savor that is the scent of summer itself. The flowers have some of the leaf aroma, and are valued for their color in potpourri. The name calendula derives from kalends, meaning the first of each month, for around the Mediterranean, golds bloom throughout the year, orange-rayed with chocolate eyes as in the variety 'Indian Maid'.

THREE CLEAN SCENTS

The freshness of various herbs has endeared them to generations. "How clean it smells," visitors exclaim, sniffing a sprig of lavender, rosemary, or angelica. Lavender in particular, "good for all greefs," as Parkinson said, has an intimate appeal. Flowers, foliage, bracts, and wood share a scent "of simple purity, the odour of the domestic virtues and the symbolic perfume of a quiet life." Of the several species, each with distinctive, aromatic foliage, only *Lavandula officinalis* and its variants are hardy enough for this climate to Zone 5. Which is a happy circumstance, for true lavender is of course sweetest and most beautiful. Found wild through the rocky Mediterranean hills, it is often called English lavender because plants grown in England produce the highest quality oil. *Lavandula officinalis* was once called *L. vera* and *L. Spica*—correct and appropriate is *L. officinalis,* meaning of the office or stillroom—that indispensable drugstore of medieval households. We plant lavender wherever the exposure is right—beside the Rose Border with pinks and iris, along paths, in the rock garden, at the tops of walls. The mauve-flushed foliage is a subtle contrast to the veiled blues and greens of other garden grays. The little shrubs, blooming before June has ended, fill all July with clouds of cool blue-violet and often send up a spike or two in September. A number of bushes give color to the garden and enough buds for potpourri and sachets as well.

Plants require full sun and a well-drained slope of soil, naturally sweet or made so. Tiny new plants take years to become mature mounds. Plants need careful pruning or they split apart into bare trunks and tufts, their chance of survival lessened. For shearing, the rule is: shape in summer after flowering, clean in spring. Tie the clippings into little bundles to bring a breath of summer to your living room when you throw them on the fire on bleak winter nights. Early in April, scratch ground limestone in under each plant, taking care not to disturb any layering branches, and remove dead branches. Look for green in the crosscut and leave that wood; new growth quickly fills in the gaps.

Six kinds of lavender have proved hardy here with this minimum care. Foliage mounds average 12 to 15 inches and spikes of bloom bring height to 2 feet or more. We have no 30-inch bushes, but farther south and in England, such tall masses are usual. The pale lavender 'Carroll' blooms first, usually by Midsummer's Eve, June twenty-fourth. The lilac-blue 'Munstead Dwarf' is next. Ours came from Shelburne Gardens, Vermont, and is the only lavender we know that is capable of surviving New England winters. The vivid light-violet flowers of 'Hidcote' bring the plant to 24 inches. It originated in the famous English garden, and is the lavender most widely distributed here. After eight years 'Twickle Purple' is still only a foot high, with the darkest flowers, a luscious violet-purple.

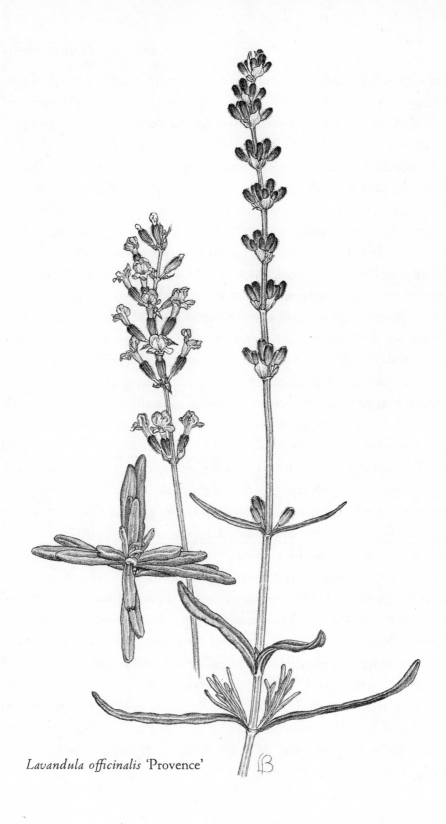

Lavandula officinalis 'Provence'

Our most richly colored lavender, 'Provence', produces freely in July with occasional spikes through summer. All forms and hybrids of *L. officinalis* smell delicious, but 'Provence' seems best. It tumbles over paving and almost surrounds the Perpetual Damask rose, 'Rose de Resht', whose nosegay flowers of intense coloring and scent accompany this handsome lavender into autumn. Our oldest bush, bought simply as *L. officinalis,* has dwelt with us for more than a decade. Wider than high, almost a yard across yet more sturdily upright than the others, it is a haze of lavender-blue wands in July, the lure of every bee.

Three more are charming but tender: *L. officinalis atropurpurea nana* grows to 6 inches and displays large bright violet flowers. White lavender, var. *alba,* is as fragrant as the others. Pink lavender, *L. officinalis rosea,* a foot high, is almost as hardy as the blues. Half-hardy spike lavender, *L. latifolia,* has a varnish scent. Tender kinds are likely to be scentless or redolent of paint thinner.

Rosemary, another fresh-smelling herb, is forever a stranger to our wet, wayward winters. In milder England it has been treasured for centuries. "As for rosemarie," Thomas More wrote, "I lette it run all over my garden walls, not only because my bees love it, but because it is the herb sacred to remembrance and to friendship; whence a sprig of it hath a dumb language." Originally the name was not Rose-mary but *ros marinus,* "dew of the sea," referring perhaps to the fragrance of the flowers, so freely dispelled that Francis Bacon noted hills of rosemary "will smell a great way in the sea, perhaps twenty miles."

Rosemary is rich in balsamic oils, possibly having more than any other herb. Crush a leaf and detect first the predominating pine, then sage, with perhaps a dash of nutmeg, something spicy. Elizabethans loved their herbs strong, indeed, *needed* them to be so. They revered this richly endowed "holy tree" and ascribed magical powers to it. The largest of the mints, it does look more like a slender yew, the narrow, gleaming needle leaves in dark contrast to the light blue flowers. Plants in poor alkaline soil and set against a wall in a *frost-free area* start popping flowers in December and continue into late May. Grown in cool windows *in full sun,* they may bloom in February and March. It is always safe to keep rosemary in a container, in summer sunk to the rim in a garden bed, in winter inside with the house plants or in a cool sunroom, guarded against excessive moisture, which is fatal.

There are three superior blue-flowered versions of *Rosmarinus officinalis:* 'Beneden Blue', with quantities of azure flowers; 'Ingram's Form', reputed hardiest and quite handsome; and 'Tuscan Blue', with the largest flowers but lacking hardiness.

The dwarf *Rosmarinus prostratus* is a gem but tender. In Southern California, it takes root wherever the little arching branches touch soil, making in time a thick springy mat, always downhill. There the bloom, light blue and ethereal, as in southern England, appears in December and lasts until May. Here in a cool greenhouse, if placed in full sun, this miniature plant flowers all winter and well into summer, and is as fully aromatic as the parent species.

The stems of angelica are familiar as candied decoration for cakes and cookies but it is the delicious scent of the leaves, lacking the menthol of the mint, that is such a fresh delight. In high shade, the biennial *Angelica Archangelica* grows to 6 feet, a massive plant like a luxuriant wild parsnip with great green-white umbels of bloom. Manufacturers have duplicated the scent, perhaps unwittingly, in lotions and cleansers. In the old days angelica was considered "that happy counterbane" to "Contagious aire ingendring pestilence," and the leaves smell clean enough to do just that.

LEMONY HERBS AND THYMES

Universal favorites are the aromatic plants with leaves of noticeably lemon scent, as lemon-verbena, the lemon thymes, lemon balm and also the citrus-scented geraniums. Lemon-verbena, *Lippia citriodora,* offers the finest. It is more lemon than a lemon tree or any of its parts, every leaf a distillation of lemon drops, a plant for children to grow up with, a talisman to take them back years later to the first garden they knew. Even the panicles of tiny late-summer flowers are fragrant.

Where winter temperatures don't often go below 20 degrees F, lemon-verbena may be grown as a die-back shrub. After defoliating frost, cut it to stubs and cover heavily with straw or salt hay. Otherwise, two or three months of outdoor sun and a cool sunny window in winter are all this tender perennial needs to grow into a shrub. You can even develop a little tree by supporting a single stem to 3- to 4-feet, breaking off lower shoots as they sprout; in a handsome tub, within pinching distance of a comfortable terrace seat or beside a much-used door, what could be more enjoyable? Use the fresh sprigs in nosegays with rose-geranium and orange mint, steeped in teas to drink hot or iced, in white vinegar for a hair rinse, in rubbing alcohol—in anything that might be enhanced by this strong essence of citrol. Curly-dry leaves of lemon-verbena combine with rose petals and flowers of lavender in wonderfully refreshing potpourri and sachets.

At Sissinghurst, V. Sackville West planted a thyme lawn and on a stone seat in her herb garden, she placed for a cushion a thick mat of thyme. A number of thymes are also redolent of lemon. *Thymus Serpyllum vulgaris,* lemon thyme, creeps but not far, concentrating on upright 4- to 6-inch shoots. It is the largest thyme we have, with shovel-shaped, shining leaves and lavender flowers. Plants are hardy if mulched long before ground freezes. Parkinson's "Embroidered Tyme, that smelleth of Pome Citron" is the yellow-variegated version of true lemon thyme, and tends to sport back to that. A form of *T. Serpyllum* that clings to the ground and has a strong aroma of lemon came to us as *T. Serpyllum aureus.* The plant is vigorous and spreads in full sun: we have one patch growing on stone that appears to have lost all contact with soil. We do not recommend 'Clear Gold', for it is chartreuse and has a lemon-varnish pungence. 'Caprilands' also smells of citrol and varnish, and may be a variant of *T. Serpyllum.* After eight years, this hardy form has become a mattress of green, sheeted with lavender from mid-May until the end of July.

Smelling only faintly of lemon-varnish and having rather a warm

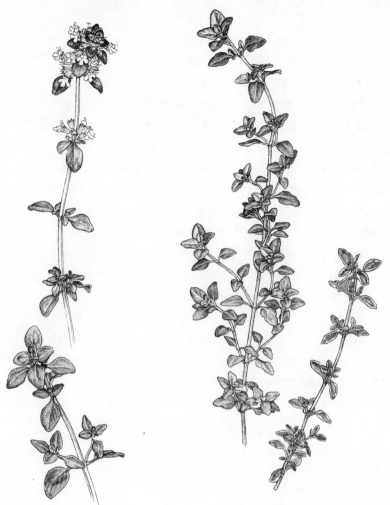

Thymus Serpyllum vulgaris

Thymus vulgaris argenteus

honey scent is one of the treasures of the garden, *T. villosus*, once called velvet-cushion. Bloom helps it reach all of 2 inches, but otherwise, it hugs the ground as snugly as white thyme. It opens countless lavender-rose flowers from early May until the end of June. Bees find these irresistible, and so do we. Others with this potent pungence include *Thymus Broussonetii*, *T. lanicaulis*, and *T. Adamovicii*, with 6-inch pillows of pink-sprigged green.

The lemon thymes are but a few members of this great tribe that inches above paving, surges over the rock garden, and carpets the ground beneath low shrubs. Every cook knows the pungence of cooking thyme, a combination of warm balsamic oils found also in sweet

224

marjoram, oregano, and the savories. The kind bought dried is French thyme, a form of *T. vulgaris*. In the garden this is a small upright bush, slender when young but gradually billowing out like some gray heather with slender leaves that dry to filings. Plants bought as *T. nitidus* have proved to be only French thyme, and neither of these has ever survived our winters.

With the same aroma that instantly connotes chicken soup and turkey dressing is English thyme, also a form of *T. vulgaris*. Plants are tumbling waves of wiry stems that build up to 8 inches or more. Where these touch ground they root, and so progress, scalloping along. This kind sometimes dies back, but where newer shoots have roots there

Ruta graveolens

Thymus Herba-barona

is life. Shear back all the wires and by July the mound will be as lush as ever. A variegated form, known by its scent and later by its tendency to sport back to the green English, is variously offered as 'Silver Thyme', 'Silver Lemon', and 'Silver Queen' but there is nothing of lemon in it.

Slowly covering a small area in the rock garden is *T. Serpyllum conglomerata;* magenta flowers decorate its dark green through August, and surprisingly, the crushed-leaf scent is good cooking thyme. Caraway thyme, *T. Herba-barona,* at first glance resembles ordinary *T. Serpyllum,* but one pinch identifies it as unique, the wonderful spicy aroma reminiscent of a Scandinavian bakery. It is a dark hardy creeper, so fast it is a hazard in the rock garden. In May, lavender flowers emerge from purpled bracts and stems are so wiry they are better cut than pulled. *T. Serpyllum aureus* and 'Caprilands' are the sorts to use for a thyme lawn, a delectable idea but a constant care.

Hard to locate is *T. vulgaris fragrantissimus,* not very hardy, even less so than French thyme, which it resembles; but shut your eyes, crush the leaves, and you may think you have picked rose-geranium. A happily situated plant will self-sow, and you may get one seedling with not only this delicious scent but hardiness as well. Here it winters with rosemary and its twin-in-scent, rose-geranium. Other tender thymes of good odor include *T. azoricus* and *T. Serpyllum micans.*

Except for the lemon thymes, you cannot depend upon pronounced odor in many forms of *T. Serpyllum.* Disappointing are red thyme,

T. Serpyllum coccineus, also *T. Serpyllum lanuginosus* and the exquisite little white thyme, *T. Serpyllum albus.* Some gardeners have
found this "extremely aromatic"; ours is scentless, but we love the
dimity of its bright green mat sprigged in late May and June with
rondels of pure white. It spreads unobtrusively through clumps of iris
and phlox, fast enough to have patches to give to admirers.

We also value lemon balm for its citrus-scented foliage. *Melissa officinalis* is actually another mint with stay-put roots and lemon-drop
flavor. Close mounds of rugose, heart-shaped leaves in bright green
look best if sheared of the taller flowering stems. A bit of menthol in
their lemon gives the crushed leaves an exhilarating savor, very good
steeped in tea, for it "strengtheneth the vitall spirits."

PELARGONIUM POSSIBILITIES

Among the sweet-leaved geraniums, in the group we designate as
citrus-scented, are some with excellent odors of lemon, while mint, rose,
and tantalizing blends of these, or hints of fruit and spice superimposed on the ever-present balsamic essences are recognized when the
bruised leaf releases minute globules into the air.

The scented geraniums make fine window plants but too soon they
outgrow average quarters. Then we start again with the so easily rooted
cuttings, often parceling out our big plants to friends with large sun
rooms. Set around one great glass-enclosed and heated corridor, these
tender plants fulfill their destiny as shrubs.

In the garden in summer our window plants, still in pots, are sunk
in the border or grouped in tubs where they flourish enormously. Those
we plan not to bring in again are planted directly in the garden. They
are a summer's joy as we brush the foliage in passing or stand among
the plants when the strong sunshine releases the fragrant oils. These
are stored in the several-celled hairs that cover every green part or in
the tiny cavities that pit the leaf surfaces.

Some of the rose-geraniums contain such a high percentage of geraniol that it has been used as an adulterant of the expensive attar of roses. Old-fashioned rose-geranium, *P. graveolens,* has always been loved. 'Attar of Roses' is truly delicious, its name no exaggeration, for few flowers other than the Queen herself, and no leaves that come to mind, flaunt such true rose perfume. 'Red Flowered Rose' offers a little less scent but charming bloom imaginatively combining the best of *P. graveolens* and *P. fulgidum* 'Mrs. Taylor'. The small flowers are rose-red brushed black, gay all summer and lovely from January on for winter nosegays.

A favorite for foliage, 'Variegated Mint Rose', is definitely mint-cooled rose, with the lemon eclipsed. 'Little Gem' is grown for flowers rather than fragrance, the scent more pungent than roselike. In 'Dr. Livingston' or 'Skeleton Rose' the perfume is slightly more lemon than rose, of excellent quality. 'Snowflake' is only faintly scented. What is known today as 'Large Leaf Rose', *P. capitatum,* probably was the species grown more than 150 years ago for its roselike oil. Plants may differ considerably in the strength of their rose scent.

Fruit odors that might elude the neophyte can be detected in many pelargonium species by those who have grown them for years. Everyone is not sufficiently sensitive to pick up aromas of apricot, ginger, coconut, or strawberry, and those who do are not always in agreement in their identification of what that "something fruitlike" is that they distinguish over the predominant balsamic oils. While the names of the apple-scented *P. odoratissimum* and the nutmeg-scented *P. ×fragrans* describe their supposed fragrances, we find they have a base predominantly southernwood. Apple has an overtone of old apples, not the taste or smell of a sweet apple but of fruit moldering on the ground. In *P. ×fragrans* there is some pungent spiciness that is no match for the stronger eucalyptol. Nutmeg geranium has sported an interesting but temperamental white-marked form, and 'Old Spice' is a cross of the two.

No doubts exist about fragrance among citrus-scented geraniums.

They are strongly, wonderfully lemon, or exotic blends of orange and lime with other oils. *Pelargonium crispum* is the familiar lemon-geranium, with small-lobed ruffled leaves on long petioles its distinguishing characteristic. Smaller and without petioles is *P. crispum minor,* the finger-bowl geranium, one of our great favorites among the scenteds and named for the Victorian custom of floating sprigs in fingerbowls. Larger than *P. crispum* in every way is 'Prince Rupert' with deeply cut ruffled leaves, and a lovely variegated form sometimes sold as 'French Lace'. All these citrus-scented geraniums bloom in full sun with bursts of pale lavender flowers.

The essential oil of *P. ×limoneum,* the true lemon-geranium, has more eucalyptol than does little *P. crispum* and its aroma is more citronella than lemon drop. The sweet goodness of orange is found in *P. citriodorum,* sometimes sold as 'Prince of Orange'; lime-geranium, *P. ×nervosum,* has more bite, less sweetness to its scent. Surprisingly large lavender flowers festoon a close-branched plant. Another variation of delicious citrol, with a hint of mint, occurs in the lemon-balm geranium, *P. ×melissinum.* This handsome sturdy plant with small double purple-brushed lavender flowers soon becomes a large shrub, too big for the winter window but useful as a filler in summer borders.

The mint-scenteds are an indispensable delight, and, forced to choose, we should probably settle for the peppermint-geranium, *P. tomentosum,* along with *P. crispum minor,* and 'Attar of Roses'. Of intriguing texture as well as odor, peppermint-geranium is so thick-piled with colorless hairs that at times the green is obscured. Unfolding leaves resemble ears of snow mice, and older leaves appear touched by hoarfrost. Mature foliage is broad, shallow-lobed like English ivy. It has true peppermint sharpness, so refreshing to sniff and delightful to feel, a perfect tranquilizer for a lively baby being changed! Indeed, children are fond of all the rose- and lemon-geraniums but mint is the favorite. In 'Pungent Peppermint', the peppermint is adulterated by some strange overtone; in 'Joy Lucille' the mint is stronger.

Mentha spicata

THE REFRESHING MINTS

Geraniums of mint scent are but a few of the herbs that offer this delightful odor. There is the amazing mint family with representatives among lavender, basil and thyme, rosemary, sage, hyssop and savories, marjoram, beebalm and oregano—an endless assortment of oil-rich foliage; and, of course, the invigorating mints themselves. Squared stems, paired leaves, and two-lipped flowers mark them all. There are so many kinds, you will probably select only three or four. The larger mints, while naturally denizens of streamside and low ground, need moisture in the garden only when newly set; once established they withstand dryness as well as their gray-leaved cousins. Except for two or three species, garden mints as a rule grow to about 2 feet, branching into taller bloom by July.

All mints contain menthol, either alone or blended with other oils. Purest is peppermint, *Mentha piperita,* so full of the camphorous menthol that its slender petioled leaves are almost too hot to nibble. Paradoxically, leaves rubbed on the skin give an icy cold sensation and children are fond of rubbing face, neck and arms with the leaves to feel the coolness and repel mosquitoes. Black mint, *M. piperita vulgaris,* with darker leaves smells the same. Spearmint, *M. spicata,* is the mint of juleps, vinaigrette sauce for lamb, and chewing gum, but the true sessile-leaved species is rare in this country. The kind usually grown for spearmint is apparently an ancient species named by Gerard, *M. Cardiaca;* seventeenth-century American botanists knew it as *M. sativa.* Passed along from one gardener-cook to another, it soon spread to many homesteads. The scent is excellent spearmint, its vigor extreme; if you can have but one mint, choose this, for most nurseries have it, though they list it as *M. spicata.* Curly mint, *M. crispa,* waved and deeply puckered, is as fully flavored.

The great woolly mint, *M. rotundifolia,* has the scent of sweetened spearmint. Pineapple mint is the name given to *M. rotundifolia variegata;* in England it is apple mint. It does have a fruity character decidedly pleasant, and perhaps this is pineapple. Apple mint here, *M. gentilis,* combines menthol with the aroma of green apples, the scent found in sweetbrier and in apple-scented geranium. In England, this is known as ginger mint.

Seldom growing above a foot is the charming orange mint, *M. citrata,* so rich in oil of bergamot that its perfume is more flowery than herbal. We read of 'Eau de Cologne Mint', a superb form, but it has eluded us; it is difficult to imagine improvement on our present orange mint. Sprigs are added to crabapple or orange jelly, as with leaves of rose-geranium, or to any summer drink; dried, they are preferable to other mints for potpourri, and brew into such a tisane as may convert you to herbal teas.

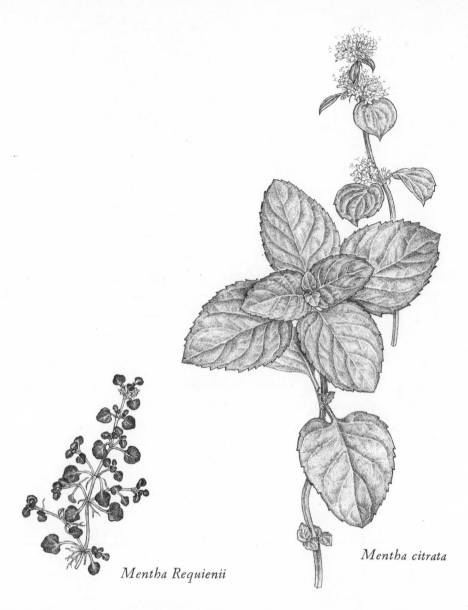

Mentha citrata

Mentha Requienii

The tiny pennyroyal, *Mentha Pulegium,* meaning "bane of fleas," is rich in camphorous menthol out of all proportion to its size; it freely casts its scent upon the air summer mornings and after rain. This diminutive loves the company of lawn grasses and seems to thrive with regular mowing, in time spreading horizontally to make an impenetrable mat. Here is an invader to cherish in a garden of fragrance. Imagine walking across such a green glacier or resting on it! And what beetle would dare deposit eggs in sward so distasteful to its grubs? Rubbed

232

Mentha Cardiaca

on skin, the leaves are even more effective than peppermint in repelling insects, and this is one of the bedstraw herbs appropriate to the Christmas crêche.

Lowest of all is the tender, miniscule Corsican mint, *M. Requienii,* with tiny leaves carrying the strong odor of pennyroyal. Such a piece of garden gossamer, only half an inch high, cannot survive exposed winters here, but grown between paving stones in shade, seeds survive to sprout in April, and carry on. To be certain not to lose it, we use Corsican mint as pot toppings for house plants grown at cool windows in winter.

Pioneer housewives cherished the wild bergamot or beebalm, *Monarda didyma,* in which mint scent merges with the Mediterranean bergamot of perfumers. The women used it as a substitute for their precious tea, hence the name Oswego-tea, and found it a "cure" for many ills. Leaves are so redolent that merely brushing past releases scent, and in earliest spring, when we scratch around to find emerging bulbs, suddenly there's beebalm in the air. Even in the dead of winter the purple-green rosettes are warmly fragrant. Years of cultivation and the help of bees have paired the scarlet *Monarda didyma* with the lavender-flowered *M. fistulosa* to produce a wide array of color forms—pinks and rose, strident magenta, royal purple—but the old wild red is still the best. White forms of either species are occasionally listed and are lovely in the night garden.

Perilla frutescens with big heart-shaped leaves as deep cut and ruffled as a fancy coleus also has a mint scent, the strong menthol overlaid with an indefinable spiciness, like mouthwash. Its deep hue and sheen of purple basil is a fine contrast to the grays of the herb garden, and it seeds everywhere.

Then there is the hardy perennial costmary or Bible-leaf, *Chrysanthemum Balsamita,* a true composite, but with the invading audacity of a big mint and much of that odor, for in this plant chrysanthemum pungence is overcome by an intriguing fruit-and-mint bouquet. Because pressed leaves kept their revivifying scent for years, early settlers put it in their Bibles and found its scent mitigation for a three-hour sermon.

234

PUNGENT AND MOSTLY PLEASING

From the composite family comes a great assortment of herbs, rich in eucalyptol, sharp in taste, pungent and refreshing to smell. The garden chrysanthemums of fall are best known, but feverfew (*C. Parthenium*) and *C. arcticum* 'Clara Curtis' have generous amounts, also.

Definitely chrysanthemum is milfoil or yarrow, *Achillea Millefolium,* with flat heads of tiny flowers in several color forms, all pleasant for summer bouquets. The deep-cut leaves are fine as Queen-Anne's-lace, and the roots spread madly. Sweet chamomile, the flowered carpeting of Elizabethan gardens, is found in this country only in the lists of specialists. If lush green mats spring up along your paths over winter and produce inch-wide daisies on long stems from May to July, they are likely to be *Anthemis arvensis,* corn chamomile, with a mild chrysanthemum odor. True chamomile, *Anthemis nobilis,* with little white daisies in May is a grayer plant, very pungent; it roots as its stolons advance. Tansy, *Tanacetum vulgare,* has the strongest, most biting aroma of all, too rank for us, but the heads of mustard buttons are useful in dried arrangements; fernleaf tansy, var. *crispum,* is a marvelously curled version. The santolinas are small shrubs with distinct pungence, sometimes more interesting than pleasant, but apparent only on pinching. Almost-white lavender-cotton, *Santolina Chamaecyparissus,* is prettiest although there is no lavender scent in it.

Sharp scents of various quality occur in the great clan of *Artemisia.* Old-man, lad's-love, and more recently southernwood, are all that hardy ancient herb, *Artemisia Abrotanum.* The aroma has great bite, almost pure eucalyptol. Mrs. Wilder loved to pair southernwood with moss-rose buds, a nostalgic combination to be sure.

Dark green simple-leaved tarragon, *Artemisia Dracunculus,* beloved of cooks, does not look like an artemisia, and its crushed leaves have a distinct flavor of anise. One of the best, the woody perennial wormwood, *A. Absinthium,* used in the production of the liqueur absinthe, (and to demolish moth larvae), has a distinct note of ether, more sweet

235

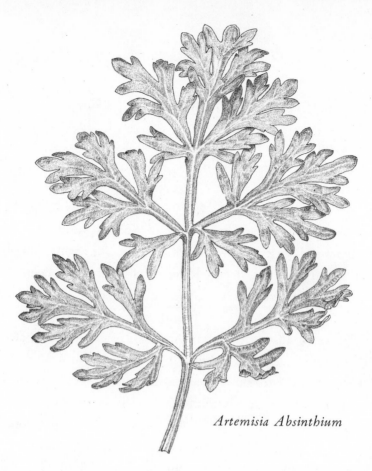

Artemisia Absinthium

than piercing. We often use long stems of the beautifully modeled leaves in sheaves of iris and sweet rocket. The Roman wormwood, *A. pontica,* with pale green filigreed leaves in a flowing mat, smells delicately of tansy. Ghost-plant or silver-king artemisia, *A. albula,* is mildly chrysanthemum. It sends up tall pale skeletons of slender leaves, popular for drying. *A. tridentata* is the true sagebrush, strongly camphorous; and there are many other aromatic Western species. The familiar dusty-miller, *A. Stelleriana,* is scentless. *A. vulgaris lactiflora,* while sharp, is too dreadful a weed to admit to the garden, in spite of the late-summer honeyed fragrance of its flowers.

FROM ROOT, SEED, AND LEAF

Many herbs offer more than garden fragrance. The dried and powdered roots of Florentine iris, the white version of *Iris germanica,* become orris, a perfume fixative; also a substitute for essence of violets. To us, orris does not smell like *Viola odorata,* yet violet sachet is mostly orris.

The thick, spicy stolons of wild ginger, *Asarum canadense,* sliced fresh, are added to moist potpourri, or cured in sand in a slow oven, as we have suggested, for use in the dry type. The perfumed ropes can also be candied in the manner of grapefruit rind—an imaginative way to cope with this woodland invader.

Seeds of cardamon, *Elettaria Cardamomum,* flavor pfeffernuesse and Christmas breads but plants are tender and grown indoors they do not set seeds. Seeds of coriander, *Coriandrum sativum*—burning the tongue like ginger, tasting also of lemon with a hint of rose—are indispensable to Indian cooking. Rye bread would be insipid without the seeds of caraway, *Carum Carvi.* From annual anise, *Pimpinella Anisum,* come seeds of licorice flavor for springerles and the liqueur, anisette. The licorice of fennel, *Foeniculum vulgare,* is in its leaves. In sweet Cicely, *Myrrhis odorata,* the anise flavor occurs in both foliage and seed.

Lovage, *Levisticum officinale,* is magnified celery flavor with a nutlike quality, delicious in chicken stock. Sweet marjoram, *Majorana hortensis,* recommended by Gerard for those "who are given to much sighing," is milder thyme, almost flowery or "sweet", while the culinary forms of *Origanum vulgare,* oregano, have tongue-burning balsams.

Garden sage, *Salvia officinalis,* the essential flavor of scrapple and sausage, was considered by Parkinson "of excellent good use to helpe the memory." Clary, *S. Sclarea,* once a remedy for maladies of the eye, is now a perfume fixative. Like these in the raw state, it smells unpleasant, an onslaught of sage and skunk. The distilled oil of clary has a grape odor, hence the old name, muscatel-sage.

14

Pleasures of Potpourri

When the fragrant garden includes roses and herbs, it can offer pleasure well beyond the months of growth and bloom, for in potpourris the delectable melange of scents can be recorded and enjoyed for a long time. In fact, it was five Christmases ago that the blue ginger jar with its scented contents was first placed on the fireside reading table and the stirred medley of petal and leaf still smells good on winter evenings. As Alice Morse Earle observed, "the subtle fragrance of a Rose can readily conjure in our minds a dream of summers past, and happy summers to come." And so we make and treasure our potpourris, souvenirs of the herb garden and the rose border. Today the word means a "little of this and that" but potpourri originally meant "a pot for rotting" from the French *pot* and *pourir*. And such it was: a jar of rose petals damp and brown; yet when properly cured and blended, rich for years to come with the warm scent of June roses, lavender and spice.

So the rotting-pot technique remains, now called the "moist

method," and it is quite simple if you grow the necessary roses. And even a small garden plot, if in full sun, can support enough bushes for at least two quarts of dried petals. Directions for both methods are given here, and once you understand the principles involved you can follow any recipe that sounds appealing.

Rose jar or sweet jar usually refers to a *dry* version of potpourri in which rose petals hold color but lose so much scent that oils of rose and other flowers are added, not once but whenever the aroma fades. This is the kind for which recipes abound; it is pretty and does not require especially fragrant roses, only those of lasting color. The oils and tinctures are obtained from a perfumer or other supplier and the finished blend can be quite expensive, nor is it ever a sampling of the essence of *your* garden.

THE ESSENTIAL ROSES

Rose petals must always form the base. Other flowers, even the most perfumed, tend to lose odor with drying, while rose petals—the right ones—hold their scent and may even seem to acquire more. The rosebuds often recommended as a fine ingredient are added not for fragrance but for the pretty color they bring to a *dry* sweet jar.

On the other hand, the buds of *Lavandula* or lavender are essential not for color but for the oil concentrated in the fuzzy calyx. Petals of pinks, mock-orange, and honeysuckle are sometimes added to moist mixtures, but if they do keep any scent, it is lost in the dominant aroma of rose. The handfuls of jasmine, violets, and orange-blossoms casually listed in old recipes make good reading but poor potpourri.

The all-important first step, then, is the selection of roses. While many gardeners prefer the everblooming Hybrid Teas and Floribundas, for potpourri these will not do. Even the most fragrant in the garden lose their scent on drying or develop an odd odor that is hardly sweet, and 'Crimson Glory' is no exception. Nor do Tea, Musk, or Multifloras endow petals with the odor we seek, no matter how fragrant they are when fresh.

The varieties richest in rose attar are the old European sorts, their hybrids as far along as the China Rose, and the more recent Rugosas. Those that flower in June give a quantity of petals within three or four weeks, while those that repeat prolong collecting through summer. We have come to prefer to do all the gathering in June, for then the petals have plenty of time to cure, lose the raw smell that develops in August, and are ready for final blending in October.

If space limits your choice to one rose for potpourri, and you have a fence or other heavy support to keep the blooming canes from breaking, select a 'Celsiana', 'Prolifera', or 'Kazanlik' (by whatever name this is offered). These three are unsurpassed. The Centifolias are next because they are less vigorous and make thinner bushes. Crested Moss and Common Moss, 'Red Provence' (or Common Cabbage, or 'Rose des Peintres'), and 'Bullata', are equally fragrant and full-petaled. The invasive patches of *Rosa gallica officinalis* in odd corners justify the trouble they cause by providing countless fragrant flowers, and don't overlook 'Banshee' with flowers as sweet as *R.* ×*bifera* itself, but with more of them on an easier-to-handle plant. The other Autumn Damasks, 'Rose du Roi', 'Rose de Resht', 'Four Seasons' or 'Quatre Saisons', and 'Jacques Cartier', provide bloom into fall, though not in large amount.

Of the Rugosas, best are 'Belle Poitevine', 'Magnifica', and 'Hansa'. Don't underestimate loud, shapeless 'Hansa'. It is tremendously fragrant, and if you cannot abide its harsh cerise, plop every one into the 'rotting pot'. Other Rugosas smell as good, but these three have the most petals and make dense plants that never stop blooming.

Of later hybrids, 'Salet', 'Zéphirine Drouhin', 'Fantin Latour', 'Général Jacqueminot', 'Reine des Violettes', 'Mme. Ernst Calvat' and 'Mme. Isaac Pereire', 'Gruss an Teplitz', and 'Conrad Ferdinand Meyer' are veritable factories of scent. There are others, certainly, but for petals by the peck, the twenty-five we have mentioned are the best we know, and by the time they are three or four years old, the bushes will richly supply your potpourri.

The time to gather flowers is in the morning after the sun has warmed them and the oils have begun to volatilize—between nine and ten o'clock on a hot day, around eleven if the weather is dull or cool. Select blooms that have just opened, or are between three-quarters and fully expanded, not faded or about to shatter. Pinch off roses with just a stub of stem and drop into bag or basket.

Indoors, have ready in any room where it can be left undisturbed a large aluminum window screen supported on two open boxes or a wooden clothes dryer. First empty the flowers onto a tray and strip off petals, discarding the green calyx or base. This is a fast, delightful job, one that children vie to help with. Next spread the petals evenly over the screen; don't be concerned if the layers seem too thick for they shrink overnight to a quarter of their fresh bulk.

THE MOIST METHOD

For the moist method, drying for about eight hours is enough, just until petals feel leathery. Next comes the preparation of the "stock." Turn the petals into an 8-quart enameled pot or a large pickle crock or any vitreous straight-sided container with a tight lid. Now comes the salting: we use kosher salt, which is coarse, free of iodine, and easy to handle. Allow one-quarter cup of salt (or a handful, as you become experienced) to two *packed* cups of half-dry petals. Sprinkle the salt over each additional layer of petals. The salt not only preserves, but extracts attar from the petals, even forming a brown essence at the bottom of the pot. After each day's harvest, thoroughly mix salt and petals and weight with a plate or saucer, whatever fits, and top with a stone or a plastic bag of sand.

At the end of June, add the fixative orris root—either the powdered form obtained from a pharmacy or dried chips made from your own iris rhizomes as explained in Chapter 13. Allow about one-quarter cup of either to four cups of loose petals. Like the mordant used to set color in dyeing, a fixative sets the fragrance, making it stable and long-last-

241

ing. Several fixatives can be used, including clary sage, but orris powder is easiest to obtain. And there is little danger of using too much salt *or* orris. The rule is, if too dry at first, add more salt; and if too moist later, check the action with orris. This forms the stock which can now be put aside, weighted and covered, until October.

Or the salting stage can continue all summer as you add fresh petals without drying but blending them in well each time. If a raw smell rises, this is to be expected; it will pass. Set with fixative in September and blend all in October. We have never had any problem with mold or mildew.

The final assembling is the great joy of making potpourri, comparable in its homely way to creating a new perfume. One fragrance dominates, others support it, while the fixative—with a scent of its own—holds all together in harmony. Rather than give a specific recipe when there are so many, we suggest proportions, and list ingredients to use and their preparation. With one quart (four cups) of stock as base, you can improvise as many combinations as you have quarts of stock, or else make one great batch.

Store the mixture in large screw-top jars to age at least six weeks before filling the potpourri jars. Containers *made* for potpourri usually have two lids, the inner one perforated to allow scent to escape, the outer one solid to retain it until you wish to uncover and enjoy the fragrance for a while. Most French jars have only the one perforated cover. However any attractive container can be used if it is glazed and has a snug lid. Ginger jars and sugar bowls serve beautifully, but we have come to prefer a rather squat vessel with a wide mouth so we can occasionally stir the contents by hand, for even though a monochromatic brown, it is pleasant to study while inhaling.

In the final mixing, one level tablespoonful of spice to one quart stock is quite enough; otherwise the scent of rose is overwhelmed. We recall that our first attempt smelled more of apple pie than flowers.

The amount of herbal lavender you add depends on how much you like it. Allow one-half cup for a hint, two cups for a half-and-half lavender-rose bouquet. Lavender buds are most fragrant just before opening, but we cannot bear to strip the bushes then so we wait until they have given two to three weeks of color.

Add dry, aromatic leaves cautiously. Some are so pungent, you must measure by the tablespoonful. Fresh leaves of special favorites may be added at the salt stage, letting your nose be guide.

Buy spices whole. Then grate or crush to a "grosse powder" with mortar and pestle. Cloves, nutmeg and mace, vanilla bean, cardamon, even ginger and black pepper can be used, also slivers of orange and lemon rind dried in a warm oven and mashed.

Large leaves napped with glands are cut to pieces and dried. This is the way to handle *Salvia dorisiana* and *S. rutilans,* 'Dr. Livingston' and rose-geraniums. Other leaves may be dried whole and stored in separate jars until October; leaves of any of these may be used—angelica, costmary, calendula, lemon-verbena, sweetbrier rose, sassafras, lemon balm, monarda, lemon and caraway thyme, and bayberry leaves and berries. A little mint goes a long way. Orange-mint is best, peppermint preferable to spearmint, and pennyroyal is potent. Culinary herbs are sometimes recommended—thyme, bay, marjoram, rosemary—but we prefer to use them in a separate mixture of herbs alone. Sweet basil is a delightful exception often added to our floral potpourri.

Every one of these ingredients can be grown in your garden, or found in pharmacy or supermarket. Do try making potpourri with these alone before experimenting with expensive extras and exotic oils. A true, moist potpourri does not need artificial additions, and after a year, it actually increases in fragrance. We came upon one recipe once that called for two gallons of rose petals, plus eleven different floral oils, one of them oil of rose. It might as well have used wood shavings instead of petals.

THE DRY METHOD

In the dry method, color and shape of flowers come first; any scent lacking in roses or lost in drying is replaced by oils. Thorough drying is essential. The rose petals left leathery on the screen should now be moved to a sheet of newspaper, otherwise when handled crumbly-dry they tend to sift through the screen. As white roses (and all white flowers) turn brown, and dark red ones turn black, fragrant pink and rose-red varieties are best. Add yellow and light scarlet petals for gaiety, and also, just for color, some tiny salmon buds of 'Margo Koster' or the dried blue flowers of larkspur.

The quicker dried, the closer the color holds to that of fresh flowers. As summer air is often too humid for natural drying, petals can be treated in a barely warm oven (150°F). Where form is important or material thick, as with rose buds, small whole roses or other entire blooms, or leaves like rose-geranium, dry them layered in a deep box of borax or silica-gel. Try to avoid anything powdered or finely ground, for as your pretty concoctions are to be used in glass apothecary jars or sachet bags, fine particles begrime glass and sift through cloth.

The lavender and leaves suggested for true potpourri may be used here as well as flowers and sprigs that would be wasted in the moist procedure. Add extras with discretion; though fragrant when fresh, most have little odor when dry, and are used only for color and interest. Try whole violets and violas, small single or double pinks, Dahlberg daisies, primroses; florets of rosemary, monarda, *Salvia superba,* lilacs; tips of thyme, lavender, and marjoram in bloom; petals of calendula, nasturtium, and chrysanthemum.

When all is dry, store each material in a separate glass jar until you have enough of everything to begin mixing; there is no problem of timing, as with the moist method. Resist the temptation to use a little of everything in your first potpourri. If rose petals form the main bulk, then add only one or two kinds of scented leaves, the fixative, perhaps a little fruit peel, fragrant beans or seeds, and two or three spices. Endless variations can be played upon this simple theme.

In dry mixtures, the proportions of spice and fixative are slightly higher because of their necessary coarse texture. Allow a mounded tablespoonful of spice, and at least half a cup of fixative to each quart of dry rose petals. It is important to allow enough fixative. For variety of scent, you may want to use—in addition to home-grown and prepared orris root—clary and calamus, some imported storax, vetiver-root, and gum benzoin. These may be purchased from potpourri specialists.

If you use only the petals of the roses that we suggest, with enough fixative no oils should be necessary. However, oils of lavender, mint, rose, geranium, orange blossom, sandalwood, lemon, and jasmine are available. These will give you an idea of the variety of concentrates you can obtain from the same specialists, to augment a weakly per-fumed blend. Use the oils with extreme care by the counted drop, only one oil to each small batch. Otherwise you may end up with something too strong for pleasure.

Once combined, the dry blends do need aging. Store them *loose* in glass preserving jars for at least three months, shaking the jars now and then. They increase in fragrance the first two years but have not the longer staying power of the moist potpourri.

The same flowers and herbs for dry potpourri can be used in sachets or sweet bags and with a like proportion of spice and fixative. The combinations are quite simple if scented leaves predominate instead of rose petals, and only one spice is added. When rose buds are used they need artificial perfuming. Organdy is the usual cloth but any kind of close-woven, sheer material may be used. Because the contents are ex-posed to air and so lose most of the scent within a year, a boost with oils or a favorite cologne becomes necessary.

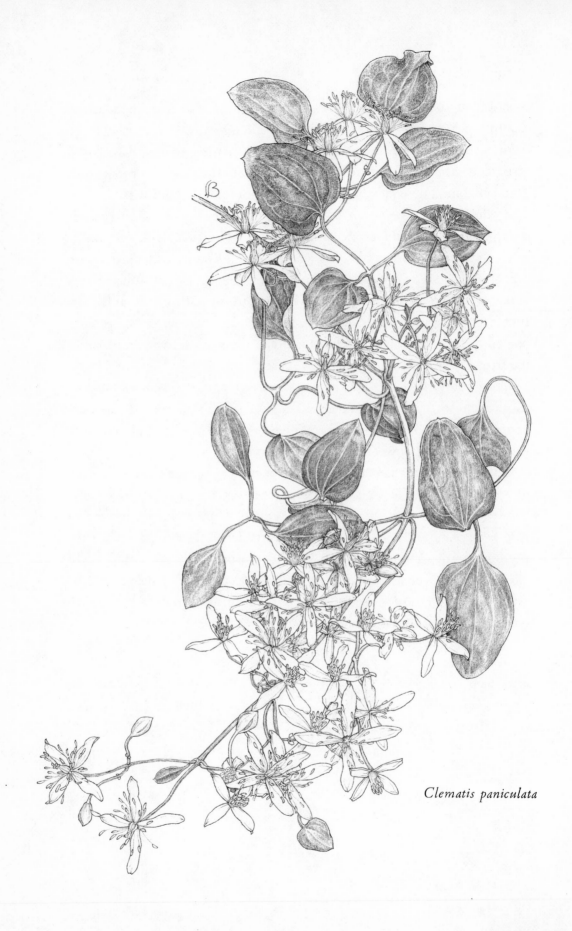

Clematis paniculata

15

Autumn Aromas

Summer slips so gently into autumn, and the warm lush scents of plants in full leaf change so imperceptibly to the crisp dry smell of those soon to fall, that until the one low branch on the great sugar maple above the rock ledge turns significantly to gold we are hardly aware of the slow passing of another year. But the purple roadside asters and the fields of goldenrod alert us, as well as the rich aromas of ripe apples burdening the hillside trees, and the Concord grapes on the arbors. The honeyed sweetness of the earlier flowers of the autumn *Clematis paniculata* now adds a pleasing musty quality to their scent.

Annuals, most refulgent now, are apparently as aware as we are of the sense of frost in the night air. The heaps of needles beneath pines, junipers, and fir trees seem more redolent in this season. Many of the most fragrant roses set some buds even after light frost may have ruined an earlier crop, and surely "the last rose of summer" does not lack for our appreciation. Finally, there comes the prevailing smell of burning leaves—to be enjoyed somewhat guiltily by the compost-minded.

Chrysanthemums come into early glory, blooming before September and until hard frost. We have occasionally come upon some with flowers of noticeable sweetness, but mainly it is the foliage that appeals to the nose. The leaves have a wonderfully bitey odor, sharp and pungent, a typical scent of fall. All the showy perennial kinds have it, and so does feverfew, *Chrysanthemum Parthenium,* now in doubled forms, all with beautifully dissected aromatic foliage.

Then there are the ferns. Many of these turn pure gold as nights grow cooler. With fresh vision, we regard the tall fronds of the royal and the cinnamon in the fern garden and the maidenhair beneath the dining-room windows. The deciduous types more than others seem to develop a peak of sweetness as they go about drying, and we discover new and delightful ferny smells as we brush by them. Most noticeable is the hay-scented fern, which is just that, redolent of clover, alfalfa, vetch, and of green quick-cured hay. Fronds pressed in books bequeath a scent to the pages that lasts for years, recalling spring and the first mowing of a lush lawn. The creeping bladder fern and the New York fern with its delicate chartreuse lances share this pleasant quality when dried or crushed. Most gifted, we are told, is a rare little species of northern limestone cliffs, *Dryopteris fragrans* with a bouquet of raspberry and peach said to linger for years on whatever it touches.

AROMATIC FALL FOLIAGES

Near the fern garden is a great, glistening mound of bayberry, *Myrica pensylvanica,* encircling itself with enough small plants to stock a neighborhood, as, indeed, this one has. The brittle leaves have a spice-and-balsam pungence that seems different with every sniff. The grainy, gray berries are full of wax; rendered and made into candles, they have a distinctive quality, a traditional Christmas scent. But fruit sets only where there are plants of both sexes. This is the superb bayberry that flourishes along the north Atlantic coast leeward of the dunes, in what appears to be sand alone. However, plants do not require seashore conditions but grow well in almost any soil. Inland they reach a dense 6 feet, seldom more. Dried, the leaves can be used to stuff small pillows in the way of pine and balsam. Several myricas grow in other parts of the country, all with crackly foliage and interesting fruit. Wax-myrtle (*M. cerifera*) of the South reaches almost tree height, while wax-myrtle of the West Coast, *M. californica,* has bronze-green leaves and purple berries. The creeping sweet-fern, *Comptonia peregrina* (*C. asplenifolia*) was once regarded as *Myrica* and indeed they smell alike, but the large frondlike leaves of sweet-fern, deeply pinnate and scallop-edged, are very different. When the sun beats down on stands of them along dusty country roads, the scent is almost tangible. Sweet-fern flourishes only in thin acid soils and must be moved in a sod. Other plants share bayberry's savor, sometimes suggesting to us the mincemeat tang of angostura bitters—which smells anything but bitter.

Spice-bush, *Lindera Benzoin,* ornaments thin eastern woodlands in fall with its red berries and big golden leaves. It has a nose-tingling cinnamon spiciness in twigs and foliage, but the tiny yellow flowers that light our woods here in early April are scentless.

Sassafras trees, *Sassafras albidum,* burgeon with odor. Leaves, twigs, bark, and roots are full of a ginger aroma that is captured to a degree in rootbeer. In the fall, the flaming cones illumine moist open woodlands here and throughout the East, the varishaped leaves—footballs, mittens, goosefeet—readily distinguishing them. And despite their long tap roots, we have had no difficulty transplanting even 3-foot plants in early leaf and almost bare-rooted. We made a row of them to espalier, and they grew mightily.

A maverick among somewhat weedy, often poisonous relatives, is harmless, sweet-smelling fragrant sumac, *Rhus aromatica.* This 4-foot suckering shrub, almost too much at home here and throughout the East, is useful for concealing unsightly situations. The three-parted foliage has a fruit-and-spice aroma, and in fall assumes the bright hues typical of *Rhus.*

249

The native witch-hazel *Hamamelis virginiana,* a fragrant, flowering transition from fall to winter, drops its golden leaves late in October. Then in November branches are massed with musty-sweet thready blooms, a delight in this month of darkening days.

OF BORDERLINE HARDINESS

Camellias are creeping north. We hear of winter-hardy plants flourishing in southern Canada, and Long Island has long been proud of many a fine specimen. The camellia is one of those challenging plants that gardeners of a certain nature just have to try. In the North it is more often grown in the greenhouse than in the garden.

Where soil is light and acid and winters not too harsh, the slender-leaved *Camellia Sasanqua* can be a dependable part of the fall garden, and some of the single-flowered forms have noticeable fragrance when smelled in hand, a subtle perfume that is Oriental yet refreshing. What *C. Sasanqua* and its forms lack in size, they make up for in number and exquisite design. Walking through the great camellia plantations at Callaway Gardens in Georgia, we were amazed to find how many had a gentle fragrance, Apple Blossom for one, a sturdy pink-and-white upright grower, and Maiden's Blush, a very pretty pale pink, single, on a pyramidal plant, sturdy enough to withstand Philadelphia winters. *C. Sasanqua* leaves when broken have a pleasing aroma that is more flowery than those of closely related *Thea sinensis,* the tea plant. The great *C. japonica* of florists and southern gardens has all form, rarely scent. Only one other has real fragrance, the highly perfumed *C. lutchuensis,* a plant for collectors with conservatories and for hybridizers.

Indispensable to our fall garden is Japanese oleaster, *Elaeagnus pungens,* with glistening foliage evergreen in the South but deciduous here. It is apparently hardy having survived intact all but the winter of 1960-61 here, and has the endearing habit of blooming in October. The very modest cinnamon-flecked, silvered flowers continue until hard frost and diffuse a musty grape-jonquil fragrance far beyond the garden. *E.*

250

pungens Simonii is hardiest, compact, with smaller foliage, 4 to 6 feet in time, but Fruitland oleaster, *E. pungens Fruitlandii,* does well here and has the most refined scent. Considered a climber but actually a weak-caned giant to 15 feet or more, *E. pungens* can be trained into a solid screen, all the more floriferous for clipping.

Early in October, as sweet-olive begins to perfume Southern gardens, mature plants of holly osmanthus, *Osmanthus illicifolius,* farther north produces along smooth gray stems quantities of tiny white flower that are extremely fragrant with a blending of jasmine and apricot. The plant does resemble English holly with its tough, dark green fiercely prickled leaves and distinctive light veining. It is hardy to southern Connecticut and can grow to 15 feet, but 8 feet is more usual with a spread as wide.

We grow the hardy orange, *Poncirus trifoliata,* for the many fruits that ripen in September. Velvety, of dull gold, and less than 2 inches across, these have a fine aromatic pungence of pineapple and bayberry, noticeable at a distance if the crop is great. In hand, the little oranges compel sniffing again and again; we set bowls of them in the hall and living room where they last through October, and make the largest into pomanders, inserting the smallest cloves into holes first punctured with a blunt needle. If the three-parted leaves are broken, they give off the expected citrol scent but the thin-textured mid-April versions of orange blossoms are at best only vaguely sweet. *Poncirus,* hardy throughout our area, seems to prefer an acid soil. Its formidable armature of 2-inch spines suggests planting for safety in a corner of masonry or on an out-of-the-way boundary.

The classic sweet-bay, *Laurus nobilis,* with flat, wavy-edged, polished green leaves of stiff papery texture offers a spicy bouquet if leaves are broken or crushed. In them we detect menthol, black pepper, and clove. A great tree in Mediterranean lands, sweet-bay is not hardy and even in the area of Norfolk, Virginia, reaches only 3 feet outdoors. Planted in a tub of moist acid soil, it makes a handsome specimen whether allowed to bush out informally or sheared to a round head.

In captivity the tiny buds nestling in each node seldom open, but there are always plenty of leaves for flavoring.

TENDER NORTH OF NORFOLK

The subtropical clerodendrums bring such glamour to fall that we overlook the coarse, rank-smelling leaves and wandering roots. Often the 5-parted bloom is set off by a colorful calyx, and some flowers pour forth the strong, marvelous perfume of nicotiana. Unfortunately scentless are the two handsome house-plant species, *C. Thomsoniae,* red on white, and *C. ugandense,* bright blue, and the fragrant ones we cherish succumb even to light frost and so must be given winter quarters indoors.

Harlequin glory-bower (*C. trichotomum*) is hardiest and most colorful of clerodendrums, a small tree that may grow 8 feet its first season. It makes an attractive espalier on a southern wall and in the enclosed city gardens of New York and Philadelphia would probably thrive as well as the fellow Chinese ailanthus and paulownia. If there is no enclosure, set it on high ground or sheltered near the house, for the light green, fuzzy foliage is sensitive to early frost. From late August until November, branches are festooned with broad cymes of little white flowers that fill the air with emanations of lily and nicotiana. Each flower leaves a polished berry of Persian turquoise, centered on stars of brilliant magenta, weighting the branches with wide flat clusters of floral jewelry. Smaller, hardier, with every part purple-suffused, *C. trichotomum Fargesii* bears flowers with a fragrance that verges on the unpleasant, and the navy-blue berries against narrow-lobed maroon stars are hardly so spectacular.

In Zone 8 and farther south where winters are milder, the fragrant belladonna-lilies, *Brunsvigia rosea,* are as important to fall gardens as chrysanthemums are to us. Often listed as *Amaryllis Belladonna,* these South African bulbs vegetate through late winter until midsummer, disappear in July, and then bloom gloriously without foliage in early fall, earning their name of naked-lady lilies. Broad umbels of rose-ribbed pink trumpets release a fine spicy sweetness, mostly cinnamon and nutmeg with an undercurrent of lily to insure carrying power. Full sun and summer drought are exactly what these bulbs need to set buds. Yellow-throated white 'Hathor' produces great heads of at least two dozen buds that open over several weeks and are exquisitely fragrant. Brunsvigias can be grown in deep pots or tubs when it is necessary to winter them indoors.

Hardier because of its heritage from *Crinum Moorei,* the hybrid ×*Amarcrinum Howardii* (*Crinodonna Corsii* in Europe) is a magnificent plant. It has the same habits of growth as the belladonna-lily but lives through winters here under a thick mulch. The flowers have wider petals, almost pure pink, and the same spicy bouquet as brunsvigia. The flowers of the smaller 'Delkin's Find' are more reflexed, and so even prettier.

16

For Cool Window Gardens

As summer draws to a close we turn with enthusiasm to the arrangement of our gardens in the house and the placement of many pot plants. It is our cold windows that offer unlimited opportunity. Here, as in a cool greenhouse, night temperatures run around 50 to 55 degrees F, and day temperatures rise with the sun as they do in a greenhouse. Depending on the cold areas available, we have enjoyed many fragrant jasmines and so-called jasmines, lemon, orange, and lime trees, acacia, sweet-olive and heliotrope, scented geraniums, and a procession of narcissus and hyacinth in bowls of pebbles. From November on all these pour forth waves of perfume, distinctive, delightful, and tantalizing in their differences.

In the course of many years—and in various houses—we have utilized cold pantries, attics and guest rooms with radiators turned off, two slightly heated but never freezing sun porches, and once a wonderfully wide, deep bay on a stair landing where a drapery was drawn at night to hold in the cold. Finally, we built a Plant Room with thermostatic control to insure the really chilly nights required by so many of our fragrant favorites.

But even a window of average size, cool and sunny, can accommodate five or six plants whose fairly constant bloom will scent a room through the winter. Of course, the less space you have, the more careful will be your selection. You will surely want one citrus and one jasmine—perhaps Meyer lemon and 'Maid of Orleans' jasmine; their delicate perfume of orange blossoms with jasmine will remind you of the Moorish gardens of Granada if you have traveled there. Include sweet-olive for its constancy, lavender heliotrope and yellow honeybells for sweetness and color, too, and select a scented geranium or a sage for an alleviating herbal aroma. Then on a nearby table set successive bowls of narcissus and French-Roman hyacinths. What unique pleasure these few fragrant indoor plants will give you—and your visitors as well.

JASMINES—FALSE AND TRUE

Many plants of fine perfume have been called jasmines although botanically they are not *Jasminum*. These include the day- and night-jasmines, or *Cestrum;* the Carolina yellow-jessamine, *Gelsemium;* and the star- and Confederate-jasmines, which are *Trachelospernum*. We have enjoyed every one of these at our cool windows with brief sojourns to the more intimate living-room. Of course, all the true jasmines are not fragrant. The hardy *Jasminum nudiflorum* and *J. Mesneyi* rarely offer a whiff of the scent which perfumers consider unique for they have been unable to produce it synthetically and must depend on living flowers for the oil-of-jasmine required in such quantity.

Queen of them all is surely *Jasminum Sambac,* the Arabian jasmine. Its fragrance, with that of *J. officinale grandiflorum,* provides the type essence we know as jasmine. Centuries ago plants were brought to China from India, Persia, and Arabia, and the flower became a supreme favorite of the Chinese, who devoted whole gardens to it and dried the flowers

Jasminum officinale grandiflorum

to add to tea. *J. Sambac* blooms throughout the year. Outdoors it becomes a shrub with long weak stems that need support to make it attractive, but indoors only occasional tip-pinching keeps buds coming. All jasmines need frequent syringing as protection from spider mites, and regular feeding.

256

Two jasmines offered are the single 'Maid of Orleans' and the double 'Grand Duke' which is less dependable. Few plants give such pleasure as a well-grown 'Maid of Orleans' sprigged with the marvelously fragrant rounds of bloom. These open pure white, then age through mauve-pink to faded maroon before dropping three days later. Though the strong scent dissipates as color deepens, the sequence is delightful. The perfume can be inhaled endlessly; it is uncloying sweetness, intense but not heavy in the way of gardenia or regal lily.

Poets jessamine, *Jasminum officinale*—easy to grow but hard to find, and of proven hardiness in the Philadelphia area—is summer flowering from July until frost. The less hardy form, var. *grandiflorum,* is the actual flower of perfumers and makes an excellent pot plant. Cymes of rose-lacquered buds begin to open in August and continue to form through most of the winter. While sprays are few flowered, the pure white blooms are comparatively large and even a single one is so powerfully fragrant it can be immediately detected, particularly in the evening.

The "many-flowered" *J. polyanthum* blooms from mid-January through February as sprigs emerge from every node and white stars open amid lacy foliage. The fragrance, considered the strongest of all jasmines, may seem so because so many flowers open at once; it is indeed powerful, but less sweet, less typically jasmine, than that of *J. Sambac* or poets jessamine. Its value is the dependable mass of bloom that comes just as winter days begin to lengthen.

It is a vine of tremendous vigor; where winters are mild, new shoots rocket up a support in a matter of weeks past second-story windows; or inside, to the eaves of large greenhouses. To confine such a one to a window, provide a 6-inch pot and some support. We have used a willow ring with success, fastened top and bottom to a bamboo stake set deep and firm behind the plant. As shoots develop, wind them in one direction and hold them to the frame with plant ties. This makes the fall cleaning-out of old growth easier.

Angelwing jasmine, *J. nitidum,* grown in Florida as a scrambling vine, in a pot becomes a tractable shrub, with bursts of bloom from shoot tips almost any time of year. The white sea-anemone flowers have a fragrance that must be sniffed up close. The Italian jasmine, *J. humile revolutum,* a shrub-vine with mildly fragrant yellow June-to-September flowers, has a reputation for hardiness and is surely worth a try at least as far north as coastal Maryland. (*J. nitidum* is sold as *J. gracile magnificum.*)

The yellow-star and Confederate-jasmines, properly *Trachelospernum,* endure a wide range of temperatures so that we have often grown them in the living room because there are not so many fragrant plants that tolerate the warmth there. But we found that they thrive with less attention to syringing in a steady 55- to 65-degree F place. (We discuss them in the next chapter.)

SCENTS OF ORANGE AND LEMON

From the Mediterranean come the oranges, lemons, limes, tangerines, and grapefruit that in this country are grown outdoors only in frostfree areas of Florida and California. We find many of them delightful pot plants though inclined to outgrow normal window space since they are naturally big shrubs or trees. The *Citrus* genus offers an assortment of odors; in every species there are four variations of the predominant oil, neroli. We think first of the scent of the blossoms. Although the various kinds are similar, perhaps the thick white flowers of lemon smell sweetest, and the broken leaves are aromatic.

The flesh or juice of each fruit also has a distinctive smell, but it is the skin itself that embodies the essence of orange, lemon or lime. Countless tiny blisters in the rind are really glands which contain the essential oil; give a sliver of skin a quick pinch in sunlight and you get a geyser of eye-watering mist. The blossoms do not smell at all the way the fruit tastes, very good yet strange, and a few inhalations satisfy. An orchard at peak of bloom is quite overwhelming.

Fruit is a colorful bonus. When plants bloom indoors, you can ensure a good crop-set by touching each flower with a dry camel's-hair brush dipped in pollen. If plants are put outside in May, they will often bloom again, and then insects do the fertilizing. Since oranges and lemons take up to a year to ripen, we often have plants with both fragrant flower and colorful fruit. Acid soil is a cultural necessity for citrus so water with a vinegar solution or feed with a soluble acid formula, and watch out for the insidious citrus scale that sucks the sap and makes leaves sticky and wet.

Citrus Limonia Meyeri, Meyer lemon, begins to bloom when plants are small, and continues in bursts from then on. Tufts of large rose-flushed buds and cupped white flowers crowd the slender branches, releasing a fragrance, strong and delicious, possibly the best of all citrus scents. If you have room for but one citrus, for fragrance as well as beauty and fruit, Meyer lemon is a wise choice. It bushes out nicely or may be trained to tree form. Many fruits set, of a size not too heavy for even a small plant to support, and they are edible.

Citrus Limonia Meyeri

Citrus sinensis 'King'

Citrus Limonia ponderosa, Ponderosa lemon, requires careful training to avoid gawky growth. It blooms prodigiously and even though
a plant may become temporarily leafless, every part will be bursting
with fat buds, rose-flushed white, in repeated spurts throughout the
year. Flowers are large and thick, their fragrance as far-reaching as that
of Meyer lemon.

Otaheite orange (ah-tah-hee′tee), the little *Citrus taitensis,* has dec-
orated florists' shops for decades, because it remained small and was
easily trained. In repeated bursts, the tiny mauve flowers come in small
clusters along the stems. They are mildly fragrant but sufficient to

perfume a window lightly and often, and eventually become dull, round fruit.

Better in every way is the Satsuma orange, *C. nobilis Unshiu,* one of the sweet-fleshed loose-skinned type, bushy rather than treelike. This is such a marvelous plant we hope it may one day be easier to obtain. Buds open one or two at a time from January to March indoors and continue when the plant is set outside late in May. Not large, the all-white flowers release a surprising amount of perfume. There is never a mass of bloom but rather a sprigged effect, and each flower sets a fruit. Though many drop later, enough remain to weigh the slender branches almost to breaking. The fruit is a small tangerine, seedless, of superb quality and ripening in time for Christmas. This and other citrus are obtainable from Florida nurseries, and may even be found on special dwarfing understock.

Grapefruit, *Citrus paradisi,* and sweet orange from Indo-China, *Citrus sinensis* are also worth an experiment. In a big cold enclosed sunroom, a collection of citrus would be delightful but Meyer lemon alone at a window always gives fragrant pleasure.

THE CYCLAMENS

We wish the big tender *Cyclamen persicum* from the florist were fragrant, for in our cold plant room, plants bloom handsomely for us from Christmas until May. But there is a miniature Multiflora strain in white, lavender, and salmon-pink, that is fragrant. It is easy enough from seed, so corms very likely will also soon be available. The perfume combines sweet violet with the best of tulip-scent or freesia and is quite pervasive.

Of the hardy species, *C. europaeum* is the sweetest and this too can be grown successfully indoors, sending up a few flowers at any time in any season. Outdoors the rose-colored flowers open in July and an old corm could produce buds into September. The fragrance, considered violet-like, seems to us more like the strong aroma of sweet bread dough.

Others to try include *C. pseudoibericum,* with wide-petaled cherry-red flowers in March; the reputedly tender *C. cilicicum,* a fall-blooming pink; and *C. libanoticum,* with surprisingly large pure pink flowers in March among marbled leaves. The old favorites, *C. neapolitanum* and the tiny spring bloomers *C. coum* and *C. orbiculatum* are scentless.

THREE SCENTED EVERGREENS

We are never without three slow-growing fragrant-flowering evergreen shrubs. Through the years, sweet-olive, *Osmanthus fragrans* (*Olea fragrans*), has been a constant delight. It is a plant we always bestow upon the new homemaker planning a first window garden. Never was there an easier plant to please. Cool air, at least morning sun, and moderate humidity are its few requirements. Small clusters of tiny cream-yellow flowers begin to open in November and continue until time to set the plant outdoors in late May, all the while scenting the daylight hours with a refreshing fragrance that is sometimes apricot, sometimes, we think more like strawberry gelatin. Strong sunlight brings it out powerfully, while at night the scent subsides.

A dense evergreen shrub that may reach 10 feet in the Lower South, *Pittosporum Tobira variegata* makes a small handsome house plant for northern windows, growing slowly to miniature tree-form with almost no training but requiring acid soil. Tight clusters of buds nestle over winter in the whorls of thick shining leaves opening to nosegays of cream-yellow, loose-petaled flowers with the scent of orange blossoms.

Then there is *Daphne odora,* prized indoors as well as out. As a pot plant, it blooms cream-pink during December and January, and, as we have remarked, the fragrance is ambrosial, combining orange with coconut. This one must have a cold place, for even one night in the dry warmth of a living room ruins the flowers.

FRAGRANCE IN LAVENDER AND YELLOW

Many indoor plants of fine fragrance have white flowers so we par-

Osmanthus fragrans

ticularly cherish several with lavenders and yellows for color as well as scent, and all look lovely with our jasmines and citrus.

None is more dependable, more sweetly cheering than the tender perennial heliotrope or cherry-pie, *Heliotropium arborescens*. It is worth foregoing storm sash on one south window and even to encourage a little draught to provide the cool night air it must have. Of course, a 50-degree F greenhouse presents no problem, and there heliotrope is lovely suspended in a basket and showered every day since it wilts quickly. Grown cool indoors, it also needs syringing once a day to maintain the humidity it needs for healthy growth. Get the true species from a house-plant specialist by mail, in either lavender 'True Sweet' or white. Either will provide you with ever-spreading plumes through most of

Brunfelsia latifolia

winter. Only in the darkest weeks of November and December does blooming slow down, to start again in January. Avoid varieties bred for summer bedding with great heads of voluptuous purple having hardly any odor. We used to wonder at the popular name cherry-pie, but the first deep sniffs explain it if the cherries are maraschino, the bouquet of almond brandy, a fragrance that wins your constant affection after one winter's residence. Mrs. Wilder, Constance Spry, and other older garden writers have devoted pages to praise of their beloved heliotrope.

The flowers of the biennial German-violet, *Exacum affine,* look rather like the African-violet with five petals of intense lavender-blue yellow-eyed. Bloom appears through most of winter and the unexpected prim-rose perfume is given freely even on cold dismal mornings. Leaves are whitened beneath, sage-scented, and the fringy flowers sprout in clusters from almost every pair, and are lovely for cutting. The plant looks better for close-cropping in April. Seedlings tend to pop up in unexpected places and can be grown on to replace the short-lived parent.

Russian sage, *Perovskia atriplicifolia,* repeats garden sage in everything but height and season. Long drawn-out branching stems open tiny blue flowers in August to a towering 5 feet, effective when used among gray-leaved herbs and Rugosa roses. Actually a shrub, this behaves like a herbaceous perennial in our climate.

FRANKLINIA AND OLEANDER

A plant jewel that deserves stage center, or the most protected, choice location in your garden is *Franklinia alatamaha (Gordonia alatamaha).* In a small sunny enclosure, it commands attention for almost three months as the first large bud-pearls unclasp about the first of August and continue until frost. The 3-inch flowers are kid-textured white, crumpled and pleated, somewhat like poppy petals and always cupped. A thick brush of golden-orange stamens lights the center, unloosing a soft, distinctive fragrance the sweetest of all tea-family perfumes. Buds and flowers nest in radiating leaves, glossy green in August, polished red leather by late September, an amazing combination. The loveliest specimen we ever saw was quite old but dwarfed by over-sandy soil. Taller than wide, from top to bottom the little tree was set with hundreds of open goblets, like so many eggs sunny-side-up. Fall transplanting, rich acid soil, full sun, adequate moisture, heavy mulching, and cool nights get franklinia through an always slow start.

We have also enjoyed this in the living-room but have moved it to the cold plant room at night.

Brunfelsia latifolia, called kiss-me-quick or yesterday-today-and-to-morrow, is often distributed, we think, as *B. calycina floribunda.* The flowers, formed similar to those of nicotiana, are clear lavender-blue, aging to white within a day or two but remaining on the plant, so that a

Mahernia verticillata

large plant in full bloom, with clusters in several tints of violet against deep green leaves, looks like a piece of old chintz. The fragrance is strong, that blend of gardenia-clove-jasmine found in many white flowers of the tropics. Blooming steadily from the turn of the year into summer and amenable to window culture if given rich soil and regular feeding, this brunfelsia is another winter dependable and will develop into a little spreading tree seldom taller than 2 feet. The fragrant flowers of most *Brunfelsia* species have the habit of opening one color and fading to another. While they are not night-blooming or night opening, their fragrance is strongest then. The West Indian *B. americana* (lady-of-the-night) and Peruvian *B. calycina* are possibilities for a greenhouse.

Wiry, trailing and bright green honeybell, *Mahernia verticillata,* offers tiny flowers of amazing perfume, pure, pervasive lily-of-the-valley. A glass shelf at mid-window is an ideal location for the tumbling growth of this easy house plant. By February the golden bells, singly and in pairs, begin to dot the plant, sending out delightful waves of scent. The buds are so inconspicuous you are hardly aware of their existence and are surprised as more and more keep opening even into May.

The familiar mimosa of street vendors and florists in March is *Acacia decurrens dealbata,* a handsome Australian shrub with downy blue-gray leaves to set off long clusters of half-inch lemon fluffs, warm with a fragrance of honey and grape. The French grow quantities of mimosa, both for perfume and for the midwinter cut-flower trade when great sheaves of the golden flowers go north from the Mediterranean Coast. In our Southwest the beautiful mimosa is used as a street tree together with opopanax, the beloved cassie of perfumers, *Acacia Farnesiana,* even sweeter but hardly a plant for the winter window. Acacias need really cold nights just above freezing.

Also from Australia comes another shrub with wonderfully fragrant flowers, *Boronia megastigma.* The twigs are wispy and upright to 2 feet, leaves needlelike and evergreen, resembling rosemary, faintly medicinal when crushed, the plant hardly a thing of beauty most of the year. But a transformation occurs in late winter, when they are hung with little lanterns, brown-red outside, lit dull gold within, of papery texture and so long lasting that for weeks the perfume, "a combination of violets, lemon-verbena and roses", pervades the cool window or greenhouse.

B. elatior produces larger bright rose lanterns but with less fragrance. Both require very acid soil and fresh seed germinates readily.

NARCISSUS, HYACINTHS, AND OTHER FRAGRANT BULBS

We also count on a succession of bulb plantings for both color and scent in our cool indoor gardens. We schedule the familiar paperwhite narcissus according to our pleasure for Thanksgiving, Christmas, and any party-time through March. Narcissus is lovely with our Christmas greens and offers a fine fragrance among the scentless gift plants of poinsettia and cyclamen. The smell of just one opening cluster pervades a large room. Even in the warmer living room, narcissus in bloom lasts for weeks if plants are moved to a cooler place at night.

We get in a supply of various tender, cluster-headed tazetta narcissus in October. The paperwhites started mid-October begin to open the week before Christmas, requiring ten weeks then but proportionately less time as the season advances. (Bulbs kept in the refrigerator, *not the freezer,* and started as late as the first of February bloom in four weeks, looking very pretty on short stems.) Mail-order bulbs are usually 2-inch and single-nosed, but from the florist we can usually get 2½-inch singles and once we found a 3-inch bulb that produced five clusters over a three-week period. Double-nosed bulbs produce one stem from each half, seldom more.

Paperwhites need not be started in the dark, which encourages massive rooting, but at the start they *must* have constant cold, between 40 and 50 degrees. A bright window in an unheated room is better than a stuffy closet. And pebbles are still the best medium, either the small kind known as Jersey gravel or large, river-washed ovals. We save the white-and-yellow Chinese sacred-lily and the golden 'Soleil d'Or' narcissus, which are somewhat slower, for February and March when they are charming in a deep window with great jars of forced forsythia set among them.

We have tried other fragrant narcissus in bowls of pebbles and water.

Probably any good polyanthus or poetaz bulb can be so handled since the embryo flower is already formed. We selected some of the early varieties. 'Cragford' put into pebbles the first week in February and given a brief cold spell for rooting flowered by the end of the month. 'Laurens Koster' was equally satisfactory. If you experiment, you will find many that bloom well indoors. 'Grand Primo Citroniere', 'Soleil d'Or', and the late poetaz—'Geranium', 'Bridal Crown', 'Scarlet Gem', and 'Cheerfulness'—force more successfully in soil and begin to open in February.

Several small kinds, potted in fall and buried beneath a thick blanket of marsh hay or set in a non-freezing garage and watered occasionally, can be brought in to a cool north window in January and set among low ivies and ferns. 'Canaliculatus' is delightful, so is 'Halingy', both miniature cluster heads. The Campernelles rival 'Soleil d'Or' in vivid color, and the creamy 'Thalia' and unique 'Silver Chimes' are very lovely. If you prefer large daffodils, these are scented possibilities: 'Armada', 'Content', 'Carlton', 'Galway', 'Golden Ducat', 'Kingscourt', 'Moonstruck', 'Narvik', and 'White Nile'.

For November scent, of the ineffable jonquil quality but with some other distinguishing note, we have found a strange Moroccan species, *Narcissus viridiflorus*. Planted in pots of soil in late October, bulbs bloom in a month, each producing clusters of four or more spidery flowers— and they are green.

Also dependable for November and the ensuing months is the slender-stalked French-Roman hyacinth, *Hyacinthus orientalis albulus*, daintier, with smaller more widely spaced bells than those of the stalwart Dutch type, but with the same delicious scent. Reputedly, southern France is the home of the French-Roman hyacinths, but they probably bloomed in the Levant centuries before they were discovered farther west. Perhaps these were the wild forms into which the Dutch bred hardiness; the flowers have a charming "unimproved" look. Over a period of three weeks, a large bulb produces some six successive sprays of blue or white bloom. Forcing is easy because the natural flowering time is

269

December through January. First plantings take about ten weeks. Bulbs planted early in September should bloom before Thanksgiving and those started in mid-October for Christmas. We keep our plantings in the cold garage for the first five or six weeks, and find that the later the planting, the less time to flower. Bulbs may mold if kept from rooting, so it is best to plant by mid-November. But, if you want to hold some for January fragrance, store them cold, just above freezing. The fairy-hyacinths, 'Borah' and 'Blue Star', while many-stemmed and charming, have but light fragrance, and the miniature 'Rosalie' apparently has none.

We enjoy four other bulbs that cannot be so exactly timed as our narcissus and French-Roman hyacinths, but each has a special charm. The Arabian Star-of-Bethlehem, *Ornithogalum arabicum* (not *O. thyrsoides*), opens broad racemes of large, white flowers, each centered with a glistening black bead, and with the unexpected fragrance of auratum lily. The flowers fold into globes at night. Bulbs planted in October sprout within a week, but do not bloom until February.

The prairie- or rain-lily, *Cooperia pedunculata,* pours forth a heavier auratum-lily perfume from six-pointed, gleaming white stars of bloom that are rose-stained beneath. This blooms after heavy April rains all through the woodlands of Texas and Louisiana and is hardy to coastal Virginia. In the North, pots are brought indoors in October to rest dormant until February, when heavy watering renews a cycle that starts in March and continues into summer.

Tulbaghia fragrans is an intermittent winter bloomer, producing in slow succession stem after stem of small lavender-pink flowers. These also have the fragrance of auratum lily. Color and form are most unusual.

Glory-of-the-sun, *Leucocoryne ixioides,* blooms during February and March. The flowers of heliotrope sweetness are periwinkle-blue paling to starry white centers, like oversize chionodoxa. If you cut them for a bouquet, you will detect garlic pungency in the stems but this soon passes and flowers last a week or longer in water.

FRAGRANT FOLIAGES FOR COOL AREAS

The sweet-leaved geraniums, which we discuss with herbs in Chapter 13, thrive in coolness and if you have a large sunny, glass-enclosed porch, cold but never freezing, they will grow prodigiously and bloom freely, with never a white fly in attendance. In hot sun, their blended leaf scents of lemon, rose, and mint offer pleasant aromatic contrast to the sweeter perfumes of the tropicals.

Two sweet-leaved sages, large for most windows but decorative for greenhouse or bay, have unusual aromas. Pineapple-sage, *Salvia rutilans,* is a bushy shrub that from November to March produces long one-sided spikes of slender rose-red flowers. The rich green leaves are matted with hair-thin glands that release a good fruit scent when pressed, more pineapple than anything else, and a nice addition to clear jellies, in the way of rose-geranium.

Salvia dorisiana produces spikes of typical lipped bloom in pink from a neat arrangement of bracts though we cannot see them. The leaves are what we so admire with their bouquet of fruit and chicle. No eucalyptol mars this goodness and children like to sniff and feel the thick, fuzzy, heart-shaped leaves.

The classic myrtle, *Myrtus communis,* appeals to all who enjoy the aromatic sweetness of sassafras and bayberry. Myrtles belong to that closed society of oil-rich plants—lavender, rosemary, laurel, thyme—that billow over hot rocky coasts of the Mediterranean and freight the sea air with their pungencies. Sprays of flowering myrtle were traditionally used in Europe as coronets for brides, and Greek poets held myrtle sacred to Venus as they reserved laurel for their heroes. The little flower puffs of green-white stamens appearing in summer add a sweetness of their own to the herbal quality of the foliage. Besides the type with long, dark, polished leaves, and its roughly cream-edged variegated form—which grow into loose bushy shrubs—house-plant catalogues list the small-leaved dwarf myrtle, *M. communis microphylla*

271

with bright green box-like foliage, and its rather weak sport, which is neatly cream-edged. These are delightful trained into small formal trees, and undemanding at cool bright windows.

Corsican mint, *Mentha Requienii,* is so small and fragile that it is difficult to believe it belongs to the same genus as the coarse mints of the herb garden. But pinch just one leaf and there will be no question as you recognize the cool pungence of pennyroyal, like peppermint but more aromatic. Children love this diminutive creeper and are possibly its one serious pest, for they pinch often and vigorously. This tiny thing is fine to use for pot-topping under treelike citrus and jasmine. Poke pencil holes in loose soil and slip a 2-inch trailer into each; within a few weeks, new plants will spread a gossamer of green to bloom invisibly in May, and seed.

If you have a greenhouse to devote to cool-preference fragrant plants, perhaps you will have space for small blocks of annuals, some of them the most marvelously scented plants you can grow. Sweet-peas would be first choice, strains knowingly selected. At the Wisley trials in London we have walked between rows of the most beautiful flowers possible and often found no scent among them. For us sweet-peas without fragrance—a contradiction of the name—are as unacceptable as scentless roses. Stocks, wallflowers, dianthus, and sweet alyssum are other annual possibilities. In earlier chapters we have listed some fragrant varieties.

17

Fragrant Schedule
for a Living Room

Who does not enjoy coming into a room where scented plants perfume the air or opening a greenhouse door to an atmosphere of delightful odors? True, the possibilities for rooms you live in and keep fairly warm in winter are somewhat limited. Most house plants like a considerably cooler atmosphere than we do. For with this coolness goes higher humidity, another agreeable condition.

Thriving with us in the warmer, sunny living room where, except close to the fireplace, the temperature rarely goes above 72 degrees F —at the windows it always registers ten to twelve degrees less, and the thermostat is set back to 65 degrees F at night—are some plants with flowers that freely scent the air even when only one bloom is open, as gardenia and ginger-lily. Then there are those that must be of good size with a quantity of flowers if their sweetness is to be noticeable throughout a room and not just when you bend to them to savor their fragrance. Such is the bouvardia. All in all, we do not find it difficult to have a fragrant progression from October to June.

The plants we choose to grow in our living rooms have considerable tolerance though many of them do *prefer* 60 degrees F. However, with the good humidity provided by our water-filled pebble trays and pot saucers and once- or twice-a-day mistings from a sprayer that emits a cloud of moisture so fine it does not harm curtains or wallpaper, they all give pleasure to us and to our guests, who are delighted by the unexpected fragrance of our winter rooms. We also enjoy the evening appearances of many cooler-preference plants that are grown and brought into bloom elsewhere, but will tolerate a few hours of our pleasant warmth, though not much more. These include the plants discussed in the previous chapter.

CLERODENDRUMS FOR THE FALL

Two that are fragrant initiate the season. *Clerodendrum Bungei*—precariously hardy in Philadelphia and known to fortunate Southern gardeners as red Mexican- or French-hydrangea—pours forth a heady fragrance like that of nicotiana when the brilliant, starry rose-red blooms first open in September. Cashmere Bouquet is a pleasant name for *C. fragrans pleniflorum*. Indoors this requires full sun and benefits from pinching back to reduce leaf size without affecting the charming pink-flushed white clusters of bloom. If you can manage 60 degrees F for Cashmere Bouquet, the perfumed nosegays will continue to appear into December; in a warmer place, the blooming period is shorter. On the debit side, the plants of clerodendrum are hardly attractive, for the foliage is coarse, rank, of evil smell when touched.

LILY-OF-THE-VALLEY, NARCISSUS, HYACINTHS

We repeatedly enjoy the pure sweet scent of *Convallaria majalis* in the living room now that cold-storage forcing pips, or budded roots, are available from fall to spring. It is remarkable, but true, that bloom does occur exactly twenty-one days after planting. Usually we time our lily-of-the-valley for the before-Christmas months when there are few free-scented plants for a warm room, and then again for St. Valentine's Day when they appear sentimentally appropriate. The sweet scent, so delicate, is always pleasant in a winter bedroom. If you want bloom for Christmas, remember to plant pips by December third, and as soon as you receive them. A deep bowl, 5 inches or so, is essential even when roots are trimmed back a third in accordance with the supplier's directions. For a dozen plants, select a bowl about 6 inches wide. However, for the ends of the mantel you may prefer two smaller bowls of six plants each. Be sure to plant immediately; otherwise, pips mold and then rot in the plastic bags they are packed in. Grow cool up to the point of budding; then move to a light not sunny window in the living room. Flowers last longer if bowls are moved to a cool place overnight.

In the previous chapter we have praised the tender French-Roman hyacinths, smaller and more graceful than the chunky Dutch type and just as fragrant, and also paperwhite narcissus, both for growing in containers of pebbles and water. Again, just as a reminder, plant the hyacinths by mid-October and the narcissus by mid-November for bloom at Christmas. Placed on the long window sill facing east, they last for weeks. If your living-rooms are warmer than ours, move the bowls to cooler quarters overnight. You may also want some hyacinths for bleak January weeks—plant these by mid-October but grow cold till the first of January. Moved then to a light living-room window, they will soon produce flowers.

For the spring pleasure of hyacinths, usually for Easter—and at the easiest possible level of effort—we plant a number of the Dutch type outside in fall where removing them will not spoil a garden picture. When the fat green sheaths are well in evidence, usually by March, we carefully lift the bulbs and pot them in commercial house-plant soil, three or five together in a bulb pan. We set the plants in the cold but not freezing garage for a few acclimating days, syringing them

Narcissus Tazetta papyraceus

often. Then they are brought to a light but not sunny window in the living-room where the flowers of heavenly fragrance open in less than a week. This is a more carefree method than the usual potting in fall, storing for months, and forcing for weeks. It is also easy to have January and February bloom from large bulbs grown over water in hyacinth glasses. Let them root in cool darkness for four weeks, then bring to light; to draw up the stems set open-topped paper cones over the buds.

276

BOUVARDIA, NOVEMBER INTO JANUARY

Generally considered a greenhouse plant, *Bouvardia* thrives for us in the window garden, and from early in November far into January is an intermittent but star performer there with its sweet jasminelike scent. The tubular white flowers are charming associated with the clear blue cones of *Eranthemum nervosum* and the bright rose-red flowers of *Rondeletia odorata* (which in our experience does not live up to the "odorata" of its name). This pretty tapestry of color delights us for weeks on end.

The white forms of *B. longiflora*—'White Joy'; var. *Humboldtii*, the florist's favorite; and the large 'Albatross'—are the sweetest, pink and red forms being almost scentless. Growth is sprawling and needs staking, but in the center of a grouping with other plants, it can be inconspicuous. Or we support it with a double arch of heavy eighth-inch wire, bending two 6-foot pieces at the halfway point. Rarely do we come near this plant in bloom without bending down for a breath of the delectable perfume. Bouvardia, the Mexican "flores de San Juan," is one of the earliest performers of our fragrant year, always lovely by Thanksgiving and continuously so. When you grow this, be mindful about watering. Like heliotrope and cyclamen, it literally faints even at the approach of dryness. And we apply a systemic pesticide to the soil (deadly poisonous but we are careful) to prevent insect infestation. Since this one would prefer it cooler, we coddle it with frequent mistings and, when we are energetic, we move it to the cold plant room at night. We trim back growth in February to thicken it.

GARDENIA AND JASMINES, WINTER TO SUMMER

In the gardenia we find an inimitable fragrance, too "heavy" for some, to us delightful. Again we find that just one flower scents a whole room and this is characteristic of many white flowers, as Mrs. Wilder has remarked: "For the most part fragrant flowers are light in colour or white. Brilliant flowers are seldom scented, though now and again there is an exception to prove the rule. There are more white scented flowers than any others and perhaps the purples and mauves come next . . . Flowers of thick texture are often heavily scented—the Magnolias for instance, Gardenias and those of the Citrus tribe."

Few of us claim unqualified success with the gardenia. Too often the slow-as-molasses buds form in quantity and then drop before opening. Low humidity would be a fair diagnosis of the cause of this disaster. Certainly high humidity is a general requirement and full sun, also a weekly soaking of large pots in a deep vessel of water. In between we promote acidity by watering with vinegar solution—½ teaspoon to 1 quart of water—or with a diluted acid fertilizer. The difficulty is that when we fail, we apparently handle our plants exactly the same as when we succeed, except for the hardly decorative device of the perforated plastic bag that is sometimes recommended. This device does promote humidity and results in good bloom, and the bag can be removed for long or short intervals to display the plant, or flowers from a plant so protected can be cut and floated decoratively in a bowl.

In any case the gardenia is worth great effort for the fragrant winter-to-summer succession of fortunate years. We often grow a plant each of the familiar double *G. jasminoides,* the smaller-leaved but also large-flowered *G. jasminoides Veitchii* that blooms intermittently through the year, and the diminutive *G. jasminoides radicans,* blooming only from January to May.

In January a number of so-called jasmines of strong though varying fragrance begin to bloom and continue into June. Rather like the gardenia, with whorled blooms white and fragrant, is crape-jasmine, *Ervatamia coronaria,* also called moonbeam and Clavel-de-la-India. This produces an almost continuous procession of semidouble, 2-inch creped flowers, not with the usual lily essence of many tropical whites, but rather with the fresh piercing sweet scent of *Daphne Mezereum.* From January, sometimes earlier, until June, flowers open one at a time from a number of spreading bud clusters, and their perfume has rare loveliness. Plants are shrubby and need no pinching to develop into bushy masses of shining green. Rich soil, full sun, steady moisture, and enough fertilizing to support the sturdy bud production are important.

Carolina-jessamine, *Gelsemium sempervirens,* has been a joy in our living-room with golden yellow flowers through the winter, the scent hardly strong in the early months but increasing as days lengthen. A twining vine, it also requires the double wire arch. Until it is ready to grow and bloom, it stands absolutely still. Even in December it may be motionless, then suddenly off it goes.

The yellow star- and the Confederate-jasmine are trachelospermums from the Orient. Their entrancing perfume suggests both jasmine and mock-orange, and a single plant sweetens the air of a room. The yellow one, *Trachelospermum asiaticum,* brought from Japan in 1880, begins to bloom in a sunny window by late January, and thereafter is seldom without a little color even into autumn. The white *T. jasminoides,* brought from China by Robert Fortune in 1844, has long been favored by Southern gardeners. Indoors, as a pot plant for the North, it blooms a little later, producing yellow buds that open to white with starry blooms with a delightful outpouring of scent from February through April.

This pleasure is possible earlier if the Confederate-jasmine is placed under fluorescent light when plants are brought indoors in September. Even before Thanksgiving, terminal clusters start to open. Meanwhile, glossy foliage is attractive, trained to three or four plant stakes, the soil kept acid with monthly waterings of vinegar solution, half a teaspoon to a quart of water. We have also grown the variegated 'White Mist', a nice foliage contrast among the prevailing green. The pervasive perfume of the white Confederate-jasmine is even stronger than that of the yellow-star, and more like that of true jasmine.

WALKING-IRIS, WAX-PLANT, GINGER-LILY FOR MARCH

Offsets of the old-fashioned, tropical walking-iris or apostle-plant have been so generally shared among families and friends that until recently plantsmen have hardly found *Neomarica gracilis* a worthwhile item. Now they offer it, after many requests we suppose, as well as several larger flowering species. These, however, do not appeal to us since they lack the rare lily-of-the-valley sweetness of the time-honored species. We value this March-blooming plant with its purple-netted white flowers because it is more amenable to living-room heat than many other fragrant favorites. Full sun is essential for heavy bloom, and quantities of water, as well as frequent top syringing to prevent yellow leaf tips. Tight potting is important, too. Those big leaf fans are supported by quite small roots. It is interesting to follow the development of the flowers. In February, feel the center leaves of each fan for revealing thickness. In the following weeks, watch the shadow of a blooming spur inch up the leaf to emerge at last near the tip. These special leaves develop a wiry strength that allows the resulting proliferation to arch far out. When a flower bud appears, watch it; next morning it will have opened, and by evening withered away. But more will come, even two at a time and for a week or longer from each spur on well-grown plants.

Although there are a number of tuberous ginger-lilies, choose only *Kaempferia rotunda* if it is fragrance you want. This one is easy to grow provided you let the tuber go dormant in fall, potting it or starting it into growth between December and the first of March. It takes but one flower to fill a room with a perfume of lilies, a light but exotic sweetness that is never distressing. It is this scent for which the plant is named since the flowers look more like large lavender-shaded white violets than lilies. These emerge directly from the soil every other day or so. They last only a few hours, not even the day-length of the apostle plant, but each mature tuber produces a fine succession in the course of several weeks. Flowering is followed by the large patterned leaves which look handsome all through the summer.

If you are a specializing sort of hobbyist like us, you might some year choose to concentrate on hoyas for today house-plant catalogues list

Neomarica gracilis

eight or more kinds, besides the two we have long enjoyed—*Hoya carnosa,* the old-fashioned wax-plant, and the miniature *H. bella,* pretty in a basket. Their sugary sweet fragrance, stronger at night, will delight you. Try to obtain plants of some age, say four years old, or else have patience for that long. Hoyas don't rush into production but, once they are established in a warm sunny window (no outside summers for these) the two bloom prolifically from March into summer. You can also enjoy abandoned growth on *H. carnosa* if you have space in greenhouse or plant room, fastening in cup hooks in long haphazard lines to accommodate 10- to 20-foot strands of growth.

Once a plant does bloom, it produces more clusters each year, on both old spurs and new ones. Umbels measure 3 inches or more across and are made up of twenty to fifty intricate half-inch flowers. Corollas are pale pink, the crowns like waxen stars lit at center by rose-red stigmas, capped by one glistening drop of nectar. If you cut a cluster for a corsage, keep in mind that you then sacrifice the spur, for there is no proper stem. It is the spur that is the source of new flowers.

Warmth and rich potting soil suit hoyas very well, and by trying different sorts, you may succeed in having one or another in bloom all through the year. New kinds include *H. Keysii,* with gray-velvet leaves and many flowers; *H. Motoskei,* round, glossy-leaved, with white perfumed stars that continue to open for weeks; *H. longifolia Shepherdii,* with distinctive long slender leaves and small flowers of intense sweetness.

UNSCHEDULED FLOWERING

At least five other plants will add excellent fragrance to the living-room window garden, although their flowering cannot be exactly timed. When they do bloom, the spurts of flowers supplement the more definite scheduling of the others.

A tropical beauty from the mountain forests of Colombia, the glistening Amazon-lily, *Eucharis grandiflora,* resembles a short-cupped narcissus, white with a touch of cool green within. Fragrance pours from the lovely sparkling clusters, a distillation of *Lilium auratum* with some other exotic note, and the scent lasts as long as flowers are fresh, usually several days. This is not the easiest bulb to bring into production outside a greenhouse but we have done it, accepting the challenge since both flowers and scent are so exquisite. In successful years, each bulb blooms three times, and at least once in midwinter, although the time cannot be exactly determined. The performance is one of alternate periods of growth and rest, as with many flowering subjects. Plant your bulb in late summer with tip at soil level in a 5-inch pot, and set in a shaded place until side shoots sprout and growth is well established. Then bring the plant in to steady warmth, 65 to 75 degrees F, and sun, for this one really thrives on heat. To encourage you, a flower-stem or two may emerge from the gleaming, hosta-like foliage to be queen of the winter window while it lasts. If you can manage it, you will find the Amazon-lily well worth your careful attention; there is no more arresting or more richly fragrant plant for a living-room window garden. A miniature form recently listed as 'Fosteri' is just as rewarding.

Of the various species of asparagus-fern suited to pot culture, one old-time favorite is essential, *Asparagus Sprengeri,* the needle type. Highly ornamental as a green plant, on occasion it produces quantities of white flowers of small size but strong fragrance, a reminder of apricot and very like that of sweet-olive. It is an excellent roving plant to set on a bracket or high shelf, or to cascade from a hanging basket. Given scope, it grows for yards and yards, tangles in window hardware and is lushly decorative. A daily winter pleasure is to aim the mist sprayer at the lacy drapery, then watch the countless prismed droplets glisten in the morning sun. If flowers are open, the fine spray diffuses the perfume, so light, refreshing, and pervasive. Hung in half shade outside over summer, the flowers appear in repeated spurts and often set bright red fruit.

We wish we could pass on a formula to insure bloom and the bright ensuing berries that make a fine basket plant an arresting sight in fall. Age is certainly a factor. Four-year pot-bound plants can usually be counted on for fairly certain performance. The shock of transplanting may stimulate flowering on younger plants or a rest period induced by several quite cool weeks with a modicum of moisture. We cannot say. In any case, the plants themselves are easy enough to grow, their long graceful sprays always decorative in the warm window garden. There are other types to try, as the heart-leaved smilax of florists, *Asparagus asparagoides,* with little paired flowers almost as fragrant as orange blossoms; and *A. crispus* a larger needled sort than *A. Sprengeri* with scented flowers that turn into pink berries.

Doubtless you know *Stephanotis floribunda,* Madagascar-jasmine, the fragrant, waxen white stars of bridal bouquets. This Easter-lily scent with a peppery note is also possible from a big pot plant in an east window of a winter room kept at 60 to 70 degrees F. You cannot schedule the lovely waxen flowering of this one, but once a mass of stems is built up and the long shoots pinched back, buds may develop at any time of year, but more likely from spring to fall. As a foliage plant, stephanotis is handsome with strong glossy leaves. When it starts to grow, it goes like mad, inches a day. It needs rich soil and an occasional dose of a soluble acid plant food and looks well when trained around three strong stakes in a foot-wide circle on a willow frame, or on our favorite double arch. Considerable top can be built up in this way, but when you check the growth at the point you prefer, the plant sulks for weeks. Eventually it accepts the situation and the 3 feet or so of bare trained stem leafs out all along the line and then produces bloom at every node. There is vigor enough in stephanotis for a trellis or the framing of a window; but this presents a problem in summer when the time comes to transfer it to the terrace. Stephanotis produces a fine succession but in its own good time. Why it is not more frequently grown in window gardens is a mystery, for it is a choice plant of fine fragrance and available from house-plant specialists if not always from the florist.

Two forms of *Carissa*—*C. grandiflora,* standard, and *C. grandiflora nana,* dwarf, produce a wealth of white pinwheel flowers like smaller versions of frangipani, and with a similar heavenly perfume. A shrubby South African plant with dark thick leaves and heavy spines, the Natal-plum is so-called for the glossy red fruits that follow the 2-inch flowers which appear at various times on a well-established specimen. Either the large or small version will delight you as a pot plant, bushy and usually willing to bloom in rich soil and full sun in a room that is 60 degrees F at night. Again you cannot schedule this one, but the scented flowers are welcome at any time. Because high humidity seems to be essential to this plant, covering with a perforated plastic bag for a few weeks is often the means of promoting bud formation.

No plant is more familiar than the ubiquitous snake-plant, but have you ever seen a fine big specimen of *Sansevieria trifasciata* or the yellow-edged var. *Laurentii* in bloom? Occasionally our well-treated old specimens surprise us with translucent, curling creamy flowers, diffusing at night the strong essence of lily-of-the-valley, that most thrilling of perfumes. From each cluster of pale green buds along the stem, one flower opens at a time, so that blooming continues for more than a week. Even one flowering stem makes its presence known in a small room.

As with asparagus, age is probably a factor in flowering, even uncherished age. We know of very old plants, so pot-bound that no soil is visible, that bloom dependably every summer on a shaded porch; the shallow containers have no drainage holes, and the only moisture is heavily chlorinated city water. Repotting on the other hand has sometimes shocked a cared-for plant into bloom. Recently *S. parva* has come into favor with thin rosettes of slender deeply channeled leaves that grow over the pot rim and down. Once in a while it blooms, one raceme from each leaf-cluster, usually after a dry spell or repotting, but the effort almost kills the plant. The long spires of tiny flowers are miniatures of those of *S. trifasciata,* and night-fragrant, too, releasing the heady scent of *Cestrum nocturnum.*

FRAGRANT FALL-TO-SUMMER SCHEDULE
FOR YOUR LIVING ROOM

September to December	*Clerodendrum Bungei*
	Clerodendrum fragrans var. *pleniflorum*
October to June	Lily-of-the-valley (start cold-storage pips 21 days ahead of desired bloom)

The Fragrant Year

November to January	*Bouvardia longiflora*
Thanksgiving	French-Roman hyacinths (start September 11)
	Polyanthus narcissus (start mid-October)
Christmas	French-Roman hyacinths (start October 15)
	Polyanthus narcissus (start mid-November)
January	French-Roman hyacinths (start October 15 but keep cold till January 1)
January to June	Gardenia
	Crape-jasmine (*Ervatamia coronaria*)
	Carolina-jessamine (*Gelsemium sempervirens*)
Late January to autumn	Yellow-star-jasmine (*Trachelospermum asiaticum*)
February through April	Confederate-jasmine (*Trachelospermum jasminoides*)
March	Apostle-plant (*Neomarica gracilis*)
	Ginger-lily (*Kaempferia rotunda*)
March into summer	Wax-plant (*Hoya carnosa* and *H. bella*)
Easter	Polyanthus narcissus (start 2 to 3 weeks ahead)
Fragrance unscheduled	Amazon-lily (*Eucharis grandiflora*)
	Asparagus-ferns (*Asparagus* species)
	Madagascar-jasmine (*Stephanotis floribunda*)
	Natal-plum (*Carissa grandiflora* and var. *nana*)
	Snake-plant (*Sansevieria* species)

18

Other Plants to Try

There remains a multitude of plants we have yet to poke a nose into, and that we long to investigate. Growing orchids, cacti, and water-lilies requires special equipment and several years of a lifetime apiece. Then there are the tropicals, plants that need nothing less than a greenhouse this far north, and others hardy though difficult to locate or satisfy. Here is the beginning of our check list for the future.

Acokanthera spectabilis
Artabotrys odoratissimus
Beaumontia grandiflora
Buddleia asiatica
Cananga odorata
Chamaelaucium uncinatum
Choisya ternata

Coffea arabica
Drimys Winteri
Eriobotrya japonica
Eucalyptus species
Gardenia Thunbergia
Hymenosporum flavum
Luculia gratissima

Mandevilla laxa (M. suaveolens)
Michelia fuscata
Murraya paniculata (M. exotica)
Pittosporum heterophyllum
Plumeria species
Pterostyrax hispida

Sinningia tubiflora
Siphonosmanthus Delavayi
Solandra species
Staphylea colchica
Umbellularia californica
Zantedeschia aethiopica

NATIVE PLANTS

American wildlings provide another storehouse of odors. Besides the balsamic goodness of pines, junipers, hemlock and birch, there are these —some minute treasures, others trees.

Acorus Calamus
Apios americana (A. tuberosa)
Apocynum androsaemifolium
Aster cordifolius
Carpenteria californica
Catalpa speciosa
Ceanothus species
Chimaphila species
Cladrastus lutea
Cowania Stansburiana
Dicentra canadensis
Dioscorea Batatas
Dodecatheon species
Epigaea repens
Hesperocallis undulata

Layia platyglossa
Limnanthes Douglasii
Linnaea borealis
Lupinus arboreus
Mitchella repens
Monardella lanceolata
Moneses uniflora
Panax quinquifolius
Podophyllum peltatum
Pyrola species
Romneya Coulteri
Schrankia uncinata
Sophora secundiflora
Trichostema lanatum
Trillium nervosum (T. stylosum)

ORCHIDS, TROPICAL EPIPHYTIC AND TERRESTRIAL

Orchids offer a vast assortment of odors, many intoxicatingly good, a few foetid. They often have one familiar fragrance in the morning and another at night—which one is the by-product of the other is impossible to say without knowing each species' pollinating insect. For those with the facilities for growing orchids, these are highly recommended:

Aërides odoratum

Angraecum sesquipedale

Brassavola hybrids

Brassavola nodosa

Catasetum roseum

Catasetum Warscewiczii (C. scurra)

Cattleya species and hybrids, many

Chysis aurea

Chysis bractescens

Cycnoches chlorochilon

Cymbidium species, many

Dendrobium aggregatum

Dendrobium moschatum

Dendrobium nobile

Dendrobium superbum

Dendrochilum glumaceum

Diacrium bicornutum

Epidendrum ciliare

Epidendrum fragrans

Epidendrum ionophlebium

Gomesa planifolia

Gongora atropurpurea

Houlletia odoratissima

Laelia glauca (Brassavola glauca)

Laelia hybrids

Laelia speciosa

Leptotes bicolor

Lycaste aromatica

Neofinetia falcata (Angraecum falcata)

Odontoglossum pulchellum

Oncidium tigrinum

Peristeria elata

Rodriguezia venusta (Burlingtonia fragrans)

Stanhopea tigrina

Vanda luzonica

Zygopetalum intermedium (Z. Mackayi)

These hardy terrestrial orchid species need steady moisture and cool summers and are worth a long search if you have both. Many of the fringed-orchis are perfumed: native *Habenaria dilatata, H. blephariglottis, H. leucophaea, H. psycodes grandiflora (H. fimbriata)*, and European *H. conopsea*. Tiny-flowered ladies-tresses, *Spiranthes cernua* and *S. Romanzoffiana*, cover sterile fields in fall with mysterious sweetness. Large-flowered and handsome are European vanilla-orchid, *Nigritella an-*

gustifolia, our *Orchis spectabilis* and *Cypripedium Calceolus pubescens,* oriental *Calanthe striata Sieboldii,* while low chartreuse *Cymbidium virescens* is the little spring orchid of Chinese paintings, powerfully fragrant.

CACTI

Many of the intricately beautiful flowers of the cactus family have delightful odors, as do a number of succulents. Plant forms vary from diminutive buttons to rambling climbers that can take over a small greenhouse. Those from desert lands need full sun and cool nights, while others are jungle plants thriving in warmth and filtered light. Never make the mistake of supposing that cacti are satisfied with a lean diet: flowering takes food, and many need frequent waterings, always with impeccable drainage. These listed, while not strictly diurnal, remain open in sunlight, often for several days. Those starred (*) are easy to locate, while those marked (E) need epiphyllum culture. The others—thorny cacti—flower dependably indoors if grown under fluorescent light.

Astrophytum capricorne
Chiapasia Nelsonii (E)
Crassula argentea
Crassula teres
Cryptocereus Anthonyanus (E)
Echinopsis multiplex
Echinopsis polyancistra
Echinopsis leucantha
Echinopsis leucorhodantha
Erythroripsalis pilocarpa (E)

Hamatocactus setispinus
Heliocereus species (E)
Homalocephala texensis
Hylocereus extensus (E)
Kalanchoe somaliensis
Lobivia chrysantha
Neobesseya odorata
Pereskia aculeata (E)
Pseudorhipsalis macrantha (E)
Rochea coccinea

Their fragrances duplicate those of the best tropical flowers—jasmine, tuberose, magnolia, vanilla, orange-blossom—and are usually free.

WATER-LILIES

Water-lilies are often blessed with abundant perfumes, pervasive breaths of lemon, lily-of-the-valley, vanilla, even blended fruit. Best are the tropical day-bloomers, which must be wintered inside; and the hardy water-lilies, many of them descendants of our own *Nymphaea odorata*. Most night-blooming tropicals lack scent, strangely, but the gigantic *Victoria regia* and Oriental lotus, *Nelumbium Nelumbo,* in its several luscious forms, have fragrances to match their dimensions, definitely free. These are superb:

Tropical day-blooming water-lilies: 'August Koch', 'Dauben', 'Isabelle Pring', 'Jupiter', 'Mrs. George H. Pring', 'Panama Pacific'.

Hardy water-lilies (*Nymphaea*): 'Dawn', 'Exquisite', 'James Brydon', 'Lilacea', 'Loose', 'Marliac Rosea', 'Marliac White', 'Mrs. C. W. Thomas', *N. odorata minor, N. odorata rosea,* 'Pink Opal', 'Pygmaea Alba', 'Rose Arey', 'Virginale', 'W. B. Shaw'.

SOME OF THE MOST FREELY FRAGRANT HARDY PLANTS

PLANT	POPULAR NAME	TIME OF BLOOM
Buddleia alternifolia	garland butterfly-bush	Late May to early June
Buddleia Davidii	butterfly-bush	Late July to October
Buxus species	box	Mid-March to mid-April
Chimonanthus praecox	wintersweet	January to mid-February
Chionanthus virginica *	fringe-tree	Late May to mid-June
Clematis montana rubens	pink anemone clematis	Late May to June
Clematis paniculata *	autumn clematis	August and September
Clerodendrum trichoto-mum *	Harlequin glory-bower	August and September

(* *Free at night as well*)

PLANT	POPULAR NAME	TIME OF BLOOM
Clethra alnifolia	sweet-pepperbush; summersweet	July and August
Daphne Mezereum	February daphne	Late March to mid-April
Dianthus Caryophyllus * and hybrids	carnation; clove pink	May to September
Dianthus plumarius * and hybrids	cottage pink	May and June
Elaeagnus angustifolia *	oleaster; Russian-olive	Late May to mid-June
Elaeagnus pungens *		Mid-September to November
Hamamelis mollis	Chinese witch-hazel	February and March
Hyacinthus orientalis *	common hyacinth	Mid-April to early May
Ligustrum species *	privet	Mid-June to mid-July
Lilium auratum * and hybrids	goldband lily	July and August
Lilium longiflorum * and forms	Easter lily; white trumpet lily	July
Lilium regale *	regal lily; royal lily	July
Lonicera fragrantissima *	winter honeysuckle	March to May
Lonicera Heckrottii *	honeysuckle	May to October
Lonicera japonica Halliana *	Hall's honeysuckle	June to November
Magnolia Kobus and hybrids		April
Malus baccata * and hybrids	Siberian crabapple	Late April to mid-May
Muscari armeniacum	grape-hyacinth	Mid-April to early May
Muscari moschatum	grape-hyacinth	Mid-April to early May
Narcissus Jonquilla	jonquil	Mid-May
Narcissus poetaz *	poetaz narcissus	Late April to early May
Narcissus poeticus	poets narcissus	Mid-May
Philadelphus coronarius * and hybrids	mock-orange	Late May to mid-June

292

PLANT	POPULAR NAME	TIME OF BLOOM
Philadelphus microphyllus * and hybrids	mock-orange	Late May to mid-June
Phlox paniculata * and forms	summer perennial phlox	Mid-July to late September
Prunus, * fruiting forms	stone-fruits: plum, apricot, peach, cherry	Late April
Prunus Mume	Japanese apricot	March
Rhododendron arborescens *		June
Rhododendron roseum *		Mid-May
Rhododendron hybrids *: Mollis, Ghent, Knap Hill, Exbury, Ilam		Mid-May to mid-June
Ribes odoratum *	buffalo currant	Mid-April to mid-May
Robinia PseudoAcacia	false-acacia; black-acacia; yellow locust	Mid-May to early June
Rosa damascena bifera	Damask rose	Late May to mid-June and later
Rosa Eglanteria * (leaves only)	eglantine; sweetbrier	Mid-April on, in dampness
Rosa rugosa and forms		Late May to October
Rosa moschata hybrids	hybrid musk rose	Late May to October
Syringa persica laciniata *	Persian lilac	Early May to June
Syringa vulgaris and forms	common lilac	Early May to June
Tilia * species	linden; basswood	June and July
Viburnum carlcephalum *		Early May to late May
Viburnum Carlesii *		Late April to May
Viola odorata	sweet violet; garden violet	Late March to late April
Vitis riparia *	riverbank grape	Mid-June to July
Wisteria floribunda *	Japanese wisteria	Late May
Wisteria sinensis * and hybrids	Chinese wisteria	Mid- to late May

293

SOME OF THE MOST FREELY FRAGRANT TENDER PLANTS

PLANT	POPULAR NAME	TIME OF BLOOM
Cestrum nocturnum *	night-jessasmine	Three or more times a year
Citrus * species	orange; lemon; lime; grapefruit; kumquat	Three or more times a year
Clerodendrum fragrans	glory-bower	November and December
Daphne odora *		March and April
Gardenia jasminoides * and forms	cape-jasmine	Most of year
Heliotropium arborescens	common heliotrope	Most of year
Hyacinthus orientalis albulus	Roman hyacinth	November to January
Jasminum officinale grandiflorum *	poets jessamine	Three or more times a year
Jasminum Sambac *	Arabian jasmine	Three or more times a year
Mathiola bicornis *	evening stock	Summer
Mathiola incana *	stock; gilliflower	Early summer
Narcissus Tazetta * and forms	polyanthus narcissus	November to February
Nerium indicum	sweet-scented oleander	May to October
Nicotiana alata * and hybrids	flowering tobacco	Summer
Osmanthus fragrans *	sweet olive	October to June
Polianthes tuberosa *	tuberose	August to October
Trachelospermum species	star- or Confederate-jasmine	March to June; October to November
Tulbaghia fragrans *		Three or more times a year

(* *Free at night as well*)

Books on Fragrant Plants

A decade, and longer, of searching out and reading on a subject much favored by older writers finds us with a bibliography too pretentious for this modest book. Here we offer a limited list, just the books we have found most enjoyable and informative. Many are now out of print, as the dates of publication suggest, but often these can be found in horticultural or public libraries, and sometimes they can be obtained through dealers in old and rare books. A number of these titles have only a chapter on fragrance or perhaps a fairly constant reference to it in the plant descriptions.

Bowles, E. A., *A Handbook of Narcissus,* London, Martin Hopkinson, Ltd., 1934

Bunyard, Edward, *Old Garden Roses,* London, Country Life Ltd., 1936

Chalfin, Eleanor P., *The Useful Herbs,* Lynchburg, Virginia, Mutual Press, 1957

Clarkson, Rosetta, *Magic Gardens,* New York, Macmillan, 1939

Earle, Alice Morse, *Old Time Gardens,* New York, Macmillan, 1901

Ellwanger, George H., *The Garden's Story,* New York, Appleton, 1889

Fox, Helen Morganthau, *The Years in My Herb Garden,* New York, Macmillan, 1953

Freeling, Arthur, *Flowers: Their Use and Beauty,* London, Darton, 1857

Hale, Mrs., *Flora's Interpreter and Fortuna Flora,* Boston, Chase and Nichols, 1865

Hampton, F. A., *The Scent of Flowers and Leaves,* London, Dulau, 1925

Haworth-Booth, Michael, *Effective Flowering Shrubs,* London, Collins, 1951

Hill, Jason, *The Curious Gardener,* London, Faber and Faber, 1932

Hole, S. Reynolds, *A Book About Roses,* London, Arnold, 1906

Jekyll, Gertrude, *A Gardener's Testament,* London, Country Life, New York, Scribner's, 1937

———, *Wood and Garden,* London, Longmans, Green, 1899

Jessee, Jill, *Perfume Album,* New York, Perfume Productions Press, 1951

Keays, Mrs. Frederick Love, *The Old Roses,* New York, Macmillan, 1935

Lawrence, Elizabeth, *A Southern Garden,* University of North Carolina Press, 1942

———, *Gardens in Winter,* New York, Harper, 1961

———, *The Little Bulbs,* New York, Criterion, 1957

Li, H. L., *The Garden Flowers of China,* New York, Ronald, 1959

McDonald, Donald, *Sweet Scented Flowers and Fragrant Leaves,* London, Sampson Low, Marston, 1895

Moreton, C. Oscar, *Old Carnations and Pinks,* London, Rainbird Collins, 1955

Parkinson, John, *Paradisi in sole,* 1629, London, Methuen, 1904, reprint

Pemberton, Rev. Joseph H., *Roses: Their History, Development and Cultivation,* London, Longmans, Green, 1920

Rohde, Eleanour Sinclair, *Gardens of Delight,* New York, Hale, Cushman and Flint, 1936

———, *The Scented Garden,* Boston, Hale, Cushman and Flint, 1936

———, *The Scented Garden,* London, Medici Society, 1948

Sackville-West, Victoria, *The Joy of Gardening,* New York, Harper, 1958

Spry, Constance, *Garden Notebook,* New York, Knopf, 1940

Thomas, Graham Stuart, *Climbing Roses Old and New,* London, Phoenix House, 1965

Thomas, Graham Stuart, *Colour in the Winter Garden,* London, Phoenix House, 1957

———, *Shrub Roses of Today,* London, Phoenix House, 1962

———, *The Old Shrub Roses,* London, Phoenix House, 1955

Wilder, Louise Beebe, *Adventures with Hardy Bulbs,* New York, Macmillan, 1936

———, *The Fragrant Path,* New York, Macmillan, 1932

Woodward, Marcus, *Leaves from Gerard's Herbal, 1633,* London, Howe, 1931

American Rose Annual, American Rose Society, Columbus, Ohio, 1916-1965

"Roses of Yesterday and Today," catalogues, Will Tillotson's Roses, Watsonville, California, 1957-1966

Index

This index lists the main discussions of plants. Botanical names are printed in italics, cultivar names are enclosed in single quotation marks, popular (common) names are printed in roman type.

297

306